THE BUTCHER

Also by Philip Carlo

Gaspipe: Confessions of a Mafia Boss
The Ice Man: Confessions of a Mafia Contract Killer
The Night Stalker: The Life and Crimes of Richard Ramirez
Smiling Wolf
Predators & Prayers
Stolen Flower

THE BUTCHER

ANATOMY OF A MAFIA PSYCHOPATH

PHILIP CARLO

MAINSTREAM
PUBLISHING

EDINBURGH AND LONDON

First published in Great Britain in 2009 by
MAINSTREAM PUBLISHING COMPANY
(EDINBURGH) LTD
7 Albany Street
Edinburgh EH1 3UG

ISBN 9781845965075

A catalogue record for this book is available
from the British Library

Typeset in Garamond and Trixie

Printed in Great Britain by
CPI Mackays, Chatham ME5 8TD

This book is dedicated to ASAC Jim Hunt and the members of the Pitera task force out of Group 33 in the Drug Enforcement Administration's New York office – Ken Feldman, Tom Geisel, Bruce Travers, Mike Agrifolio, John McKenna, Mike Rubowski, John Welch, John Wilson and Violet Szelecky. Every day, these brave men put their lives on the line fighting the scourge that drugs are, warring with extremely wealthy, diabolical, highly motivated drug lords from all over the world.

In respectful memory of the DEA agents
brought down in the war on drugs.

Charles A. Wood
Stafford Beckett
Joseph Floyd
James T. Williams
James E. Brown
James R. Kerrigan
Spencer Stafford
Anker M. Bangs
Wilson M. Shee
Mansel R. Burrell
Hector Jordan
Gene A. Clifton
Frank Tummillo
Richard Heath Jr
Emir Benitez
Gerald Sawyer
Leslie S. Grosso
Larry D. Wallace
Octavio Gonzalez
Thomas J. Devine
Marcellus Ward
Enrique S. Camarena
William Ramos
Raymond J. Statsny
Terry W. McNett
George M. Montoya
Paul S. Seema
Everett E. Hatcher

ACKNOWLEDGMENTS

The Butcher: Anatomy of a Mafia Psychopath would not have been possible without the kind help and never-ending cooperation of ASAC Jim Hunt of the Drug Enforcement Administration. Thanks to his steel bear-trap memory and his willingness to sit down with myself and my assistant, Kelsey Osgood, for endless hours, we were able to understand and portray this very complex, epic tale involving the war on drugs – the Bonanno crime family on one side and the DEA on the other, mortal enemies both. I came to believe that Jim Hunt is a real live hero – men like him are one in a million. The agents who work under Jim, out on the streets with Jim, like him and respect him and told me they'd rather have Jim Hunt watching their backs than anyone else.

I wish to also express my heartfelt gratitude to Kelsey Osgood for her quick wit, sharp intelligence, her ready willingness to do whatever she was asked. Without Kelsey, this book would not have been possible. I also wish to thank Matt Bialer at Sanford Greenburger for his enthusiasm and encouragement, dedication and loyalty. Matt comes from the old school of literary agents – he truly cares for his clients, their work and artistic sensibilities. My thanks to Matt Harper at HarperCollins for his good cheer and excellent editorial input. Many thanks also to my family, my parents, Dante and Nina Carlo for understanding why I missed so many family functions. Also many thanks to my Los Angeles agent Jerry Kalajian for always being there and for promptly returning phone calls, for his guidance, experience and friendship. My heartfelt gratitude to my wife, Laura Carlo, for her help and support, input and understanding, for her sitting down with me and line reading, out loud, this whole book. I would be remiss if I didn't here thank the kind people at the Savoy Hotel: Carlos Mendes, Fernao, Sergio Coniglio. Also many thanks to Raf Pasquet and the wonderful, amazingly hospitable Boucher brothers, Michael and Perry. I would also like to thank the mean streets of Bensonhurst, Brooklyn, where I received most of my education, where I learned about the culture of La Cosa Nostra, its walk and talk, mindset, bloody rhyme and rhythm.

'Right now, the federal government is fighting a war on drug abuse under a distinct handicap, for its efforts are those of a loosely confederated alliance facing a resourceful, elusive, worldwide enemy.'

> – Richard Nixon, July 1973, upon creation of
> the Drug Enforcement Administration

'There's never been anyone like him. He was like a vampire. We believe he killed over 60 people.'

> – James J. Hunt, Assistant Special Agent,
> New York Field Division, DEA

'We followed him for three years. He always wore black. His face was very white. One night we saw him doing chins on a fire escape in a dark alley at four o'clock in the morning. It was an unsettling sight.'

> – Agent David Toracinta

'If anyone deserved the death penalty, it was Tommy Pitera.'

> – Federal Prosecutor David Shapiro

'Greed was the engine that fuelled his criminal enterprise.'

> – Assistant US Attorney Elisa Liang

'After what he did to Phyllis, I hated the fucker.'

> – Frank Gangi

'When he talked, he sounded just like a girl.'

> – Lenny the pizza guy

'Three men could keep a secret, if two of them are dead.'

> – Santo Trafficante, Louisiana Mafia Boss

'Just say no.'

> – Nancy Reagan

CONTENTS

- -

PART 4: TRAUMAS AND TRIALS

AUTHOR'S NOTE

C ontained in this book are particularly unsettling crime scene photos of Tommy Karate Pitera's victims. We realise the photos are horrible and shocking but we feel the hardcore reality of exactly what Pitera did, the Mafia culture that begot him, is important for the reader to see and know and experience. Exclusively, the DEA provided author Philip Carlo with these photographs; they have never been given to any journalist before.

Here, now, we enter the macabre, bloody netherworld of Tommy Karate Pitera.

CAST OF CHARACTERS

THE GOOD GUYS

Agent Jim Hunt	Pitera task force street captain
Agent Tommy Geisel	Jim Hunt's partner
Joe Hunt	Jim's grandfather
James Hunt Senior	Jim's father, DEA agent
Bruce Travers	Group 33 agent
Mike Agrifolio	Group 33 agent
John Welch	Group 33 agent
Dave Toracinta	Group 33 agent
Timmy MacDonald	DEA agent
John McKenna	DEA agent
Vinnie DeMarco	DEA informant
Maria Polkowski	DEA informant
Inspector Martin	head of Canadian Mounties in Toronto
Inspector McDonald	head of Canadian Mounties in Montreal
Joe 'Dish' Senatore	DEA informant
David Shapiro	Federal prosecutor
Elise Liang	Federal prosecutor

Andrew Maloney	US attorney
Matthew Mari	criminal defence attorney
David Ruhnke	criminal defence attorney
Cheryl Mackell	criminal defence attorney
Reena Raggi	judge

THE BAD GUYS

Tommy Pitera	Bonanno family capo
Frank Gangi	Pitera associate
Billy Bright	Pitera associate, Gangi's partner in drug dealing
Shlomo Mendelsohn	Israeli drug dealer, Pitera associate
Anthony Bruno Indelicato	Bonanno family member
Joseph Bonanno	former head of the Bonanno family
Anthony Spero	Bonanno family underboss
Alphonse 'Sonny Red' Indelicato	Bonanno family member, father of Bruno
John Gotti	Gambino boss
Eddie Lino	Bonanno war captain
Frank Lino	Bonanno capo, Pitera boss, Eddie's brother
Angelo Favara	Pitera associate
Judy Haimowitz	Pitera associate
Arthur Guvenaro	Gangi and Bright's drug-dealing associate
Talal Siksik	Israeli drug dealer, Pitera associate
Moussa Aliyan	Israeli drug dealer, Pitera associate
Richie David	Pitera associate
Joey 'Pizza' Tekulve	Pitera associate
Vincent 'Kojak' Giattino	Pitera associate
Manny Maya	Pitera associate
Frank Rubino	Eddie Lino business associate
Lloyd Modell	Pitera associate aka Lorenzo Modica

THE BUTCHER

Frank Martini	Pitera associate
Carlos Acosta	Colombian drug dealer
Fernando Aguilera	Colombian drug dealer
Paul Castellano	former head of the Gambino family
Joe 'Butch' Corrao	Gambino family member
Ross Gangi	Genovese captain, Frank Gangi's cousin
Richard Leone	Pitera associate
Hector Estrada	Queens-based drug dealer
Vincenzo Lore	Canadian drug dealer
Giles	Canadian drug dealer, fugitive
John Gotti Jr	son of John Gotti, drug dealer
Greg Reiter	Gotti Jr associate
Michael Harrigan	former Gotti Jr associate
Mark Harrigan	Michael's father
Thomas Carbone	Pitera associate
Michael Cassesse	Pitera associate
Andrew Miciotta	Pitera associate

THE INNOCENTS

Phyllis Burdi	Frank Gangi's girlfriend
Celeste LiPari	Tommy Pitera's common-law wife
Barbara Lambrose	Tommy Pitera's girlfriend
Sophia Gangi	Frank Gangi's wife
Marek Kucharsky	Russian boxer
Andy Jakakis	friend of Frank Gangi
Joey Balzano	Brooklyn guy
Wilfred 'Willie Boy' Johnson	government informer
Solomon Stern	Richard Leone associate

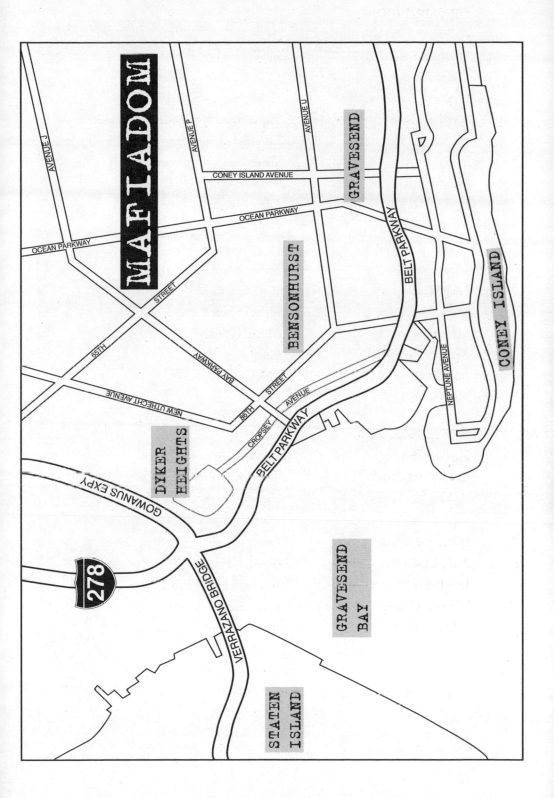

Courtesy of the DEA

PROLOGUE

Gravesend, Brooklyn, is a 7,000-acre swathe of land sandwiched between Bensonhurst and Coney Island. The area initially drew its name from a small graveyard located at McDonald Avenue and Neck Road. Beaten and battered and worn down now, the graveyard is still there today. Gravesend was settled by the Dutch in 1640. Between the years 1641 and 1645, the Dutch had a campaign to rid the area of its indigenous peoples, and they remorselessly murdered over 1,000 American Indians; they beheaded them, dismembered them and burnt them alive at the stake in the years before the area became an English settlement.

Gravesend was strategically close to estuaries fed by the nearby Atlantic Ocean. It was well located for importing and exporting various goods and commodities. The forests of Gravesend were abundant in all manner of game, moose, deer and beaver, wild pig and huge numbers of rabbits. (Nearby Coney Island is Dutch for 'Rabbit Island'.) The waters of the Atlantic were teeming with many varieties of fish. During the summer months, the pristine, unpolluted Atlantic literally boiled with huge schools of anchovy, cod, mackerel, bluefish, bass, fluke and flounder. Tons of succulent lobster and blue claw crabs were there for the taking. Mountains of oysters, mussels and clams were easily accessible. The vast, blue skies of seventeenth-century Brooklyn were filled with edible fowl – quail, duck and goose. The dark, fertile soil was ideal for bountiful crops. With the exception of the brutal and unforgiving winters, Gravesend was a place of sweet abundance.

As Brooklyn grew to be a large, bustling metropolis, so did Gravesend. In the early twentieth century, the New York Mafia began using the more desolate areas of Gravesend as a convenient dumping ground for bodies. The Five Points Gang, Joe 'The Boss' Masseria, Salvatore Maranzano, Lucky Luciano, Murder Incorporated, the five New York crime families – Genovese, Profaci, Bonanno, Lucchese and Anastasia – all gladly used Gravesend as a convenient place to leave their victims – stabbed, ice-picked, butchered, beaten, battered or shot to death.

Up to the day of his arrest, Sammy 'The Bull' Gravano had his office smack in the heart of Gravesend, at Highland and Stillwell Avenues. The Lucchese, Genovese, Gambino, Colombo and Bonanno crime families all had secretive black-windowed social clubs in Gravesend and Bensonhurst. Here, mafiosi played cards, drank strong espresso, planned new crimes, murders and hijacks, and settled disputes. Thus, Gravesend, Brooklyn, took on a more sinister, morbid connotation to its inhabitants and the people in nearby Bensonhurst and Coney Island. Here, people minded their own business. Here, no one saw anything. The citizenry could readily be likened to the three wise monkeys . . . they saw no evil, spoke no evil, heard no evil.

Because Gravesend and its neighbour Bensonhurst had larger populations of 'made men' than anywhere else in the world, including Sicily, one of the by-products of their work – bodies – was always a concern. Where to hide them; how to get rid of them permanently; whether or not to blatantly leave them out in the open. These were decisions that either had to be made quickly, on the spot, or planned in advance. As vacant lots all across Brooklyn were filled with two- and three-storey red-brick homes, the impromptu burial grounds of the area systematically disappeared. The mob, as a collective whole, had to look for new places to hide their victims.

Thus, it was logical that nearby Staten Island came into play. On Staten Island, there were still huge tracts of uninhabited land, blackened swamps, fields covered with tall green grass in the summer that turned a golden, wheat-like hue in the winter. Here, too, were thousands of acres of thick forests of oak, hickory, maple and beech trees. More importantly, though, were the state wildlife sanctuaries which were protected by the government from any kind of development. No construction was allowed; no utility lines would be laid. Surrounded by hundreds of acres of empty land, there was little threat someone idling by would stumble across a body or members of the mob burying one. Inadvertently, the government had invented the perfect place to get rid of bodies for the Mafia, and it didn't take long for particularly cunning members of La Cosa Nostra to take advantage of this convenience.

Always wily, always quick to exploit a situation, the Mafia turned Staten Island's wildlife sanctuaries into its private burial grounds. Interestingly, all five New York crime families used the sanctuaries. One would think members of the mob would keep secret cemeteries private, not tell anyone about them, but just the opposite proved true. They actually shared the sanctuaries with one another. Members of all the five families came to Staten Island with bodies in the trunks of their cars. They drove Cadillacs and Lincolns, Mercedes and Jaguars and arrogantly made their way to private burial grounds scattered all over Staten Island, in the south, the north, the east and west. They were so sure and confident that they often came across the Verrazano Bridge in broad daylight with bodies and long-handled shovels in the trunks of their cars, as Sinatra, Tony Bennett, Dean Martin and other golden oldies came from their radios. Never speeding, always carefully abiding by traffic rules and regulations, signs and lights, they made their way to these prearranged burial sites, sometimes singing along with Sinatra. Occasionally, there were graves already prepared; most often, however, shallow graves would be quickly dug in the secret-holding sanctuaries.

One such place was the William T. Davis Wildlife Refuge, some eight miles as the crow flies from the great-grand Verrazano Bridge. A caporegime in the Bonanno crime family out of Gravesend, Brooklyn, had made this bird sanctuary his private burial ground. Here, there were bodies that had suffered tremendous trauma while the person was still alive – here were bodies that had been neatly cut into six pieces: the legs, arms, head and torso all separated from one another by skilful cuts that showed no tears. Whoever dismembered these bodies was experienced, methodical, as cold and efficient as a butcher in the Meatpacking district of lower Manhattan.

Here, there were no tombstones.

Here, there was no reminder of the many who had lost their lives.

PART 1

SEEDS

SANCTUARY

It was 6 June 1990. The skies over Staten Island were clear and unblemished, as blue as the eye of a dove. An unusual caravan of police slowly made their way off the Staten Island Expressway and towards the William T. Davis Wildlife Refuge. It was a task force comprised of crack, hard-faced DEA, FBI and ATF agents, as well as hardcore NYPD organised crime detectives. Prosecutors from the Brooklyn DA's office were also present. Each of these prosecutors, agents and detectives was tense and uptight. What they were doing today, the reason they were approaching the William T. Davis Wildlife Refuge on Staten Island, was the culmination of three and a half years of hard work, blood and sweat and tears – literally.

In the second vehicle of this solemn caravan sat DEA Agent Jim Hunt, the man in charge of a DEA task force that had been pursuing a notorious Bonanno capo by the name of Tommy 'Karate' Pitera. Hunt was the man in charge of all the DEA personnel involved in this particular investigation; he was the eye of the storm, the skipper of the ship. Hunt was a six-foot, thickly muscled Irishman; he had a pale, handsome countenance and large, all-seeing Paul Newman blue eyes. A stoic, exceedingly dedicated third-generation cop, Jim took his work very seriously, was highly motivated, tenacious, though he was quick to laugh and quick to smile with no strings attached. He would gladly help a colleague or friend in need.

Hunt had an unusual sense of fair play for a cop. As much as he hated drug dealers, drug abusers and bad guys, he empathised and sympathised with some of their plights. Hunt viewed drug abuse more as a medical problem. He well understood that while some people can have a social drink or two, others become alcoholics . . . the dregs of society. What Jim Hunt was after, what he had his sights on, were the drug lords – those in faraway places, distant lands, who had learned to manipulate the system in such a way that they had become some of the wealthiest people in the world. The drug lords not only usurped the rule of law but also gleefully defecated all over it. These foes, these enemies, were not only in distant lands. They were here, also. Home-grown. The Mafia, the bosses and capos of each of the families, was dealing in drugs, Jim knew.

What was particularly unusual about this group of law-enforcement agents serpentining through Staten Island that June day was that they were all cooperating with each other. Most often, there is a fierce, bare-knuckled competition between the FBI and the DEA, the NYPD and the ATF; they were competitors in perpetual pissing contests, not colleagues. But this case was so unusual, the stakes so dire, that each of the agencies had made peace and were truly cooperating with one another on a large scale – a rare thing.

Sitting alongside Hunt was his fellow DEA agent and partner, Tommy Geisel. Geisel and Hunt were so close that they were more like brothers than partners in the war against drugs. For years, they'd been trusting one another with their lives. Geisel was a large, broad-shouldered, strapping individual. He had, in the parlance of the DEA, 'brains, balls and brawn', a phrase commonly used within the agency to describe the type of men they were looking for. Geisel was the kind of guy that Jim wanted in his foxhole, and there was no one else he wanted watching his back. Throughout the DEA, these two were known as 'the Perfect Storm' by their colleagues.

Accompanying this variegated army of police, there was also a bad guy – someone who wore a black hat, who would draw the curtains back and reveal the true horrors that even this group of law enforcement would soon be shocked and stunned by. He was tall and thin; his nose resembled a Toucan's beak. This bad guy was nervous and unsettled to the core of his being. Over the last four years, he had become, quite literally, unhinged – pushed to his limits by mind-numbing violence and unspeakable barbaric acts, as people around him were tortured, cut up and summarily discarded.

Some 13 months ago, ASAC Hunt had heard that a Bonanno family capo, Tommy Pitera, was leaving bodies on Staten Island. An Israeli drug dealer named Shlomo Mendelsohn had got himself in trouble and offered to give up the whereabouts of Pitera's cemetery. The only problem was Shlomo couldn't remember exactly where the cemetery was located. He had only been there once and it was at night. He had never been to Staten Island before the time he went with Pitera to dispose of a body. At one point during their quest to find Pitera's cemetery, Shlomo had even said, scratching his head, 'I'm thinking maybe it was New Jersey, not Staten Island.'

Shlomo was deeply immersed in selling huge amounts of cocaine in Manhattan, but Staten Island and New Jersey were completely foreign to him. Though Shlomo had seemed sincere and truthful, he had stepped up to bat and struck out.

Now Jim Hunt was back with another man who said he knew where Pitera's victims were. Hopeful, though wary, Jim's keen blue eyes moved left and right as the caravan slowly crept forward. As they approached a desolate street, the bad guy said, 'Here . . . here, this is it! I'm almost sure.'

The problem was that, like Shlomo, this bad guy had only been there in the dead of night. Daylight cast the stage of horrors that existed here in warm, welcoming light. That June day was cloudless, and the sun shone with such brilliance most all the agents donned sunglasses. It looked more like the south of France or a Mediterranean island than a Mafia burial ground.

The caravan moved right. Like a giant anaconda coming to a sudden stop, all the vehicles became immobile. Serious-faced and curious, each of the law-enforcement professionals stepped from their air-conditioned cars. The humid hot air struck them like a wet towel. As though on cue, an unruly gang of crows noisily cawed in different trees spread throughout the William T. Davis Wildlife Refuge.

Concerned about contaminating the area, losing potential evidence, all the agents and NYPD cops began to put on white jumpsuits made of a thin, malleable paper. Having a good, easy rapport with the informer, Jim Hunt asked, 'Where?', his eyebrows raised sceptically.

'Oh man,' the informer said, his brow creasing, the weight of the world suddenly on his shoulders. Sweating, licking his lips, smoking a cigarette, the bad guy moved into the thicket of poplar and elm and pine trees spread out before them. He had a worried look about his face. He seemed confused – lost. He took about 30 cautious steps into the sanctuary, stopped, looked around as some 25 pairs of cynical, wary cops' eyes regarded him with a mix of trepidation and curiosity.

He began moving east, stopped, turned around and moved west. He looked down. He scratched his head. He regarded Jim Hunt. He liked Hunt. He wanted to please him. Hunt was a straight shooter and the bad guy knew that whatever Hunt promised him, he would get. It was already agreed that the federal government, because of his cooperation, would put him and his family into the Witness Protection Program. He had no reason to lie. If he had any future, he had to cooperate with the feds. He knew he had to give them what they wanted.

'The problem,' the informer apologised, 'is that I was here at night. It's very hard to tell one spot from another. You know, it's, like, really the same.' He looked down at the ground. It was covered with a carpet of dead leaves and foliage. The thick smell of wet soil and mildew hung in the humid air. There was nothing to indicate that humans had been buried here; no bald spots, no sudden bursts of greenery – no telltale sign of human death. The crows continued to caw. Their ruckus was distracting. A chain smoker, the informer lit one cigarette after another. Beads of sweat ran down his face. Jim called an impromptu brainstorming session between all the law enforcement there that day. They, as a collective body, believed what the informer had said. They knew Pitera was murdering people as though he had a God-given right, as though he had a licence to kill, and that the informer had no reason to lie. They decided that until proven otherwise, they'd believe him and move full out until they found Pitera's victims. Hunt and Geisel believed that Pitera had killed over 60 people.

The NYPD set up a command centre. Uniformed cops were posted all around the bird sanctuary, roughly 25 acres in size. They knew that once the news media got wind of a Mafia burial ground, they'd have reporters sniffing around like hungry hounds within hours. Finding bodies buried months and years ago here, without coordinates, without landmarks, would be no easy task, like looking for the proverbial needle in the haystack, though none of that was going to dissuade any of the hardcore law-enforcement professionals there that fateful day. They continued looking without luck. The fierce June sun reluctantly dropped below the line of trees. Long shadows appeared. Silently, dusk descended onto the sanctuary. The sounds of crickets and frogs came from every direction at once. Large flocks of sparrows chattered rapidly. The birds, troubled and nervous by the cops' sudden presence, knew the secrets that their sanctuary held.

Foul flesh, silent screams and nightmares. As dark continued to envelope the sanctuary, agents and police there decided they would start up the search again the following morning.

DARK SECRETS

Mechanised, organised, as succinct as a well-run military operation, the Pitera task force gathered at 8 a.m. the following morning.

Again, the skies were clear. The birds that dwelt in the sanctuary made a racket. They were used to peace and quiet. They did not like the hurly-burly gathering around their homes. Above, a pair of red-tailed hawks circled over the sanctuary, hunting for prey, hunting the abundance of food they knew lived below.

It was decided that the first thing the strike force would do was bring in cadaver dogs. Given the circumstances, this seemed logical. When the dogs arrived, unremarkable mutts anxious to please, anxious to find the rotting bodies they would receive rewards for, they made their way into the sanctuary. They moved north and south and east and west in prearranged grids. This went on all that day to no avail. Everyone there was sure that if there were bodies, these dogs would find them; they had proven themselves in the past.

Nothing.

Not willing to accept defeat, the task force brought the dogs in a second day. They worked slower but still found nothing.

How, the task-force members wondered, could the dogs miss the scent? Some of the victims here were buried several months ago. Some of the victims one year, some two or even three years ago. The stench of death, the stench of putrid meat, organs, should still have been real and tangible – outright offensive – but the cadaver dogs seemed oblivious.

At a meeting back in Manhattan at the DEA's office on West 57th Street, the task-force members sat down and brainstormed some more. They questioned the informer's validity. They discussed the probability of his being mistaken about the William T. Davis Wildlife Refuge. They consulted maps to see if there were other bird sanctuaries nearby, to see if there was another logical explanation. There wasn't.

One of the task-force members talked about a machine a man in California had developed that could find bodies. His name was George Reynolds. They kicked the idea around of bringing him out, and then contacted Reynolds. He assured them seven ways from Sunday that the machine worked. It had proved itself over and over again, he said. Cops, fellow colleagues, attested to the machine's working. At great expense, Reynolds and his machine were brought to New York and driven out to the bird sanctuary. There was excitement in the air. Finally they'd have the proof, finally they'd have the sorrowful remnants of Pitera's handiwork. As some 30 members of the Pitera task force looked on, the man and his machine searched for bodies. It was hot and humid. Everyone was sweating. The crows were back and they made an awful racket. All that day, the man diligently searched and he, too, found nothing. Jim Hunt soon gave him the boot and sent him back to California.

This, combined with the heat, combined with the failure of the informer and the dogs, was discouraging. Was the informer pulling their legs; would he try to cut himself a deal for crimes he committed that they, at this point, knew nothing about?

These were not, however, the type of people who gave up easily.

They were all alpha males and females, tenacious investigators, the type that would not let go. They were experienced – the best of the best.

Often with police work, it's more than facts and figures, names and places, the who, what, when, where and why. Often it's just a gut feeling, something deep inside that points the way, that has a voice and direction of its own. And almost all of them there, working the sanctuary, the Pitera case, felt in their gut that they were on the right trail; felt in their gut that they had discovered the Jeffrey Dahmer of the Mafia – that they had discovered a serial killer who was a capo in a Mafia family, and they would work this case tirelessly, to the very end, wherever it took them.

The following day the task-force members, wearing white jumpsuits, were back at the sanctuary. They were now doing it the old-fashioned way, the way their fathers and grandfathers had looked for bodies. They secured four-foot-long metal probes pointed at one end and with a five-inch handle at the other that would enable the task force to literally probe the ground.

Again, going back to basics, they drew precise, neat grids on different sections of the sanctuary and, working two and a half feet from one another's shoulders, they began to walk in a straight line, every foot or so jabbing the probes into the ground. Luckily for them, the dirt was soft and readily accepted the probes. For all that day, back and forth, quiet and solemn, a joke now and then – mostly macabre ones – the strike force moved. Towards the end of the day, as the fiery June sun began to set, the strike force prepared to break for the night. They had come across rabbits and raccoons, skunks and weasels, but no bodies.

An NYPD detective out of the Brooklyn Racket Squad named Bobby Povone made his way away from the group, sat down on a rock and lit up a cigarette. He, like most of the law enforcement there that day, believed that there were bodies buried here. He had been hearing for years rumours about the Mafia burying bodies out on Staten Island. Why not here? It seemed the perfect place. There wasn't a house or human being anywhere nearby. It struck him as ironic that the federal government had created, in a very real sense, a place where the Mafia was able to hide bodies, bodies that would never be found because the EPA – Environmental Protection Agency – wouldn't allow the birds to be disturbed.

Slowly, reservedly, Bobby moved back towards the group, a tall, wiry, resolute individual. He kind of haphazardly, though pensively, probed as he went, pushed down, found nothing, withdrew the probe. He had moved some 20 feet when the probe suddenly struck something hard, but giving. He pulled out the probe, pushed it back down, pulled it out, pushed it back in still again . . . something was there; something not indigenous to the ground.

'Hey! Hey! Over here!' He signalled to the others. They moved towards him. 'I think I've got one.'

3

IT'S GOOD TO KNOW KARATE

Thomas Pitera was born in Gravesend, Brooklyn, on 2 December 1954. His parents, Joseph and Catherine, were hard-working people of modest means. He had an older sister named Theresa and a large, close-knit extended family. Joseph Pitera was a candy salesman. With samples of his wares secreted in the trunk of his car, he drove throughout the five boroughs selling Mary Janes, Pixie Sticks, Red Hots, Lemon Drops and Bazooka Gum. The Piteras hailed from southern Italy, the Campagna region. They were good Catholics, and Mrs Pitera attended church on a regular basis.

Tommy Pitera was an unusual child. He had thick, jet-black hair, piercing blue-grey eyes, a strong jaw line and high cheekbones. Without wanting to, without meaning to, his intense stare and black hair drew attention to him, attention that he didn't want, attention he would grow to disdain. As a boy, he was thin and pale, shy and withdrawn. Tommy had a particularly high-pitched voice that sounded more like a girl's than a boy's. It could readily be likened to Michael Jackson's voice, though it was even more falsetto.

Given his frailty, combined with his small stature and cartoonish voice, Tommy was an ideal target for Gravesend bullies, food for hungry carnivores. This was an extremely rough-and-tumble neighbourhood – one of the toughest in all of America – filled with thickly muscled labourers and blue-collar workers. The young Tommy Pitera couldn't have been in a worse place. Here, people did not turn the other cheek. Here, if you were abused, you struck back hard with bad intentions. Here he who struck first was victorious. He who was left standing was the winner. Gravesend, Bensonhurst and Coney Island were all particularly tough neighbourhoods. You could liken these areas to concrete jungles filled with predatory creatures: those who readily fed on the weak, those who took advantage of the lame and the unaware.

On a daily basis, often several times a day, neighbourhood bullies picked on Tommy. They made fun of his voice, his clothes, his walk. He was slapped or kicked for no reason. He was mocked and spat on for no reason. In short, the young Pitera had no peace, had no solace, had no way to strike back, had no friends. Not wanting to appear like a crybaby, a sissy, he said nothing to his mother and father about the abuse he suffered on a daily basis.

Frequently when he came home from school, he was on the verge of tears. In fact, he often cried alone in his room because of the grave injustices he suffered at the hands of the neighbourhood miscreants. Like most who are mistreated, Tommy fantasised about striking back, hurting those who abused him – getting even. As he got older, those fantasies became tangible realities and, unbridled, they grew to monstrous proportions. The abuse and ostracism caused in the young Pitera an antisocial mindset, a feeling of being alone in the world, a feeling he could not shake. It was him against them; he felt as though he was on an island alone and unloved. Whenever possible, he would readily express his feelings of anger in the only way he could – striking back and taking revenge in diabolical ways. He stole, as an example, the little league baseball equipment and sold it on the street. He did this not only for the money he was able to make but also, more importantly, it was his way of getting back at the establishment, it was his way of undermining, setting fire to, what he could not become a part of. In a very real sense, it was Pitera's way of saying, 'Fuck you, world.'

Tommy attended Boody Junior High School on Avenue S. When recently queried, teachers there had very little recollection of him. He was so quiet, so shy, so put-upon that he seemed to disappear into the woodwork. It wasn't unusual for Tommy to sit at his desk and stare out the windows, imagining himself a valiant, badass fighter, a champion of the downtrodden. Because of his unusually high-pitched voice, it was difficult for him to make friends. In this tough, macho world, boys who spoke like girls didn't have a chance. Even girls in his classes made fun of him, mocked him, imitated his voice. As days melted into weeks, and weeks into months, the young Tommy's inner turmoil, animosity and hatred grew and grew. What was in him could readily be likened to a bubbling cauldron getting hotter and hotter still.

The young Pitera particularly liked a popular television show which would end up playing a large part in his life. It was called *The Green Hornet* and featured the brilliant martial artist Bruce Lee as Kato, the Green Hornet's sidekick. Fascinated, fixated, Tommy watched Bruce Lee fly through the air, slide down poles, beat bad guys into submission before they knew what had hit them. He threw amazing kicks. His punches were lightning speed. Yet he was always respectful, particularly towards women; he was a gentleman. This, too, appealed to the young Pitera's sense of fair play.

Naturally enough, Tommy became interested in martial arts. He viewed it as a way for him to be left alone and, if need be, strike back with great force. It was no secret now to Tommy's parents that he was regularly bullied, and when Tommy told his mother and father he'd like to take karate classes, they acquiesced; they thought it would be a good thing for the boy. They understood the obvious – if the bullying continued, it might have a long-term negative effect on their son.

With great enthusiasm, Tommy began going to karate school in Sheepshead Bay, practising kicks and punches, turns and jumps with the dedication of a cloistered monk. He quickly moved to the head of his class. What was motivating the boy, what was driving him, was that karate gave him strength – an almost religious calling. When, in 1969, Bruce Lee's first major feature film – *Marlowe* – came out, Tommy Pitera was hooked on martial arts for life. He became a zealous devotee of throwing accurate punches and kicks. He accepted all the constraints placed around martial arts: you were never to pick a fight, you were always supposed to avoid trouble; to turn the other cheek was the righteous thing to do.

However, when Tommy watched Bruce Lee beat sneering bad guys to a pulp, he felt justice had been done – street justice. Inevitably, Tommy's muscles began to grow, become more defined. His skinny arms were replaced by strong sinew and muscle tissue. His fists flattened out and widened from constantly hitting heavy bags. His knuckles grew to disproportionate size. His stomach became cut up. The leg muscles between his hips and knees thickened and defined from endless practice kicks.

As Tommy entered high school and moved through the classes, he was a very different boy. He walked with his head high and his shoulders back – defiant and arrogant. He feared no one. In his feet and hands, he felt he had weapons that he could use quickly, discreetly or indiscreetly as he chose. He began to think of himself as a human weapon. He knew, as an example, that professional boxers were not allowed to fight outside of the ring, that the hands of professional boxers were thought of as weapons.

Now, when neighbourhood bullies started with him, made fun of him, they were confronted by a completely new person. Suddenly, the Tommy they used to abuse without response was kicking and punching them from three directions at the same time. He was tough; he was fearless. It didn't take long for neighbourhood punks to walk around Tommy when they saw him coming. Despite the disapproval of his parents, who didn't want Tommy looking like a 'hippie', Tommy also let his thick, straight black hair grow down past his ears and to his jaw line. His father and mother didn't like the long hair. They wanted him to get it cut. For the most part, Tommy was a good son, an obedient boy, but in this he would not listen to them. Bruce Lee had long hair and so Tommy wanted it, too.

Still, Tommy Pitera had that awkwardly high falsetto voice. Previously, when in a new classroom, when a question was posed by a teacher all the students would look in his direction. Now, though, no one made fun of him, no one mimicked him. This voice would be a curse Tommy had to live with all his life, an imperfection that no amount of martial arts training could alter.

What he did do, almost as a way of balancing this feminine voice he'd been cursed with, was train harder and harder. He approached martial arts as though it would be his life's work. Tommy's karate teachers were proud of him. They saw in the boy a ferocious appetite to fight. They saw a particular acumen in the boy: not only in the punches and kicks he was throwing, but also in his speed; he was hard to hit. Some of his teachers, who were ten, fifteen years Tommy's senior and had a hundred pounds on him, were astonished by how ferocious he was when he fought.

'His punches stung as though you'd been hit by a hammer,' one of his teachers recently explained. The resentment and pain that had been a daily part of Tommy's life had been replaced by animus and anger.

As well as training for hours every day, Tommy lifted weights. His body took on the demeanour of a labourer; of a man who worked carrying heavy crates all day, every day. Tommy stood in front of a mirror in his parents' home and marvelled at his muscles, moving slowly this way and that, admiring how his body had changed.

Inevitably, Tommy began fighting in martial arts competitions. Here he was pitted against boys his own age and weight, and he ate them up. It seemed that there was a full-blown ferocious man inside the teenage boy. He had a pent-up anger, hostility, that, when expressed, was a very difficult obstacle to overcome. It wasn't just a matter of physical strength. It wasn't a matter of larger biceps or thigh muscles, calf muscles. It was something inside the boy's head that would inexorably grow and become a fearsome entity. The endless taunts, abuse and beatings he had endured had planted a kind of dragon seed in him that would grow into something horrifying and unspeakable.

Not only did Tommy bury himself in martial arts, but he also began to read voraciously about war in all of its shapes, strategies and tactics. He learned how to torture, how to take apart bodies, where to strike for the maximum effect, where to strike to cause death, how to kill. When Tommy read these words, written carefully by learned men from all over the world, he felt that he was becoming part of an underground culture – a sophisticated society that was wiser and more in touch with the truths of life. His daily martial arts workout, his lifting weights, his reading and watching of violent movies, particularly martial arts films, was a combustible, dangerous recipe for disaster, chaos.

The fact that the young Pitera was growing up on the streets of Gravesend and Bensonhurst added jet fuel to the fire inside him, teeth to the dragon. Here was the largest concentration of Mafia members in the world; this was ground zero for the American La Cosa Nostra. Here was a culture in which the killing of human beings was the norm; here was a culture in which murder was as inevitable as the changing of the seasons. A young boy in this environment could not help but see and know and feel the tangible elements of the Mafia, which were as much a part of the place as pizzerias and espresso cafes. Tommy Pitera came to admire the mafiosi he was surrounded by. They were on every other street corner. They drove fancy cars. They sported silk suits and expensive Italian shoes and were always well barbered, cared for. They were a kind of aristocracy for that place and that time, exuding power and a feeling of danger – things Pitera was drawn to.

For the most part, Pitera was a loner; he was ideally suited to what they wanted. Tommy inevitably began fantasising about going that way, becoming a respected mafioso. He knew that, even with his Mickey Mouse voice, nobody would make fun of him any more; that people would speak to him respectfully, look the other way when they saw him coming. That if you fucked with Tommy Pitera, you would be dead.

To some, this might seem like a fanciful stretch, but when you look at bullied young boys taking up firearms all over the country and attacking their schoolmates and teachers, killing them, killing them without guilt or remorse, killing them in the light of day, you can begin to understand the hateful seed that had been planted and was growing in Tommy Pitera. They say the soul of a man is in his eyes. Well, when you now looked at Tommy Pitera, you saw hooded, bright blue eyes that had the cold, flat depth of ice. One could readily liken his eyes to those of a predatory animal that knows no fear, an animal that would readily tear open your throat – it's in its nature.

Martial arts gave Tommy Pitera a calling. It gave him a belief system that would, he was sure, serve him well for life. Naturally competitive, he became so adept at throwing punches and kicks and avoiding being hit that he won contest after contest. When a large martial arts bout was held in Brooklyn's Sheepshead Bay, Pitera competed. In order to win his weight class, he had to fight seven different opponents and, ultimately, beat them all. This was no small task. There was not only a substantial cash prize, but a large amount of prestige also went along with the win. Tommy was also offered a 'scholarship' to go and live in Japan and study under one of the country's most revered martial arts masters. For the young Pitera, this was an exciting, monumental event.

Initially, Tommy's parents didn't like the idea, but they changed their minds and gave him their blessing. They felt it would be good for the boy; he would further learn discipline and strengthen his character. The trip would give him a rare opportunity to see the world outside of Brooklyn, an opportunity that few boys in the neighbourhood were afforded. His winning the tournament and the prospect of travelling to Japan further bolstered Tommy's commitment to martial arts. He surrounded himself, immersed himself in, martial arts, and he embraced the eastern culture's way of thinking and behaving. Interestingly, he also embraced eastern cuisine. He began eating sushi before it was fashionable – he shied away from Italian food with its emphasis on dairy products and pasta.

When finally the day came for his trip, the Piteras drove their only son to Kennedy Airport and, tearfully, said goodbye to him. He was not only going to a foreign country; he was also going to a country where they didn't speak English, a country far removed from anything he had known. They were worried for him, concerned.

However, as Tommy made his way to the gate, there was joy, a quiet rejoicing, in his every step. Tommy was not sure where this trip would lead, but he viewed it as an exciting adventure that would bring him in touch with the best martial artists in the world. He felt blessed. All the bullying; all the barbed, vicious taunts, the slaps and punches and kicks he regularly suffered, were now a thing of the past. The plane taxied and took off.

Tommy Pitera was soon high above Jamaica Bay. The sun was setting and it laid a flaming blanket on the wide expanse of the Atlantic Ocean. Tommy Pitera of Gravesend, Brooklyn, was soon speeding towards Japan and his violent destiny at 500 miles an hour, the dormant dragon in him slowly awakening.

THE MAKING OF A
DRAGON SLAYER

As Tommy Pitera made his way to Japan to learn the finer points of martial arts, DEA Agent Jim Hunt was 17 years old. Though he didn't know it yet, Hunt had being a cop in his blood. Of course, he knew his father and grandfather were both dedicated to law enforcement, but he had no personal connection to their careers, to their morality, their sense of right and wrong – to their dogged adherence to the rule of law.

His grandfather, Joe Hunt, emigrated to America from County Roscommon, Ireland, in 1913. He heard that there were jobs that paid well in the mines of Montana. After arriving in New York, travelling with fellow Irishmen he made his way to Montana by way of trains. The work in the mines was backbreaking and bone-twisting, under the worst, most dire of circumstances, but Joe Hunt did not complain. He did what was required of him. He was a genuinely tough man, nearly six feet tall. He had black hair, dark eyes and chiselled cheekbones. In his mind, calluses and sweat went hand in hand with making a living, getting somewhere in life.

News of the First World War hit Montana like a bomb. Though Joe Hunt hadn't been living in the States long, had only been exposed to backbreaking, menial labour, he felt it was his inherent duty, obligation, to go and fight in the war to end all wars. He travelled, via rail, back to New York and without hesitation joined the army.

As it happened, Joe Hunt was wounded in hedgegrove country in France, shot and gassed; because of the gassing, he would have respiratory problems his whole life. He was given several medals and an honourable discharge. He heard, through family and friends, that there were civil servant jobs available in New York – specifically, openings for policeman. This, in a large way, appealed to Joe Hunt, so he found his way back to the cobblestone streets of New York and joined New York's finest.

A large, tough man, Joe was ideally suited to work the rough streets of New York. He readily passed the physical and psychological tests and he began walking a beat, carrying a club and wearing a .38 on his hip. Joe quickly took to the job. He liked putting bad guys behind bars. He felt he was protecting not only society but also its weaker members – children and women. He felt he was the difference between chaos and order. It was the roaring twenties, and drinking and living in excess were the norm, making Joe Hunt a very busy man. Despite the realities of the age, Joe dealt with the curveballs life threw without regret, attributes he would instil in his sons. A dedicated family man, Joe returned home after work everyday, and weekends found him with his family. The murders, the violence, the amazing brutality men showed one another were all left at the door. He never brought the job back home, to his wife and children, one of whom was named James.

When Joe Hunt retired, he was a happy, content man. He had found his niche in life and he felt he had served society well. Since he was only 52 years old, he opened Joe's Stroll Inn bar on Crescent Avenue in Queens. The bar was frequented by many in law enforcement and Joe's Stroll Inn prospered. The problems in Joe Hunt's lungs, by way of gassing during the war, gave him a severe case of emphysema, which ultimately stole his life away.

Like his father before him, James Hunt I, known as Jim, was born to be a cop, but, as it turned out, he was a natural born fighter as well; not bar-room brawls, not with strangers over supposed or real insults; he was not an argumentative individual who was easily offended. Jim was a boxer, a very tough middleweight. He began boxing in the Golden Gloves and knocked out everybody he confronted. He was fast and agile, and had a wicked left and right, both capable of knocking out an opponent. He was thickly muscled, with no fat on his body. If he'd had his way in life, he would have chosen to be a professional fighter, and he had been moving in that direction. He liked the discipline and regimentation. He liked being the best at what he did, a quality that he would have for the rest of his life. This was an attribute that would make him one of the most successful and famous law-enforcement individuals in the annals of American crime history.

Jim gladly joined the army and went to war when the Second World War broke out. He had come to love America, the freedom and equality it readily afforded its citizens. He would gladly lay down his life for America. Its enemies were Jim Hunt's enemies.

Inevitably, Jim began boxing in the army. He quickly rose up the ranks and became an army middleweight champion. This was no small feat given that there were nearly one and a half million men in the army – he had tremendous competition. To be a boxing champion in the United States Army back then immediately elevated a boxer to rock star status, though star status and adulation did not at all interest Jim Hunt. He was a true sportsman, loved boxing, and was in it for the sport and competition. The army was filled with men who not only wanted to fight but also wanted to kill. When there were boxing matches, held in England before the invasion, it was always standing room only. Boxing was by far the most popular pastime for fighting men. The stringent competition only furthered Jim's aspirations to box professionally, to make boxing his life's calling. Jim knocked out most everyone he was pitted against.

As it occurred, the reality of war, the reality of fighting an enemy as consistently tough and resistant and belligerent as the Germans were, struck home during the Battle of the Bulge. This was close, hands-on fighting which took place over a period of some 32 days, mostly in the Ardennes forests between Belgium and France. These lush, thick, fertile forests were a terrible place to make war. The American forces were up against highly motivated, deeply entrenched German soldiers whose ferocious fighting acumen took a terrible toll on the American soldiers. There were some 80,000 Americans killed, maimed or captured during the campaign; 19,000 were confirmed dead. It was on this bloody stage, man killing man, that James Hunt was severely wounded. As he made his way across an open field, he was brought down by machine-gun fire. All around him, men lay dead and dying, their blood being quickly absorbed by the fertile soil. James looked up to the sky and cursed in anger. He didn't want to go down like this, lying there injured, helpless, as his buddies continued towards the enemy. At first, there was no pain; the natural endorphins of the body kicked in. But soon a hot, angry pain bit into his legs and all James could do was grit his teeth and wait for help.

After a long, torturous convalescence in hospitals both in Europe and stateside, James Hunt was confronted with a life-changing reality. Because of the injuries to his legs, his knees, he could no longer box, his doctors told him. This was a hard blow for a man who had been in superb physical condition all his life, who was endowed with the natural athleticism of an Olympian. Yes, with therapy he could walk all right, but running full out was impossible.

With boxing no longer an option, Jim turned towards the only occupation that interested him – law enforcement. When he heard about a new federal agency whose job it was to stop the sale and use of illegal narcotics, his interest was piqued. He saw an opportunity

to get in with a meaningful, well-funded federal agency and begin
from the bottom up. He saw a way to contribute positively to society.
Jim Hunt viewed drugs as the scourge of society. He knew women
prostituted not only themselves but also their children for drugs. He
knew men robbed and stole and even murdered, without conscience
or remorse, for drugs. The name of this new agency was the Federal
Bureau of Narcotics (FBN). He joined the FBN and, through
diligence, hard work and a keen, fair sense of what was right and
what was wrong, James made a lot of arrests.

As well as being physically superior, James was a particularly bright
man, a deep thinker, an intellectual who was a voracious reader. He
also had a photographic memory, could remember the names and
dates and places of most all his arrests. It was uncanny. He was the
sharpest knife in a drawer filled with sharp knives. In the FBN, James
Hunt was able to put all these talents to use, and he quickly rose up
the ranks. He was admired and respected by not only his colleagues
but also his bosses. They saw in Hunt a rare individual who had both
street savvy and an abstract, intellectual approach to bringing down
bad guys, drug dealers – mafiosi.

Gangsters had learned, during Prohibition, that providing goods
and services outlawed by the government could be very lucrative.
They began to think of narcotics as they had once thought of illegal
alcohol. There was a huge demand for substances that took away
pain; for substances that made you feel good, for substances that
added lust and fuel to sex. Cocaine became known as an aphrodisiac.
Heroin took away all ills, pains, discomforts – failures in life. Men
and women, America's youth, were dying all over the country because
of drugs.

It didn't take long for organised crime, for the Mafia, to see the
great moneymaking potential in illegal narcotics. In that the Mafia
was already deeply immersed in all things illegal, it wasn't a far throw
for them to not only pick up the ball, but carry it and run far as
well. Through the American Mafia's connection with mafiosi in

Sicily, contacts were made to get heroin from Turkey to Sicily and, ultimately, to the United States for distribution.

These Italians developed amazingly ingenious ways to bring heroin into the States, disguising it in cans of olive oil, in crucifixes and tall religious statues. They turned pure heroin into moulds of candied fruit, painted and coloured and sculpted perfectly. Suddenly, the United States government was facing a heroin epidemic coming out of not only Sicily, but all of Italy. Starting in 1956, the Mafia realised that Canada would be an ideal place through which to get heroin into the country. There were thousands of miles of un-policed border, desolate forests, slow-moving rivers.

As the Mafia's tactics for narcotics trafficking evolved and became more sophisticated, James Hunt found himself at the epicentre of the war on drugs. He made arrests of major men in the Mafia, personally putting the cuffs on Carmine Galante, a very dangerous war captain in the Bonanno family, a bona fide psychopath. Along with his partner, Frank Waters, Jim arrested the head of the Genovese family, Vito Genovese. Genovese, a tall, gaunt, dead-eyed man with high cheekbones and a wrinkled, hard face, was fond of a particular steak restaurant in Germantown, on East 86th Street. He often ate at this restaurant. James Hunt and Frank Waters managed to have a Puerto Rican informer by the name of Nelson Cantaloupes convince a Genovese captain that he was on the up-and-up, one of them, cut from the same cloth. In turn, the captain brought Cantaloupes to meet Genovese at the restaurant. Genovese gave Cantaloupes his blessing to sell drugs, as Frank Waters and James Hunt sat at the bar watching them, the restaurant crowded. The two government men blended in as well as the bottles behind the bar. With this observation, Genovese was arrested and sentenced to ten years hard time, though his heart gave out before his time was up and he died in prison, forlorn and forgotten – a very angry man.

As a part of this same case, Hunt and Waters arrested an up-and-coming Mafia star, a former boxer named Vincente 'the Chin'

Gigante, who, in years to come, would be made the infamous head of the Genovese family.

Shortly after the arrest of Vito Genovese, James Hunt hooked up with a new partner. His name was Arthur Mendelson, a quiet, unassuming man but as tough as rusted barbed wire. Together Hunt and Mendelson were an extremely effective combination. Both Second World War veterans who had been wounded in battle, the pair became known as 'Death and Destruction' throughout the agency. James Hunt was also known as 'Jim Hurt', for when perps tangled with Hunt, defied him, got tough with him, they were, inevitably, hurt. Jim's reputation grew by leaps and bounds. He became one of the most respected and revered men in the history of the FBN, which by that point had been renamed the BNDD (Bureau of Narcotics and Dangerous Drugs). As the battle to keep illegal drugs out of the country, out of the hands of the weak and needy, out of the hands of the addicts raged, the BNDD was expanded by Richard Nixon in 1973 and renamed yet again: the Drug Enforcement Administration, better known as the DEA. The DEA was well funded, focused and had the support of both parties (Republican and Democrat). Any politician who wasn't supportive of the war on drugs would be committing political suicide. Both liberal Democrats and conservative Republicans lined up behind and supported the DEA.

Here, for the first time, was an agency whose sole purpose was to stop the importation of drugs, the sale of drugs, the distribution of drugs. This was no easy task, and the amounts of money at stake were colossal. For the most part, the men and women of the DEA were straight shooters, but the temptation to steal was great. There would be, sometimes, millions of dollars in crates and paper bags there for the taking. There, too, would be hundreds of pounds of cocaine, heroin, tons of marijuana – all tempting agents who had mortgages, often struggling to pay the bills, feed their families. However, compared to police departments in large cities across the country, other federal agencies, the DEA garnered a very good reputation.

It was their job to extinguish the firestorm of drug abuse that had spread across the country over the last several years. It was no longer a disenfranchised group of society that delved into drugs – musicians, blacks, those on the down-and-out. Now drugs were becoming popular, indeed fashionable. As the appeal of drugs increased, so did the demand for them. Bold men with bold plans, unafraid of the punishment, unafraid of being arrested, saw the opportunity to get rich and went for it.

One of the more notorious of these individuals was one Frank 'Superfly' Lucas, a large, strapping black man from the south, by far the most successful, dangerous drug dealer in New York – in fact, in America. He was cagey and surrounded himself with killers and good attorneys. He also killed anyone he thought might be an informer before they ever had a chance to talk. He managed to develop a trusted relationship with the Gambino crime family. They supplied him with all the heroin he could sell. The Gambinos, in turn, secured the heroin from the Bonanno crime family. In January 1975, Frank Lucas finally went down. James Hunt helped orchestrate and put together the extensive investigation against Lucas and was there the blistering cold night Lucas was arrested at his home in Teaneck, New Jersey.

Busts like Lucas and Gigante helped Hunt rise to be second-in-command of the DEA's office in New York, but there was always more work to do. More dealers to catch, more people who belonged behind bars. For every Frank Lucas who was caught, there were a dozen others waiting in the shadows to take his place.

THE APPLE DOESN'T FALL FAR FROM THE TREE

Though he had become one of the most talented lawmen in the country, Jim Hunt Sr always remembered a valuable lesson he'd learned from his father: Jim did not bring his work home to his wife and three kids in Cambria Heights, Queens. Jim was a family man, and he kept his home life and his work life as separate as possible. Still, he did let his children know about the perils of drugs. He did let them know the difference between right and wrong. He was not overly strict, but he kept a close eye on his two sons, Jim Junior and Brian. The Hunts also had a daughter, Colleen. She had strawberry-blonde hair, was attractive and people readily warmed to her. She would later become a very popular on-air reporter in the New York metropolitan area. She was tenacious and always seemed to ask the right questions.

There was one time, Jim Hunt Jr remembers, when he and some friends had got very drunk on cheap wine called Boone's Farm. When Jim stumbled in that evening, his father was there. All he did was make sure his son got to bed and stayed put. The following day, however, Jim Senior bought a whole case of Boone's Farm and put it in the basement. He told his 16-year-old son that he could go in the basement with his friends and drink all the wine he wanted to, drink to his heart's content. He said, 'If you've gotta drink like that, do it at home. I don't want you drinking and getting drunk on the street like some forgotten bum. You get your friends and you drink here.' Still hungover, Jim Junior was not at all interested in drinking, but he took a good lesson about public intoxication away from this incident.

Like his father, Jim Hunt Jr excelled at sports. He was a natural-born athlete, particularly well coordinated, had a thin, muscular physique that responded well to all types of sports, including boxing. Jim Senior had taught his son the rudiments of fighting early on. He told him where to place his feet, how to throw a left and how to throw a right with maximum effect. He also, perhaps more importantly, taught him how to avoid a punch by moving his head.

Several times, at a local club Jim hung out at – Dizzy Duncan's in New Jersey – there were fights and brawls. Inevitably, Jim got involved in these altercations and broke them up, pulled combatants apart. Before he knew it, he was offered a job as a bouncer. The money was good, his friends were there and he had access to girls . . . lots of girls. What made Jim stand out was that he was always cool under pressure, his head seemed to rise above the fray. He was particularly good at talking guys out of fighting one another, though, if need be, he was just as adept at knocking out people who wouldn't listen to reason. Jim Hunt was about reasoning – not brawling.

As weeks and months went by, still living at home, Jim began to think seriously about a career other than as a bouncer; he couldn't help but think of law enforcement. After all, his grandfather and father, as well as uncles and cousins, were all cops who were highly respected and honoured by their friends and colleagues. The more Jim thought about law enforcement, his getting between the bad guys and the innocents, the more the job appealed to him. He thought about what branch of law enforcement he would join and, like his grandfather, cousins and uncles, he decided on the NYPD. He knew, too, in the NYPD he would have good health benefits and an excellent pension plan. He also knew that he'd quickly rise up through the ranks. It was no secret that Jim was particularly bright and knew the ways of the street well. He had no doubt that in due time he'd be giving orders instead of taking them; that he'd make sergeant, lieutenant and captain quickly. At that juncture in his life, Jim had no desire to get married or have a family. He saw the rudiments of married life as something that were not, at that point, for him. Women readily took to him, though; they sensed the goodness in him. They, too, felt that he could be trusted. Plus he had a glib tongue and a constant twinkle in his eye when he was around pretty women. He was, in a word, charming.

Jim Hunt went and spoke to his father, and his dad thought Jim's turning to law enforcement was an excellent idea. Jim applied to the New York Police Department, took the physical and began the six-month course at the New York Police Academy on East 20th Street, looking forward to the prospect of serious police work in the great city of New York. To Jim, New York was the heart and soul of the world and he looked forward to protecting society from its degenerates, miscreants and criminals. On his way to the academy, as Jim read about different crimes in the newspapers, he was appalled at how women and children were put-upon, beaten and battered and raped. This was during the height of the drug epidemic that was plaguing the United States, and street crimes were off the charts.

Jim excelled at the firing range. He became a crack shot. He knew the .38 revolver the police department issued was a tool of his trade, a tool that could save his life, his partner's life . . . an innocent's life. Every week, he spent extra hours at the pistol range, perfecting his shooting prowess. When, towards the end of the course, Jim was asked where he'd like to be placed, he purposely picked one of the toughest known precincts in all of New York City: the 34th Precinct in Washington Heights. Jim was not about to go through the motions. He wanted to be in the epicentre of where crime was happening on a large scale, to be in the action. When he started at the 34th Precinct, he was assigned to walk a beat, precisely what he had wanted.

With his fair skin and red hair, Jim Hunt stuck out in Harlem like a carrot in a cabbage patch. He had a pleasant baby face, a warm, beguiling smile and he quickly made acquaintance with shop owners and residents on his beat, many of whom would become his friends. Jim knew good police work was, to a large degree, about having your ear to the ground, having informants, having both eyes wide open. He let the word be passed all along his beat that he would welcome information about crimes and keep the source a secret. Like this, little by little, Jim heard about robberies, assaults, drug deals, murders and unspeakable sex crimes. He began to shine. As well as being clever, easy to talk to, easy to warm to, Jim Hunt was fearless. Often he'd make an arrest by himself without a second thought. He had a gun. He knew how to use it well. And he was very good with his hands. Yet if he needed back-up, he'd call for it. He knew a good partner was worth his weight in gold.

As much as Jim liked police work, walking the beat, he came to realise that his opportunities for promotion were inherently limited at the NYPD. Jim began to think of leaving the force. He heard through family that there were positions open in the Secret Service, so he went to their offices at One World Trade Center, took the exams and passed with flying colours. Next he had to be interviewed by a senior Secret Service agent. These interviews established if any given individual was adequately qualified to be in the Secret Service; that is, capable of protecting the president and other political luminaries of the United States. A senior agent named Jack Sullivan interviewed him and said, 'Jim, I like everything about you. You did great on the test. You're the kind of guy we're looking for, but I don't know if you'll like the job. I don't know if we are what you're looking for.'

This caught Jim off guard. 'Why is that?' he asked.

'Jim, what we do is not hands-on. I'm telling you this as a friend, as though you were family – what we do is all about waiting, watching. What I think you're used to, what I think you want is to be in the action, to be out there making arrests, chasing down bad guys, running over rooftops.'

Jim Hunt smiled. 'Well,' he said, 'you're right.'

'Well, Jim, that's not what we do,' Jack repeated.

Jim Hunt thanked him and the two men parted. As Jim made his way down the elevators, his mind went towards the DEA, his father's home turf.

Jim Hunt Jr was soon enrolled in the four-month course given by the Drug Enforcement Administration at Quantico, Virginia. His class trained alongside the new class of the FBI. The DEA and the FBI were sister agencies. Though they were supposed to be working harmoniously, hand-in-hand, they were often at odds with one another, competing with each other to see who could piss the furthest.

Though Jim was only 26 years old, he was serious beyond his years. Jim knew the job was about life and death, but that did not distract or dismay him in the least. He concerned himself with doing the job well. At the DEA Academy at Quantico, there were plaques to commemorate agents killed in the line of duty. These men were thought of as heroes, but to Jim they were heroes and more – they were good, decent family men who had been struck down and killed before their time, for all the wrong reasons.

Jim was a natural loner. He had come to rely on himself, his own resources – he was brought up that way. His father had taught him to deal with life's twists and turns with his own two hands; he had taught him to think on his feet.

Jim was anxious to get out of the Academy and hit the streets. He had no idea where he'd be assigned as such, for the DEA had offices in pretty much every major city in the world, but he hoped to be assigned to New York. He still viewed the Big Apple as the heartbeat of the world – and its tarnished soul.

After Jim had finished his classwork, his wish was granted when he was assigned to New York. He immediately began working out of the DEA's office at 555 West 57th Street, just off 11th Avenue. It was a large white office building with a car dealership on the ground floor – innocuous. The DEA occupied just three floors in the mostly commercial office building, but from these three floors they were fighting a multitude of battles in the war on drugs. Here, strategies were put together; here, groups were assigned to fight on different fronts.

Jim Hunt took to the DEA like a duck to water. When he first arrived, he was assigned to Group 33. Comprising handpicked, serious, seasoned DEA agents, Group 33 had seen and done it all – it was the place to be. They were on the frontlines, in the trenches, in the war on drugs, the best of the best that the DEA had to offer. These were dedicated, highly motivated men and women who believed in their hearts that drugs were the undoing of society – an evil tantamount to the plague. Of all the different groups in all the different DEA offices in all the world, Group 33 was by far the most successful. They moved at 200 miles an hour. Ran on high-octane fuel. They had a singular purpose in mind and they had become particularly good at carrying it out.

It was no secret who Jim's father was and he was greeted warmly. At this juncture, his father was literally a hero in the DEA, a legend within the agency. Jim had some big shoes to fill, but that never entered his mind. He was not the kind of man who would compete with his own father. He would do his best and let the chips fall where they may. However, Jim Hunt was particularly suited to the DEA: he was street smart, quick-witted, personable and genuinely tough. He was also a consummate actor.

One of Jim Hunt's first cases was the infamous Pizza Connection Case, which involved hundreds of players, all of whom were mafiosi, the majority of whom hailed from Sicily. From the year 1975 to 1984, the Sicilians cleverly, diabolically brought some $1.6 billion worth of heroin into the United States. Always shrewd, always audacious and deadly, taking advantage of whatever situation presented itself, they began selling heroin across the length and breadth of the United States. Many of the players, coincidentally, owned pizza places, thus the operation became known as the Pizza Connection Case. One of the busiest locations was Al Dente's Pizza in Forest Hills, Queens. Here, you could get a slice or a Sicilian piece of pizza, veal Parmigiana and meatball heroes, calzones and zeppolis, and amazingly pure Turkish heroin.

Jim was brought in towards the end of the case. Working shoulder to shoulder with Group 33's veteran agents, Jim learned quickly. Through the ingenious, clever use of wiretaps, surveillance, infiltration and informants, the DEA, with the help of local police jurisdictions and the FBI, put together a monumental, airtight case that would end up with 18 out of the 22 defendants convicted. These were no small, would-be mafiosi. There were major players involved, cunning Mafia superstars, including family heads Gaetano Badalamenti and Domenico Lo Galbo. One of the reasons the prosecutors managed to get so many convictions was that they turned the boss of bosses, the Caruso of the Mafia – Tommaso Buscetta. He was, by far, the most important mafioso to ever become an informer. He knew more about the intimate workings of the Mafia than most of the five bosses put together. Having someone of his stature, importance, with his amount of knowledge regarding the inner workings of the Mafia, was a groundbreaking event; it would teach prosecutors a very good lesson. They came to know that if they could manage to get the heads and bosses of any given family to talk, they, the prosecutors, could bring down the whole house of cards.

This case opened Jim's eyes to the workings of the Mafia and how dedicated and diabolical his adversaries were. He came away from the Pizza Connection Case with a sense of satisfaction; he had accomplished something important. Had the heroin the DEA intercepted made it to the street, thousands of lives would have been marginalised, squandered, lost. Little did Jim Hunt know that he would soon be up against an adversary, a monster of the night far more evil than any of the mafiosi associated with the Pizza Connection Case. There were dark skies, thunder and lightning just over the horizon swiftly moving towards Jim Hunt.

6

CHERRY BLOSSOMS
AND SAMURAI

Tommy Pitera loved Japan. He especially liked how polite the people were to one another, and their thoughtful approach to food and art – but particularly their mindset regarding martial arts. Here was a society, a culture, a way of life that had been founded on the samurai, the ultimate machismo culture. Though the samurai were long gone and forgotten, their way of life was still very much a part of modern Japanese thinking. In a very real sense, the Japanese's success in business, their world domination of business, had to do with the samurai approach to life, to work. The Japanese thought of themselves as a superior people; they thought of themselves as smarter, wiser and more resilient. Through the consistent application of intellectual pursuits, higher education and the samurai way of thinking, they believed they could conquer the world.

The world, as such, got a foul-bitter taste of the samurai warlike thinking when the Japanese attacked China's Manchurian Province in 1931. We witnessed barbarism on an unprecedented scale, unspeakable torture and rape and murder the norm. Arrogantly in broad daylight, in squares all over Manchuria, shaking, quivering Chinese were beheaded. This was not done in secret, in forgotten places or prisons. It was done defiantly, openly, for all the world to see and know. Chinese women were systematically turned into prostitutes to satisfy the Japanese soldiers' cravings for sex. However, there was no quid pro quo. The women received nothing but brutal rape after brutal rape after brutal rape. The Japanese soldiers felt they had an inherent right; that they were samurai and they could take from and do whatever they wanted to whomever they pleased. It became a known fact that the Japanese soldiers turned their libidos on the young; the raping of prepubescent girls and boys, the sodomising of them, was the norm, brutally real.

The great expatriate writer Pearl S. Buck documented in her unforgettable novel *Dragon Seed* the destruction of a Chinese family at the hands of Japanese soldiers and how a seven-year-old boy in the family was repeatedly raped by a group of soldiers. The young boy grows up to be a fierce partisan fighter.

There was no rule of law. No country interceded, stepped in and tried to stop the daily brutality. Year after year it went on, fuelled by the twisted interpretation of the samurai way of thinking. In 1937, Japan attacked China on a full scale, all-out war. Unchecked, unchallenged, the Japanese now conquered the whole of China, a huge country with an enormous population. The Japanese gleefully raped and stole and pilfered as they went. They were like a plague of locusts that left nothing alive in its wake. All was dead.

The Japanese began to believe that they were – *invincible*; that they were above the laws of men. This, fused with the samurai belief system, made them a very dangerous foe. They were without conscience and remorse, and took great pride in their brutality, in their indifference to life.

When, on 7 December 1941, the Japanese bombed Pearl Harbor, they did so truly believing that they could, surely would, beat America at war. Again, fused with the samurai way of thinking, they believed that the Americans were soft, that they would not fight, that they would quickly give up and Japan would control North America. The Japanese obviously underestimated not only America's resources but also America's willingness to fight. In reality, when the Japanese attacked Pearl Harbor they awakened a 'sleeping giant', they awakened a fighting machine the likes of which the world had never known. As the two countries fought horrific battles all over the South Pacific, it became obvious that because of the samurai code the Japanese would never give up, that they would fight to the death. An outgrowth of the samurai culture was the kamikaze – a fighter pilot who gladly steered his plane into enemy ships. They were able to do devastating damage to Americans. It did not come about so much because of the bomb-laden planes the Japaese flew but because of the mindset of the kamikaze pilots, who gleefully gave up their lives. An enemy only too happy to die was a difficult adversary. In Washington, it was decided that the only way to end the war would be to drop atomic bombs; it was commonly believed, understood, that the Japanese would never give up unless they absolutely had to.

This warlike mindset, obsession, the Japanese had would not allow them to give up. Thus America dropped two atomic bombs, one on Nagasaki and one on Hiroshima, quite literally blowing the samurai belief system into oblivion. Faced with this overwhelming, devastating power, the Japanese finally surrendered – unconditionally.

After the Second World War, a new way of thinking swept over Japan. The Japanese became a society of pacifists. They had no army; they wanted no army. They became a world power again not through military prowess but through financial genius. The samurai culture reared its head again, but this time it was applied to business rather than war. For many Japanese, it was still something to be revered and proud of and so the direction of this belief system took a new path; it became part of an individual's or corporation's mantra rather than an army's. Martial arts schools opened and flourished across Japan.

Japanese martial artists became world famous, held in high esteem and thought of as rock stars.

It was into this modern take on the samurai culture, into this world, that Tommy Pitera entered when he landed in Japan. What drew Pitera to this place, to this mindset and culture, was the steely, stoic warlike approach to life the samurai not only lived but also embraced with all their being. In a sense, the samurai warrior was a mirror reflection of old-school mafiosi – respect, honour, bravery were all intricately woven between these two spartan, warrior-like mentalities. Pitera thought little about what the Japanese did to the Chinese in the Second World War. What drew him to Japan, what drew him to the samurai way of life, was the Japan of old; the Japan where men lived and died by the sword. He was there to study martial arts. He was there to make the world of the samurai warrior his. He would become a samurai warrior; he would be fearless and remorseless and unbeatable. Invincible. The killer in Tommy Pitera had flown halfway around the world to find a comfortable place to develop, grow, learn. Here the dragon would find nourishment and sustenance – become a dangerous creature of the night.

Wide-eyed and innocent, though with war on his mind, Pitera showed up at the martial arts school in Tokyo, Japan. He studied under Japan's most revered senseis. Every day Tommy showed up at class and worked out with a fervour and dedication that were religious. Seven days a week, he fought with his hands, his feet and various Japanese weapons: tonfa, nunchucks, bos and katanas. His muscles, which had been toned already from his years of training, became rock hard. His facial features changed. His cheekbones became higher. The teenage fat melted off his face; it became more angular and defined. His stick-straight black hair grew even longer and contrasted with his blue-grey eyes, making him an unsettling sight.

Though his effeminate voice stayed with him, nobody made fun of him. Here, Pitera was respected and thought of as a champion athlete, a fighter. Pitera ate mostly fish and rice and seaweed, and there was little fat on his body. For entertainment, he read voraciously, books about war, martial arts – how to kill. He read about where to stab and slash and cut for the maximum effect. He studied killing people the way a dedicated student involved in physics studies numbers. He became obsessed with not only winning every fight he fought but also winning decisively, irreversibly – killing his enemies.

For the first time in his life, it seemed like he had discovered a place in the world where he fitted in. When it was time to go, he wasn't ready to leave and instead went to work in a chopsticks factory to help underwrite his stay and make ends meet. His mother and her sister Angelina Bugowski came over to visit him. They were both impressed by the change in his physical appearance, how he had matured, how much he had grown and how much he thought of the Japanese culture and people, his grounded sensibility. Now when Pitera fought in tournaments, he always won. Even his sensei shied away from him in fights. When he hit people, he broke bones, traumatised flesh and muscle and sinew, left his opponents covered in black and blues – contusions.

Like all championship fighters, Pitera inevitably began to think of himself as invincible. He no longer walked, he strutted, head high, shoulders back, his chest out – defiant. Now, it was he who looked down on people; now, he was an alpha male, a predator, a burgeoning dragon.

Tommy Pitera became so absorbed in his life in martial arts, in the culture of Japan, the days went by unusually fast. In no time, the young man had been there some 27 months. He had learned everything he could, developed himself into a fighting machine. His muscles were much like those of a thoroughbred horse; it looked as though steel cables were alive under his flesh.

Still, he was not sure what he wanted to do with his life. Could he make a living at martial arts? Perhaps he could open a martial arts school, though he was not the type that had either the patience or inclination to teach. He was, by nature, self-centred and was not apt to teach what he had learned through hard work, blood and sweat.

Tommy Pitera knew it was time to come home, time for him to return to Brooklyn. Even he, back then, there in Japan, had no idea he would end up one of the most feared assassins the Mafia had ever known – a capo in the Bonanno crime family, a killer who would take a place of honour – infamy – in the Mafia's hall of fame.

7

THE BONANNOS

The history of the Bonanno crime family goes back several hundred years, beginning in Castellammare del Golfo in Sicily. Back then, the Bonannos were men of 'respect'; educated, wealthy landowners – not a ruthless gang of killers and thugs. They were a family that comported itself with heads high – with pride.

In 1903, Joseph Bonanno emigrated with his family to Brooklyn, New York. A particularly bright, ambitious young man – hard-working and not afraid to take chances – Joseph Bonanno quickly made a go of it in his new country. He was a tall, good-looking, affable individual, though tough when necessary. Through family connections, he met the higher-ups in La Cosa Nostra. The organisation was then thought of as a group of Italians who banded together to prosper, to make a living, to benefit their families in what they viewed as a hostile, unwelcoming society. It was no secret that Italians were not allowed in unions, that Italians were thought of as an ignorant, backward people who ate too much spaghetti, drank too much wine, were oversexed and gruff. There was such open animus towards the Italian immigrants that the Statue of Liberty became known as the

'Statue of Spaghetti' because steamboats coming from Italy had to pass the statue on their way to Ellis Island. Even the venerable *Herald Tribune* regularly referred to the Statue of Liberty by this slanderous nickname.

Through these connections, Joe Bonanno became involved with Salvatore Maranzano, a seasoned, scheming, extremely tough mafioso. In the young Joe Bonanno, Maranzano saw a particular brilliance, a ready willingness to follow orders, a willingness to do whatever he was told, a willingness to put La Cosa Nostra before all things – no questions asked. He was, Maranzano knew, a rising star with tremendous potential. In 1929, a bloody war broke out between Joe Masseria and Salvatore Maranzano. The conflict, which became known as the Castellammarese War, claimed many lives. Joe Bonanno fought diligently and well on Maranzano's side. Ultimately, Masseria was murdered with the help of Lucky Luciano and Tommy Lucchese.

With the guidance and good business sense of Lucky Luciano and Salvatore Maranzano, the New York Mafia was divided into five families: Mangano, Maranzano, Luciano, Profaci and Anastasia. Luciano and Maranzano devised a clever plan in which the different crime families would be given different territories and rackets that they would run autonomously, as though successful corporations. The Italians were inspired by men like Henry Ford, Carnegie, Rockefeller and Joe Kennedy, who they thought took hold and manipulated circumstances to their advantage.

Luciano, however, was not happy with the way Maranzano had divided up different rackets and, moving with the lethal speed of a rattlesnake, struck and killed Maranzano. To people in the know, it seemed inevitable that one of these two men would kill the other. There could be only one boss of bosses; there can only be one alpha male in a wolf pack, and so Maranzano went down. The fact that Joe Bonanno was able to work well with Luciano after he had killed his mentor spoke volumes about him. Bonanno was not about revenge –

was not about getting even. Though revenge was surely in his Sicilian blood, he saw the wisdom of peace; he saw the wisdom of looking the other way and forgetting what Luciano had done.

Peace reigned. Everyone prospered.

The outlawing of liquor, Prohibition, had enabled all the five families to make staggering amounts of money. Joe Bonanno quickly managed to develop a large network of stills and distributors. In a short period of time, he became a very wealthy man; to him, the selling of alcohol was no big deal. He believed if men wanted to have a drink, they had every right in the world – that was their business. The fact that it was an illegal substance meant little to Joe Bonanno.

Narcotics – cocaine, heroin and marijuana – were outlawed very much like alcohol had been. La Cosa Nostra initially saw nothing wrong with supplying society's need for narcotics. For them, it was just an extension of bootleg alcohol. After all, Joe Bonanno was quick to point out, Joe Kennedy – a pillar of the community – was a bootlegger, yet no one pointed a finger at him, called him names or prevented him from becoming an ambassador to England. Indeed, years later, when Joe Bonanno wrote his memoir, he used a picture of Joe Kennedy in the book, likening himself to what Kennedy had been – a bon vivant, a man of the world.

More than any other Mafia group, the Bonanno crime family dealt in drugs, and they did it more openly and defiantly than any other borgata. With his deep roots going back to Sicily, Joe Bonanno had little difficulty finding sources for high-grade heroin in nearby Turkey. With the help of Sicilian counterparts and, later, French gangsters out of Corsica and Marseilles, Bonanno and his contemporaries discovered clever new ways to bring heroin into the United States.

In 1956, Joe Bonanno travelled to Italy. He had with him his top capos, including Carmine 'Lilo' Galante. Bonanno was received in Rome as though he were a highly respected ambassador from the United States. Red carpets were laid out for him. Bonanno and his entourage then travelled to Sicily and there he was embraced as though Italian royalty. Dressed to the nines, he posed for the local media like a movie star. He and his entourage stayed at the Grand Hotel et des Palmes, where they wined and dined like kings. Nothing was too good for them – the best food, wine, grappas and champagnes. The black prince of the Mafia himself, preternatural Lucky Luciano, joined Bonanno and company and over a four-day period, working day and night, the logistics of exactly how heroin would be brought to the States were perfected.

Bonanno put feared, psychotic street capo Carmine Galante in charge of bringing heroin into the States via Canada. After their trip to Italy, Galante went to Canada and set up a network based in Montreal that enabled the Bonannos to get their hands on all the pure heroin they wanted.

They made a fortune. Let the good times roll. Heroin spread across the country like some insidious disease that showed no mercy, that destroyed everything in its wake. In all walks of society, heroin users became mere shells of who they had been: women and children were sold for the drug; desperate junkies would sell everything that wasn't nailed down. They robbed their own mothers without a second thought or conscience. People were found dead on New York's Park Avenue, as well as in tenements and on tobacco roads throughout the country.

Washington lawmakers could not help but see and know and feel the problems in their district, in every town and city and state. There was a clamour for change. Newspaper editorials from California to New York demanded more stringent laws. The public outcry was such that politicians could not ignore their constituents and much stricter laws governing the importation and sale of heroin were quickly and with little debate enacted.

Initially, the Mafia had thought of heroin as they had thought of alcohol. The Mafia misunderstood the way the law, the courts, Washington would respond to the selling of heroin. The penalties for selling narcotics were far stiffer than they had been for bootlegging; the penalties were now as harsh as, or even more so than, those for murder.

With the change in laws, La Cosa Nostra was forced to re-examine, take a closer look at the issue. The full Mafia Commission, comprising the heads of each family, had a meeting to decide whether or not they should deal in drugs as a group. Ultimately, it was decided that they would not deal in drugs because the penalties were so stiff, the punishments so severe that sooner or later their kind would turn on one another – cannibalise each other – they knew. In theory, this was a wise decision; however, many men in La Cosa Nostra did not adhere to this mandate. Vito Genovese, Carmine Galante and The Chin Gigante were all arrested for dealing in heroin and sent away with stiff sentences. Genovese got ten years, Carmine Galante received twenty years and Vincente the Chin ten years. None of these Mafia superstars ratted anyone out – they stayed stoic and silent and did their time. Even though La Cosa Nostra's members faced serious time behind bars, retribution from their contemporaries, they continued to deal drugs. The profit was enormous. It was nearly impossible for them to look the other way, especially when they saw other ethnic groups throughout the tri-state area selling drugs and becoming filthy rich.

Too tempting to ignore, selling drugs became something La Cosa Nostra did 'off the books'. Any given individual who was made, who was a mafioso, could sell drugs, but he had to do it covertly, secretly – *off the record*. Captains and consiglieres, underbosses and bosses all took the money and looked the other way, acting as though they were deaf and dumb and blind.

They saw nothing wrong with what they were doing.

The Bonanno borgata was the only family that openly defied the Commission, the other families. The Bonannos were a large family and had many tough soldiers and war captains – the baddest of the bad. None of the other four families would challenge the Bonannos because they knew it would result in a long, bloody war. It became a kind of laissez-faire situation. The Bonannos sold drugs. Everyone acted as though they weren't. In reality, the Bonannos were doing, more or less, what everyone else in La Cosa Nostra was doing, just more openly, defiantly . . . brazenly. The Bonannos – feared, prosperous, and powerful – were always looking for good men.

Such was the state of affairs in 1976 when Tommy Pitera boarded a 747 in Tokyo, Japan, and returned to the United States, returned to Brooklyn's Gravesend/Bensonhurst; his home; his roots. Here, the Bonannos were deeply entrenched. Here, they had social clubs. Here, their soldiers, lieutenants, capos and bosses lived, brought up their children, bonded, married, celebrated holidays and prospered. Here is where they lived out the American Dream.

PART 2

KILLERS FEAR HIM

8

THE GREEN HORNET
AND THE BONANNOS

In the 27 months Pitera had been living in Japan, he had matured considerably beyond his years. This was no longer a frail boy trying to overcome various inferiority complexes. He was now a confident man, opinionated, well read in the history of war; well read in the destruction of human beings. While in Japan, he had not only studied martial arts using fists and feet of fury but had also mastered the different accoutrements. Tommy Pitera's hands were now weapons. His feet were weapons. However, more important than anything was his mindset. He was, he had become, he had moulded himself into a killer. He had come to view killing, the martial arts, as a literal art form. There was no room in this art form for conscience, sympathy or remorse. Consistent with the samurai way of thinking of old, Tommy Pitera had become a remorseless killer of men.

Oddly enough, he showed tremendous deference and respect to women – his mother, his sister, girlfriends. They were all treated well by Pitera. He was no longer shy, quiet and withdrawn. He no longer blended in with the furniture. Now he looked people directly in the eye and walked with his head high – stoic, hard-jawed, dragon-eyed.

He thought about what exactly he would do in life, how he would make his living. Pitera wanted the good things life had to offer: a fancy home in a nice neighbourhood; he wanted his parents to be proud of his achievements; he wanted his friends to look up to him. With no family connections, trade or particular business training or acumen under his black belt, Tommy Pitera's prospects were minimal. Again, he thought about teaching martial arts, thought about opening his own school, but this did not excite or interest him beyond an occasional fleeting daydream.

Inevitably, Tommy Pitera came to a crossroads. One road led to the dry, mundane destiny of his father; the other road, red with blood, led to power and riches, respect and adulation. Born and raised in Gravesend, Tommy Pitera was known and readily accepted by the mafiosi who saturated the neighbourhood. The respect and trappings mafiosi had as a matter of course were things Pitera wanted. How could he not? The straight life was not for him. A nine-to-five gig, for him, was anathema. The thought of taking the subway to work every day was . . . nauseating. Naturally enough, given who he'd become, what he was about – the fire-breathing dragon within – he began hanging out in mob bars, social clubs and restaurants in Gravesend and Bensonhurst and there rubbed shoulders on a regular basis with Mafia soldiers, lieutenants, captains and even bosses. They warmed to him – he warmed to them. It was no secret that he was a martial arts expert, and soon Tommy Pitera became known as 'Tommy Karate'.

Mafiosi have an amazing penchant for giving one another nicknames. Some of these names are hilarious: Sally Socks, Vinnie the Nose, Vincente the Chin Gigante, Anthony Gaspipe Casso, Vinnie Beans, Sammy the Bull, Vinnie Gorgeous, Anthony Bruno Whack Whack, Carmine the Snake, The Mad Hatter, Kid Blast Gallo, Crazy Joe Gallo, Lilo Gigante, Sonny Red Indelicato, and on and on. These names were also a good way to hide the true identity of any given mafioso; they confused the cops, they confused the FBI. But amongst themselves, they all knew who they were.

In order to become a made man in any of the New York crime families, you must take an oath, on a saint, swearing allegiance to the crime family above all other things – even one's own family, parents, wives, children. There are also a knife and a gun on the table at which the oath is made. In addition to the made men, there is an outer core of men known as associates, who actively work with the Mafia. Associates are protected by the family they are involved with; they are, in a sense, surrogate members of the family. If any given associate does particularly well, exhibits loyalty, dedication, willingness to follow orders blindly, that associate could very well be nominated to become a fully fledged made man.

One of the made men that Tommy Karate Pitera began hanging out with was a deadly, erratic psychotic killer – one Anthony Bruno Indelicato. It would be Indelicato who would open the door into La Cosa Nostra for Tommy Pitera. Bruno was one of the premier killers in the Bonanno family. He killed so readily, with such aplomb and such ease, that he actually became known as Whack Whack. Bruno was tall and thin and muscular, had a dark complexion and a large beguiling smile that seemed to stretch from ear to ear. Women were readily drawn to him. Contrary to Bruno's good looks, he began balding prematurely – when he was in his mid-20s – and had difficulty coping with the loss of his hair. This stone-cold killer, who shot, stabbed and beat people to death, was more concerned with his hair loss than the terrible destruction he wrought upon his many victims. He had an abundance of vanity, but no conscience . . . no morality. Hair, for him, represented masculinity and virility. In fact, he was so preoccupied by his hair loss, so put out by it, that his constant complaints to fellow mafiosi drove them nuts. Bruno was one of the first people in the New York tri-state area to get a hair transplant, but it didn't work. As well as having developed an inferiority complex regarding his hair, regarding his appearance, Bruno was a dedicated cokehead. This was a very dangerous thing for a made man to be.

The Mafia, as a whole, viewed drug users as unreliable, potential trouble, weak links in a carefully put-together, very strong chain. Bruno came from a family with close Mafia ties. His father, 'Sonny Red' Indelicato, was a respected capo in the Bonanno family, while his uncle, Joseph, was also a capo in the Bonanno family. As a result, people looked out for Bruno and constantly warned him to stay away from drugs. He kept promising he would and he dutifully went to rehab. Upon his release, he was as handsome as a movie star and as charming as a seasoned car salesman. However, Bruno would go back to his old ways – snorting and smoking cocaine, while acting completely out of control.

Bruno's drug use did not deter Pitera from pursuing a friendship with this erratic killer. Bruno and Pitera were very tight and quite fond of one another. Together they made for a volatile mixture, to say the least. One could readily liken it to mixing arsenic and cyanide. Bruno and Tommy were cultural contemporaries, both of them blindly dedicated to the rules and laws and mandates of La Cosa Nostra, not society.

Fuck society!

Fuck its rules and regulations. These two lived to a different beat, a rhythm they heard only in their heads.

With Bruno's assistance, blessings and encouragement, Pitera became a Bonanno associate. Pitera was eager to please, and others in the family quickly took a shine to him. He had all the right moves, comported himself perfectly, said all the right things. With Bruno's support, Tommy Pitera earned his bones (committed a murder) and killed for the Bonanno family. Dismemberment, the taking apart of bodies for easier disposal, was one of Bruno's specialities. Inspired by Bruno, fused with the amazing, innate knowledge that Pitera had of bodies, of taking them apart, of where to cut and where to saw and where to separate trunk from limb, victims of the Bonanno crime family were soon being neatly cut into six pieces and buried in forgotten lots and flatlands around Brooklyn.

THE BONANNO VAMPIRE

Through Bruno's friendship and affection for Tommy Pitera, Tommy met all the luminaries in the Bonanno crime family – Joe Massino, Anthony Spero and all its capos. Spending time with these men and learning from their ways, Pitera began to fuse the samurai mentality that he had developed in Japan with the Mafia mindset. The Mafia's amazingly violent, unique forms of machismo and the samurai's deadly precision created a highly lethal and dangerous combination, setting the stage for a tragedy of Shakespearean proportions.

As much as Pitera liked Bruno, he saw in him a potential for trouble on a monumental scale. Bruno's drug abuse had become legendary. Pitera, at all costs, would avoid the trappings that Bruno Indelicato had got himself into; he would never, he vowed, become a drug addict; he would never, he vowed, let a chemical steal him away from his goal: becoming a highly respected capo in the Bonanno family.

At this point, Pitera had come to believe that his future would be with the Bonannos, and he warmed to the idea. He viewed them as a lean, mean fighting machine. He was particularly fond of Bonanno bosses Joe Massino and Anthony Spero, thinking of them as omnipotent, protective, surrogate fathers. Unlike his own father, who was an easy-going man, willing to accept his lot, they were men who took life by the throat and made it what they wanted it to be. They were bold. They were forthright. They were a success. They were both feared and respected. In that Pitera had been born and raised in Gravesend – was a true neighbourhood boy – he had been readily accepted, trusted by the Bonannos. He was one of them, coming from the same mindset, gene pool.

Now, when people crossed the Bonannos, when murder was necessary, Pitera was dispatched and he made people disappear with incredible precision, acumen and expertise. People died. Pitera embraced his role as assassin the way a great actor would embrace playing King Lear or Macbeth, even dressing the part when necessary. To fool his adversaries, to blend in, Pitera took to dressing as an Orthodox rabbi. Guised like this, he was able to get near his marks and strike them dead before they knew it. When the guise of a rabbi wasn't appropriate, he would dress as a woman and kill men looking for romance, who instead got a bullet to the head, cut up and buried in forgotten places.

Throughout the Mafia, Pitera was garnering a reputation as an assassin extraordinaire. Now when he entered a room, people looked and pointed and spoke in respectful, hushed whispers. As the Bonannos were deeply immersed in the selling of drugs, it didn't take long for Pitera to become a sleek, swift, dangerous vessel for the distribution and sale of heroin and cocaine.

THE PERFECT STORM

J im Hunt's boss, Fred Sandler, asked him if he would go talk to a new entering class. 'Tell them what to expect; tell them what we're about. Don't pull any punches. Tell it like it is,' Sandler said. As ordered, Jim went and spoke to the rookies. He explained how the agency's modus operandi was based on infiltration and surveillance.

'The best thing you can do is find people who want to cooperate. You bust Joe on Monday, he offers to help, the following Monday you're arresting two other guys. You can compare it to a spider's web: it starts in the centre and it goes around and around and around, and the wider it gets, the more people we bring down; the wider it gets, the more tentacles we have. The more tentacles we have, the more arrests. We are about arrests. We are about bringing down the bad guys. We have one job and that's arresting drug dealers!' Jim said.

There were a few questions and the meeting was over. As Jim was about to leave, one of the men approached him. Glancing up at the large smile on his face, Jim instantly recognised him. It was Tommy Geisel, a bouncer that Jim had worked with years before at Dizzy Duncan's nightclub in New Jersey. Geisel was a large, strapping man, fast-moving and nimble on his feet, muscular and strong as a Brahma bull. Like Jim Hunt, Geisel wanted to be a federal agent, wanted to help in the war on drugs. Together they had fought with patrons who drank too much, who wouldn't listen to reason, who were intent upon being violent. When these patrons came up against Jim and Tom, they inevitably ended up being knocked out.

'Jim,' Tommy said, smiling. 'Remember me?'

They shook hands and embraced. Jim wished Tom luck at the academy, said that when he graduated, he'd recommend him to his group – Group 33 – if he liked. Even Tommy, who wasn't yet an agent, knew what Group 33 was about, knew he wanted to be a part of what they were: the action, the real deal.

When, after the four-month-long academy programme, Tommy Geisel was ready to be assigned, he reached out to Jim Hunt, reminded him of their conversation. Jim immediately went to his boss and told him about Geisel, told him that he thought he'd make a 'very good' agent. 'The guy's got it all,' Jim said. 'Brains, balls and brawn.'

'Trust him with your back?' Sandler asked.

'Absolutely.'

With that, Tommy Geisel was soon assigned to Group 33 and wound up as Jim Hunt's partner – and like this the Perfect Storm was formed.

In preparation to work the streets, work cases, both Tommy and Jim radically altered their appearances. They were all about blending in, getting bad guys to trust them. Jim grew his hair long and sported a funky, rust-coloured Fu-Manchu moustache. He wore jeans and cowboy boots and could pretty much blend in anywhere. Tommy, likewise, grew his hair long, a scruffy beard and took on the guise of Dennis Hopper in *Easy Rider*. Like this, Jim and Tom went out into the world, its streets and avenues, and made arrests. They were soon the most successful team in Group 33.

ARMED, DANGEROUS
AND AGGRESSIVE

The esteemed, controversial head of the Bonanno crime family, Joe Bonanno, was in retirement. He had bought a particularly comfortable, spacious home in Arizona and lived there with his family, staying out of the daily hands-on running of the crime family. His old street capo, Carmine Galante, who had been arrested by Jim Hunt's father, was nearly finished with 12 years of his sentence and was soon to be released on parole. From prison, he had been insistently ranting and raving, threatening and demanding, saying that he was going to kill Carlo Gambino. Gambino had become the boss of bosses, a very powerful man. Galante had no fear of him. Galante sent word from prison: 'I'm going to make him suck my dick in Times Square.'

Carmine Galante was an out-of-control, bona fide psychopath. He had no conscience, scruples or reservations about blowing the brains out of either a real or imagined foe. When his old nemesis, Frank Costello, died, Galante ordered his mausoleum blown up, from jail. While in prison, Galante was examined by a psychiatrist, who diagnosed him with 'psychopathic personality disorder' – an understatement.

The network of dedicated thugs that Galante had put together had no compunction about selling heroin and was still viable; the foundation he laid, at the behest of Joe Bonanno and Lucky Luciano, was so strong and well put-together that it was still up and running. These were men who, at another time, might have been strikebreakers, bootleggers, killers. Interestingly, it was not only they who were at Carmine Galante's beck and call, but also their brothers and their cousins – relatives through marriage. In other words, in order to belong to this fraternity, you had to be a relative or go back many years.

From jail, with a vengeance that bordered on obsession, Galante planned his comeback, the engine of which was heroin. He planned his becoming the boss of bosses. He was going to sell heroin – openly, boldly and without reservation. Fuck the other families. Fuck the DEA. He was willing; indeed he was happy to go against the dictates of the full Mafia Commission. He didn't respect them. He thought they were soft. In time, he planned to kill them all. As he paced his cell in Lewisburg, as he finished his last days in prison, he plotted in his mind the deaths of all the Mafia bosses – Philip Rastelli, 'Cockeyed' Philip Lombardo, Tony 'Ducks' Corallo and Carmine Persico. Fuck, he'd kill them all.

Like this, the stage was set for a monumental, bloody war that would rock the foundations of the Mafia from Bensonhurst, Brooklyn, to Castellammare del Golfo, Sicily. True to his word, when Carmine Galante was released from prison in 1974, he immediately went about putting together his plan. Within weeks, pure grade heroin was coming into the United States because of his connections in Sicily and Montreal and because of his fearless, audacious belief that he could do whatever the hell he wanted. Not only did he and his faction of the Bonanno family start openly selling drugs, but they also openly defied the mandates of the Commission.

'Fuck them,' Galante told anyone who would listen, his words echoing throughout Brooklyn like some kind of religious mantra.

Additionally, Galante began having members of the Gambino family murdered. Leaving no clues as to who was committing the killings, he brazenly brought down Gambino soldiers and captains. Meanwhile Carlo Gambino died of natural causes, in his sleep, disappointing Galante no end. 'The cocksucker wouldn't even give me the pleasure of killing him,' Galante told confidants.

Galante's intention was to eliminate the competition. It was no secret in La Cosa Nostra that the Gambinos were selling drugs – Carlo's brother Paulo was suspected of running the operation – nor that the Gambinos were bringing high-grade Turkish heroin from Sicily. This was, of course, all off the record.

The acting head of the Bonanno crime family, Philip Rastelli, was not up to the task of fighting Carmine Galante. Galante was as tough as a junkyard dog. He had come up the hard way. Born in East Harlem in 1910, he had first worked for Vito Genovese as his chauffeur and private assassin. Eventually, Galante began driving Joe Bonanno around and ultimately was made a capo de facto of the Bonanno crime family – a street boss. He acquired the name 'Lilo' because of his penchant for smoking Italian cigars known as 'guinea stinkers'. People in the know said that Galante killed over 50 people. People in the know said that Galante even murdered a cop. He kept his hair short and wore glasses. He weighed 155 pounds.

Always on guard, always expecting trouble, he went about the business of building a large heroin enterprise while plotting and planning the deaths of his enemies. He murdered as though he had a state-issued permit to kill. Galante was so out of control, attracting police and press scrutiny, that there was a sit-down of the crime Commission at which it was decided that he had to go. This would be the second time in the history of the American Mafia that the head of a family would be ordered killed; the first was Albert Anastasia.

People sent from the Commission approached Bonanno captain Alphonse Sonny Red Indelicato and told him that he was either with them or he was dead. They informed him of the Commission's decision that Carmine Galante had to go, that Galante was causing problems for them all; that if he didn't help, he would be taken out within 24 hours.

Sonny Red had been expecting this. The handwriting was on the wall in blood red. He was surprised it hadn't happened sooner. He knew which way the tide was moving; he did not have to be threatened or cajoled any further. He readily agreed to cooperate however he could with the killing of Carmine Galante. One of the men chosen to be a part of the lethal hit team put together to kill Galante was Anthony Bruno Indelicato – Sonny Red's son and Tommy Pitera's inspiration, mentor and friend.

A seasoned killer himself, Carmine Galante was not an easy man to bring down. He knew the dance of death; he knew not only how to protect his back but also how to avoid being put in a position where gunmen could readily reach him, hit him. He always travelled with several men who were armed and, he thought, loyal to him. As with most megalomaniacs, Galante did not realise his bullying and threatening and killing were coming back to haunt him: not only was the full crime Commission behind his murder, but all members of the Mafia in all places wanted him dead as well.

It was a particularly warm day: 12 July 1979. There were no clouds above Bushwick, Brooklyn. Galante chose to have his lunch that day in a trusted cousin's restaurant, Joe and Mary's. This was a good example of how Galante insulated and protected himself from would-be assassins – he was always wary. Bushwick, Brooklyn, was an Italian enclave. Most of the stores catered to the Italian community. There were Italian bakeries, pork stores, pizza places and restaurants all along Knickerbocker Avenue. The smell of fresh espresso, freshly baked bread and pizza seductively wafted through the air. In the pork stores, huge wheels of cheese, provolone and parmigiano enticingly hung in the windows.

Galante arrived for lunch with two of his men in tow, Lenny

Coppola and Cesare Bonventre. Bonventre was a traitor, a would-be assassin; he would make sure the hit went smoothly, on time. When Galante and his party entered the restaurant, waiters bowed and scraped and treated him like he was Italian royalty. This was a thing Galante had become used to and coveted, the deference he received as an elite mafioso. The garden was at the back of the restaurant. It was some 70 feet through the long, narrow room. Though the garden was not air-conditioned, it was shaded by large umbrellas. As is the Italian custom, Galante would eat his meal in courses. Towards the end of the meal, Cesare got up to make a phone call. Galante lit up a cigar.

Word was soon passed to the hit team that Galante was in place. With the quick, lethal expediency of a military operation, they were on the move. Soon a light-blue Mercury sedan, a stolen car, pulled up in front of the restaurant. There were three men in the car. They were Bruno 'Whack Whack' Indelicato, Dominick 'Sonny Black' Napolitano and Russell Mauro, all large, broad-shouldered men.

This was where Bruno Whack Whack showed his true colours, showed his amazing balls and audacious moxie, for when he stepped from the automobile, pulling down a ski mask as he went, he was carrying a full length, blue-black shotgun. It was a little after twelve noon. Shoppers crowded the sidewalk. Rubbery waves of heat rose from the ground. Cars and buses drove by. Bruno was the lead man. He acted as though he was invisible. Without reservation or hesitation, he and the hit team moved to the restaurant, grabbed the front door's handle and arrogantly walked in. They knew Galante was sitting in the back. They walked straight towards him, moving swiftly, as one, as though a robotic killing machine. Nothing could stop them now. They were invincible. Bruno was able to quickly discern Galante sitting in the yard. Patrons saw Bruno and the hit team, the guns they carried, and desperately scrambled to get away.[*]

* It should be noted here that Richard Kuklinski, aka 'the Ice Man', would later claim to have been involved in the Galante murder, though it turned out to be untrue.

Bruno was as tight as a coiled spring. This man was a professional killer. He did not feel nervous or frightened or scared. He knew this murder would resonate throughout Mafiadom; he knew, too, that this killing would bolster his reputation as a man of respect. He also knew he would be made a capo for what he was about to do.

Galante saw them coming. Guns were drawn, raised, pointed. With a thunderous roar, Whack Whack Indelicato cut loose with the 12-gauge shotgun. The other members of the hit team also fired shot after shot after shot. Whack Whack fired again. Carmine Galante went down in a heap of torn flesh and broken bones, never to rise again. Also killed were his cousin Giuseppe Turano and his zip bodyguard Leonard Coppola. The attack was so sudden and violent Coppola never had a chance to draw his weapon. As Galante lay there, his glasses askew, he still had the cigar he was smoking clenched in his teeth – clenched in a death grip that would be memorialised in the most famous photograph of a Mafia hit ever taken.

Bruno and the hit team turned and, calmly, not running, made for the front door. Bruno carried his shotgun straight down. He let his right leg block it as he walked. It seemed a natural extension of his lithe body. They hit the sidewalk, took the seven steps to the street and arrived back at the car. Bruno opened the door, put the shotgun inside, grabbed the roof of the car and got in. Slowly, the car pulled away. Bruno and the hit team abandoned it in Gravesend, where it would later be found by police.

The jungle drums of the Mafia echoed loudly and insistently all that day and night. Word of Galante's murder spread far and wide with the speed of a bullet. Mob guys all over the United States, all over Italy, learned what had happened. Toasts and cheers were made. For them, for La Cosa Nostra, this was a good day. A proverbial thorn in all their sides had been removed, irrevocably and irreversibly. Again, La Cosa Nostra showed its killing prowess, showed that it kept a clean house, that it would even kill its own if need be.

Wide-eyed, though not surprised, Tommy Pitera heard about the murder, heard that his friend and mentor had been part of the hit team. Pitera was proud – proud to know Bruno, proud to be his friend.

A short time later, Bruno Whack Whack Indelicato showed up at the Ravenite Social Club in Manhattan's Little Italy. He had obviously been sweating and looked dishevelled, like he'd been through the mix. Boldly and with great audacity, he had been sent to kill, to wreak havoc – and kill he had. FBI agents watched surreptitiously from rooftops and vans as Bruno was greeted by not only fellow Bonanno crime family members but also half a dozen Gambino members. This was an oddity. This immediately proved to law enforcement that the hit on Galante was a collective effort – a cooperative killing. The bad guys all smiled. They kissed and hugged Bruno Indelicato. Even the second-in-command (underboss) of the Gambino family was there, Aniello Dellacroce, and he hugged and he kissed Bruno Whack Whack with obvious respect and admiration.

Whack Whack was the man of the hour. Whack Whack was a hero. Whack Whack had lived up to his name in a large way. His father could not have been more proud of him. All the mistakes Bruno had made with drugs and his erratic behaviour were forgotten. With this one deed, the slate was wiped clean. He was the Mick Jagger of the Mafia. With good cheer, laughing, patting one another's backs, they all went inside, disappearing into the black hole that was then the Ravenite Social Club.

Salud!

Salud!

Salud! could be heard over and over again as passers-by moved in front of the club.

The following morning, on the front page of every newspaper, was the shocking black-and-white, amazingly graphic image of Carmine Galante lying there dead, with half a cigar clenched in his teeth and his glasses all crooked. The big badass Carmine Galante was no more – the wicked witch was dead.

Unlike the common misconception, mafiosi are very open and candid, bragging about who killed whom, when, where and why. They could be likened to old women talking over the backyard fence. They seem to take it for granted that if they talk amongst themselves it will go no further.

Pitera marvelled at the newspaper reportage of the very dead Galante. He marvelled at the audacious aspects of the murder. This was so foreign, so unlike what he had been exposed to in the Far East in Japan. There was nothing subtle or delicate or discreet about the murder of Galante. It brought home just how brutal, though effective, the way of La Cosa Nostra was. This murder, and the secretive, violent underground society of La Cosa Nostra, drew Pitera further towards it, the culture, mindset, walk and talk. More than ever he wanted to be not only a part of it but also an important part, a central part. He knew if he comported himself with pride and dignity, acted as though he was a man of respect, they would be drawn to him. You cannot go knocking on the door of any given capo and say, 'Let me in.' They must see you and like what they see; you have to prove yourself. It didn't take long for Pitera to get a chance to do just that.

Murder is the only way to become a made man. Murder is the one thing all mob guys have in common, a secret bond. There is no statute of limitations on murder and at any given time anyone who kills can be culpable in the eyes of the law, no matter how long after the crime. Taking that into consideration, it was easy to understand why La Cosa Nostra demanded blood on the hands of anyone who took the oath of omerta. If they broke their oath, if they betrayed their colleagues, they were vulnerable and culpable, more than likely dead.

When it ultimately became time for Pitera to earn his bones, he was given a name, address and photograph of the mark. Without reservation, he shot to death a man on a residential Brooklyn street. He didn't know who the man was. He didn't care. He was told to commit the murder and he did it, coldly and efficiently. He felt no remorse – no guilt. It was business. A way of life.

After Pitera committed this murder, he was one of them. Until he was sworn in, however, he would not officially be a made man. He could now work with the Bonanno crime family, was an extended part of it – though not an official member yet. He was an official associate. If there were disputes involving him, the family would back him. If there were sit-downs involving him, the family would back him. Pitera was no longer a lone alpha wolf trying to satiate himself; he was now part of a clan, part of a pack of wolves who would protect him, watch his flank and watch his back. That is, if he behaved, if he toed the line.

Bruno Whack Whack Indelicato would hasten Pitera's career considerably. After Whack Whack had committed the Galante killing, he was given his own borgata and made a capo. This was a reward for a job well done. Whack Whack was now, throughout La Cosa Nostra, a superstar. He had audaciously killed Carmine Galante in broad daylight.

As stone-faced Brooklyn homicide detectives questioned all the patrons of Joe and Mary's, questioned the people on the streets, bus drivers, shop owners, cab drivers, they kept coming up with blank stares, as though all the people of Bushwick were deaf and dumb. The people of Bushwick all knew who had been killed and the last thing any of them wanted was to be involved in the murder on any level. Many had seen who had got out of the Mercury sedan, but none would say who it was. The killing of Galante seemed, at first, like the perfect hit. But its brazen attitude rubbed the men and women of the NYPD – in high and low positions – the wrong way. The murder had been committed with such hubris, was so in-your-face, that they felt personally affronted and offended.

'How dare these guinea cocksuckers think they can do something like this and get away with it,' was the utterance heard throughout station houses in New York. With an unusual vigour, the NYPD went looking for Galante's killers. They didn't have to look far. They soon learned that Bruno Indelicato, Russell Mauro and Sonny Black Napolitano were part of the hit team, and Galante's associates, Cesare 'CJ' Bonventre and Baldo Amato, were in on the plan, but proving their involvement was another matter. Initially, the police believed that Sonny Red had paid to have Galante killed. This would turn out to be false.

As the cops were trying to solve the murder, the rest of the Bonanno family was preparing for war. Galante was barely in the ground before people began vying to fill the void his murder had left in the organisation. Sonny Red was part of one of the factions that would soon be at war for control of the Bonanno family. Philip Rastelli, temporary head of the family, was on the other side. War lines were drawn in the sand.

Everyone had hoped the transition would be smooth but Rastelli, presently being kept in the federal house of detention, was intent on keeping control of his position in the family and would not acquiesce to the crime Commission's mandates.

Born on 31 January 1918, Philip Rastelli was a stubborn man who refused to see the reasoning of not only the crime Commission but also most all of the Bonanno capos. Having said that, it wasn't long before they were shooting at each other, killing one another.

The last thing anyone in La Cosa Nostra wanted now was a protracted, bloody war between different Bonanno factions. There were numerous sit-downs between Bonanno captains and other families all over Bensonhurst. Try as they might, the collective effort of La Cosa Nostra seemed to be failing and still more dark clouds filled with lightning and thunder gathered over Brooklyn, gathered over Gravesend, Bensonhurst and Dyker Heights.

One of the more powerful men in the Bonanno family, Joe Massino, more than anyone, some say, tried to avoid war, tried to work hard for peace. But each of the Bonanno captains was strong-willed and obstinate, and refused to walk the path of diplomacy, refused to listen to reason, even though there was more than enough to go around.

Massino, with the help of the Gambinos – John Gotti's crew – resorted to war, and hit teams brought in from Canada set up and murdered Alphonse 'Sonny Red' Indelicato, Philip 'Phil Lucky' Giaccone and Dominick 'Big Trin' Trinchera. They were buried, somewhat haphazardly, in lots in an undeveloped area of East New York near Queens. This was unprecedented in the history of La Cosa Nostra. Captains were akin to generals and three noted, talented generals all struck down at the same time was news – an event.

What happened next was an interesting illustration of just how cooperative Mafia families are with each other. When it was time to get rid of these three captains, a van was driven by Joe Massino and associates to Howard Beach. There they met Gambino members Gene Gotti – John's brother – Fat Angelo Ruggerio and John Carniglia. Carniglia was a gorilla of a man and no doubt was brought along for his digging talents. Soon, graves were dug in lots between Ozone Park and East New York and the three Bonanno captains were unceremoniously laid to rest. One of the bodies, that of Sonny Red, was found a mere 19 days later in a lot at 1 Ruby Street in South Ozone Park. He had on a $5,000 Cartier watch. The bodies of Dominick Trinchera and Philip Giaccone were not found until 2004.

It didn't take long for Bruno Whack Whack Indelicato to learn that his father had been taken out. Bruno had been very close to his dad. They were, in a sense, more like best friends than father and son. For Bruno, the loss – the methodical, treacherous murder – of his father was the most traumatic experience in his life. He was a pressure cooker about to explode, but even he, a stone-cold killer, knew he could do nothing to avenge his father's death. If he so much as lifted a finger in retribution, he'd be dead in a New York minute.

The news of his father's death brought home the hardcore, bloody reality that Bruno himself was in danger; he had no doubt that hit teams were actively searching for him as well. Bruno, along with his good friend Tommy Pitera, hightailed it out of Brooklyn and they barricaded themselves in a secluded house way out on the edge of Long Island. Pitera had brought with him an army duffel bag filled with guns. He was dedicated and he was loyal to Bruno and he would fight to the death on Bruno's behalf. Meanwhile, word was sent out that if Bruno was willing to let go of what happened, he could continue running his borgata and do his business without trouble from the new regime. As a secretive, surreptitious dialogue went back and forth between Bruno and Joe Massino, Pitera methodically cleaned and oiled his guns over and over again. Ultimately, an agreement was worked out, and Bruno and Pitera were welcomed back into the fold.

Cocaine.

Bruno Whack Whack Indelicato wound up finding solace and comfort in cocaine. It wrapped him in a warmth of numb indifference and took him to another place far removed from the mean streets of Gravesend and Bensonhurst. He moved to Miami and there, with different girlfriends, stayed holed up in his house for days on end on long, protracted cocaine binges.

While Tommy Pitera empathised and sympathised with his friend's loss, he ultimately lost respect for Bruno because of his drug addiction. In the world of La Cosa Nostra, the excessive abuse of drugs and/or alcohol was tantamount to a cardinal sin, a potential death sentence. Though most all mafiosi in their 30s, 40s and early 50s dabbled in drugs, few, if any, of them were serious drug abusers. Once more, those around Bruno began to view his drug habit as a serious problem, a liability that was a one-way ticket to the grave. Theirs was a world where men had to be sharp, at the top of their games, lean and mean and ready to strike at the bat of an eye. Drugs, everyone knew, made you stupid and unreliable.

With the changing of the guard and a new faction taking over the Bonanno family, Tommy Pitera rearranged his alliances. He came to the attention of powerful underboss Anthony Spero. Spero was a large man with dark hair, a dark complexion, good-looking in a rough way. He was respected by most everybody. It was hard not to like Spero; he was fair, smart and exceedingly well versed in the ways of the street. Surprisingly, one of his more lucrative enterprises was fireworks. He had huge warehouses of them and made $4–5 million annually just from their sales. On Bath Avenue, every 4 July, Spero would put on amazing firework displays. He spent several hundred thousand dollars on fireworks to be blown up there in the streets. The cops looked the other way. Not only did he supply the fireworks for free, but he also gladly provided enough food to feed all of Bensonhurst, and feed all of Bensonhurst he did. Later, John Gotti would try to co-opt and copy what Spero had done, but his firework shows paled in comparison to the earlier displays of generosity and patriotism.

Not only was Anthony Spero liked and respected by the people within the confines of the Bonanno clan, but all the captains of all the families also knew him and liked him, respected him. He was particularly close to war capo Greg Scarpa, of the Colombo family. He was very close to Anthony 'Gaspipe' Casso, superstar of the Lucchese family. Spero was about diplomacy, building bridges, though when murder was called for he would readily and quickly push the button.

With the death of Sonny Red Indelicato and the loss of Bruno into a storm of cocaine, Tommy Pitera became closer to Anthony Spero. It was ultimately Spero who would allow Pitera's dream to come true: the thing that Pitera wanted more than anything in life was to be made, to get a button, to be a bona fide member of the Mafia. Everyone liked him, respected him. The murders he was assigned had been carried out quickly and efficiently and he had kept his mouth shut about them. He was exactly what La Cosa Nostra was looking for. With the blessing of Anthony Spero, the books were opened and Tommy Pitera was nominated to be inducted into the Bonanno family.

Word was sent out to all the five families in the New York tri-state area; word was sent out to mafiosi across the country. 'Does anyone have any reason why Tommy Pitera shouldn't be made?' was the question asked. No one objected. Pitera had created a good reputation for himself.

The ceremony was held in a two-storey red-brick house in Bensonhurst, off Bath Avenue. Anthony Spero decided that he would place Pitera in the borgata of Bonanno capo Frankie Lino. Lino had Mafia in his blood. His brother, Eddie Lino, was one of the most feared men in all the Mafia, both in Sicily and in New York. He, too, was close to John Gotti, was in the Gambino family. It was said that Eddie Lino had personally killed more people than ten mob guys put together.

Frankie Lino was a pudgy individual with a high, broad forehead; his eyes, nose and mouth were too close to one another, as though they were rudely pushed together while he was still in his mother's womb. He attended Lafayette High School in the heart of Gravesend, Brooklyn. His marriage had been arranged for him by his parents and Vito Genovese.

By the day Pitera was made, Frankie Lino had become all grey, his hair so naturally curly that his nickname was, appropriately enough, 'Curly'. Consigliere Anthony Spero was there. Several men that were to be made were also present, all dressed to the nines. For them, this was being baptised, receiving communion and confirmation. This was what they had all wanted all their lives and it was about to happen. The ceremony, created in Sicily and brought over by immigrants at the turn of the twentieth century, was simple and to the point. Pitera, repeating the Sicilian pledge of omerta, swore that the Bonanno crime family would come before his own family. He swore, too, that if he violated this oath, he'd burn in Hell, as was a portrait of a saint now burning in his cupped hands. Pitera stood ramrod straight, his chest puffed out, his head high. He knew when he left that room no one would ever make fun of him again, no one would ever knock his high-pitched voice. Even now, standing there, reciting omerta, he was speaking in this distinct falsetto voice. If it wasn't so solemn and serious, it would have been outright comical to hear him talking like that – more *Saturday Night Live* than La Cosa Nostra.

With the ceremony completed, they shook hands heartily and kissed on the cheek, embracing one another. Afterwards, they all went out to dinner at a popular La Cosa Nostra hangout, Tommaso's, on 86th Street. There was no laughter, no patting on the back. It was a quiet, solemn dinner in which hushed toasts were made in hushed tones.

'Salud.'

'Chindon.'

Thus, the dragon was born.

12

GRAVESEND: THE CEMETERY

Inevitably when dealing narcotics, some people don't pay. They get caught up in the trials and tribulations of life and don't realise that the non-payment of drugs could very well lead to a death sentence. If, as was common knowledge, you fronted an amount of drugs that were not paid for, soon everyone would be doing it; soon the dealer would be out of business. To stay in the business, people had to keep their word, people had to own up to the agreements they made. No one believed this more than Tommy Pitera. He came to view the selling of drugs as though he were selling his own respect. For him, it became a very personal enterprise. If he gave you drugs and you didn't pay him back, you were stealing away his livelihood, you were stealing away the reputation he had worked hard and diligently to acquire. He took his place in the family very seriously. For him, his position in the family was something to be revered, not merely respected and spoken about in whispers.

According to those in the know, Thomas Salerno had taken several ounces of cocaine on consignment from Pitera. He paid a little late, though he paid. Pitera gave him more cocaine and, again, he paid a little later, but still paid. Pitera warned him about paying on time. Apparently what Pitera said fell on deaf ears, because the third amount of drugs Pitera fronted Salerno were not paid for. Pitera sent word for Salerno to come see him. He didn't come. When Pitera finally met up with Salerno, he managed to convince him to go for a car ride, which ended up with Salerno being shot in the head.

Pitera thought it would be funny to leave the dead Salerno in his car right next to Gravesend Cemetery. When the body was found by police, there was no connection to Pitera, but soon word spread on the street of exactly what had occurred and why; people in La Cosa Nostra nodded knowingly, as the police scratched their heads and wondered who had committed the murder.

Like this, Tommy Pitera began killing people who were not paying for drugs on time. He not only killed those he personally had fronted drugs to but he also murdered for associates of his in the Bonanno clan. He soon became the go-to guy for murder, not just within that family, but for all the families. With each murder, Pitera's reputation grew. Pitera became so adept at murder, comfortable in that guise.

Now, for the most part, Pitera wore all black. He shunned daylight, came out mostly at night, and his face grew pale and waxy. His light skin juxtaposed with his black clothing gave him a vampire-like appearance. He was quiet – sullen. This further fuelled the fear people felt towards him. This further fuelled the rumours that were being passed all over Brooklyn: that Pitera was a remorseless killer; that he was dismembering his victims, neatly cutting them up into six pieces, and disposing of them at various burial sites.

It was said that he had cleverly discovered that land in bird sanctuaries could not be disturbed; that building and construction would not be allowed. It didn't take long for him to put two and two together and realise that burying a body in such a place would just about guarantee the body was never discovered. It was also said, people in the know have recently revealed, that Pitera had an autopsy table in the basement of a building he controlled.

Pitera married a Brooklyn woman named Carol Boguski and had a male child with her. They named the boy Charles. This, however, was an ill-fated marriage and soon the couple separated. With the proceeds Pitera made from dealing drugs, he opened two bars: one in Cypress Gardens called Cypress Bar and Grill and another on Avenue S and West 8th Street called the Just Us Lounge. It was a residential street with few stores. More than being a moneymaking enterprise, it was a place for Pitera and his people to meet and arrange for drug sales; in reality, more a place to sell drugs than alcohol. That's not to say they sold drugs over the bar or out of the bathroom. Deals were consummated here. Agreements and handshakes were made here. The physical passing of drugs happened elsewhere.

Now when Pitera walked into a Brooklyn restaurant frequented by mafiosi, conversation slowed; people stared and pointed. Tommy Pitera had become what he always had wanted to be: feared and respected, a man not to be taken lightly. Pitera still practised martial arts, but now it was more to keep in shape, to keep well coordinated. He was a vain man and did not want to develop a stomach or jowls. He continued to read voraciously about killing human beings, war and destruction, and acquired books on how to dismember bodies. He diligently studied where to cut and slice, deepening his knowledge of how to neatly take apart a body.

BUY AND BUST

The war on drugs had not just heated up; it was now being fought at a feverish pitch. The Drug Enforcement Administration's Group 33 had never been so busy. They were up against some of the most devious criminals of all time, who hailed from Italy, Colombia, Mexico, Jamaica, Afghanistan, the near and Far East, Turkey and France. These were highly educated, highly motivated, particularly bright men who had ready, well-trained armies of cut-throats at their disposal. Modern business practices were perfected and scaled down to fit the drug lords' needs. They had scores of boats and planes, and even submarines. They were busy constructing tunnels that ran from Mexico for several miles into the United States.

The men and women of the DEA fought a heroic battle, tooth and nail, hearts and souls, but no matter what efforts they made, how many sacrifices they were willing to make, it was never enough. Drug lords were like mushrooms after a heavy rain: they popped up everywhere and you could not stop them. They were so effective that they literally created new words for the English language. As an example, the phrase 'Colombian necktie' meant that the throat was cut and the tongue pulled

out through the slit. It was a horrible, unsettling sight and would last
with whoever saw it for the rest of their lives. All the drug cartels, in their
own ways, were particularly dangerous; however, the most dangerous
were the Mexicans, Colombians and the Dominicans. For them, life
was cheap. Most all these individuals, all these drug lords, came up the
hard way, were from the streets, were ruthless in the extreme and they'd
kill you as soon as say hello to you. Murder, for them, was arbitration,
conciliation. Reasoning, for them, was a bullet to the head. Might was
right. When the Colombians wanted to kill one man, they would not
only kill him but also murder his entire family – men and women and
children – the very old as well as the very young.

Because they were able to use phoney passports and various forms
of identification, these were particularly hard adversaries to bring
to justice, for they were mobile, came in and out of the country as
readily as a turtle's head went in and out of its shell. Once the blood
was washed from their hands, they could go through customs with
impunity.

For Jim Hunt and Tommy Geisel, the war on drugs was a daily part
of their lives, an intricate part of who they were. For them, it was not
a newspaper article or a blurb on television. They, far more than the
public or press, knew the true, heinous nature of the fire-breathing
beast they were fighting. They saw the bodies, the crime scene photos.
They heard the stories in great detail about what occurred, how and
when.

Several times a month, the DEA would make huge busts. One
would think, considering the amount of drugs they confiscated, that
they'd slow the flow of narcotics, put a dent in it. Just the opposite
occurred. No matter how many busts they made, there seemed to be a
never-ending supply, mountains of drugs in far away places that were
cleverly brought into the United States using unsettling amounts of
imagination and creativity.

Hunt and Geisel worked so well together they could readily be
likened to a bow and a fiddle in a maestro's hands. They were not

only fearless but also, more importantly, street smart. From studying how colleagues were shot and murdered, they had learned well what not to do. Any bad guy that went up against Jim and Tommy was the one in danger. In Group 33 and all throughout the DEA, they became . . . famous – respected.

They were moving at 200 miles an hour.

'They were the best,' a former colleague by the name of Bruce Travers recently said.

On a regular basis, they made busts using professional informers and snitches, drug users and street people. Every night they were out on the street, looking to collar bad guys all over the tri-state area, looking to win a battle in the war on drugs.

Still, no matter how careful they were, with all the resources of the DEA behind them, people were hurt, killed. A good example of just how dangerous their job was, how they were truly putting their lives on the line, happened at 133rd Street and Amsterdam Avenue. This was an area known as a Dominican enclave. Of the three worst groups, the Colombians, Mexicans and Dominicans, the most violent at the time, the most apt to pull the trigger of a gun, were surely the Dominicans. They were less about business and more about overt brutality as a matter of course. They were thought of by the DEA as the most dangerous of all the bad guys they chased. Jim recently explained that he had busted Colombians with kilos on them and no guns, but Dominicans with two ounces and three guns.

Group 33 received word through a Colombian informer that some Dominicans he knew had kilos of cocaine to sell. This was a classic ploy the DEA used to catch drug dealers. It was called 'buy and bust'. Through negotiations that often went back and forth for days, weeks or even months, a buy was set up in which the DEA would provide money and bust the dealer, most often through an intermediary, an informer.

The Dominicans had rented a stash house in a tenement on 133rd Street. The drugs were supposed to be in the apartment. It was a little after midnight. The informer told Jim and his team, all-told eight agents, that the cocaine was in the apartment.

'Are you sure?' Jim asked, always wary.

'They say it's there,' the informer said.

Jim well knew that they could be running into a situation where the Dominicans were looking to rob them; that there were no drugs; that this was, in fact, a rip-off. It had happened before. DEA agents were killed in situations in which they thought they were buying drugs only to have the dealers turn on them, shoot them dead and steal the money.

It was a risk they would have to take that night. Would they be facing a compliant dealer or a dangerous predator? There was only one way to know for sure. The Colombian informer, Jim and Tommy and the rest of them knew, had proven himself reliable in the past. With that, Jim and his team headed into the tenement and started going upstairs cautiously, guns drawn. They were in plain clothes but had badges on chains around their necks. Unfortunately, just as they were moving up the stairs, the Dominicans were coming down. They were startled by the agents and hightailed it back up into the stash apartment. Jim and his people ran full out, got to the landing and burst into the apartment. As they went, Jim grabbed one of the Dominicans and brought him to the ground, cuffed him and handed him off in fluid, amazingly fast movements, almost as though it was a magic trick, all the while the agents yelling, 'Policia! Policia!'

Jim and Tommy Geisel now ran to the back of the apartment, looking to get the other two. In the far rear room, there was a window open and a fire escape. The agents could see a bad guy making for the window. Jim bolted forward and dived on the bad guy. Tall, wiry, very strong, every sinew and muscle in the man's body fought Jim as he continued to shout, 'Policia! Policia!' Wanting to end this quickly, Jim struck him on the head with his pistol, but the dealer furiously fought back, and their life-and-death struggle continued. The bad guy didn't acquiesce; Jim was forced to strike him over and over. The bad guy knew there was a hidden assassin whose job it was to kill, to kill indifferently, to kill efficiently, and the bad guy wanted nothing to do with the murder of a cop.

As Jim grappled with the man, Geisel had been searching the kitchen and now he moved back towards the bad guy. As Geisel went to help Jim, some ten steps away, DEA Agent Bruce Travers, a dark-haired Irishman with a muscular build, opened a closet door Tom and Jim had passed. At first glance, he saw nothing. He was about to close the door when he thought he discerned, in the weak light of the stash apartment, a human form and, suddenly, the outline of a gun – pointing at him. As he raised his own gun, there was a deafening explosion. The bad guy was low in the closet, pointing the gun up when he fired. He had in his hand a .357 magnum. The magnum's slug tore into the bottom of Bruce's jaw, drilled through his face and came out right below his eye. Bruce went down. He didn't quite look human any more. In the darkness and in the life-and-death havoc, Jim Hunt did not know who was firing.

'That us or is it them?' he called out.

The assassin in the closet now stood straight up. Though he had just shot a cop in the face, he was not finished. He could see from where he stood the doorway, and outlined in the hall light was the informer and two of Jim's guys. Without hesitation, he raised the .357, took a bead on the informer and fired. The informer went down, muscle torn and shredded, bones broken.

Tommy Geisel and Jim Hunt now aimed at the closet and opened fire with equal ferocity. Between the two of them they fired 21 rounds. In the small, hard confines of the tenement, the shots were loud and resonating. The assassin was hit three times. Neither Tommy nor Jim knew that a steel support pillar for the building had stopped most of their rounds. Had the pillar not been there the assassin would surely have been dead. As it was, he survived.

Jim Hunt was very fond of Bruce. He viewed him as a younger brother, an eager, trusted protégé. He was one of the nicest, most giving men Jim had ever met and here he was now, lying on the floor, a remnant of who he had been, his face destroyed, a large pool of blood surrounding him. Knowing that seconds mattered, knowing that Bruce's life was hanging on a thread, Jim and Tom picked Bruce up and seemed to fly down the stairs. An ambulance was summoned, but they could not wait. They knew in that time they could lose their brother. They put Bruce in the back seat of an unmarked DEA vehicle and sped over to Columbia Presbyterian Hospital some 30 blocks away, at points in time hitting 110 miles an hour. As they went, they called DEA headquarters, who in turn called the hospital, and word was sent that a cop had been shot – shot in the face.

When they pulled up at the emergency ward at Columbia Presbyterian, there was a team of a dozen nurses and doctors waiting for Bruce. He was slipping in and out of consciousness. He wanted so badly to tell them that he had another gun strapped to his ankle, that he didn't want to get shot while the orderly was taking it off, but he could not talk. His tongue was destroyed. His situation was so dire, his life precariously hanging by a thread, that doctors were forced to cut open his trachea, giving him a tracheotomy right there in the street. A plastic tube was forced down his throat and his lungs were given desperately needed oxygen. He drifted off into a coma-like deep sleep.

In no time, some 50 anxious, worried DEA agents had gathered at the hospital. They were as close as brothers and sisters and they stayed there all night long. Because of the brilliant efforts of the surgeons and nurses, Bruce's life was saved. Higher-ups in the New York office of the DEA arranged for a plane to pick up Bruce Travers' parents in Boston, where he was born and raised, and flew them and his brothers and sisters and fiancée to Teeterboro Airport, where they were taken in an SUV with a souped-up engine, sirens screaming, lights flashing, to Columbia Presbyterian.

When later that day Bruce woke up, he was in a fog, though he could make out his whole family gathered around the bed. His father took his hand. 'You're going to be all right, son,' he said. 'You're going to be all right.' Bruce had no idea how his family had so quickly been summoned, but he was grateful, deeply and profoundly grateful. He tried to talk but could not.

When in Washington DC President Reagan heard what had happened, he insisted on placing a call to Bruce. He wanted to talk to him. The phone at his bedside rang. Bruce's father answered. He was shocked to hear President Reagan on the other end. He explained that Bruce couldn't talk, so President Reagan told Bruce's dad that he was 'extremely grateful' for what he'd done, that he and Nancy sent their support and love and prayers. Everyone was very touched, very moved. Mr Travers thanked the president and hung up.

'It's a hell of a thing,' Mr Travers said to his son. 'A hell of a thing.'

Jim Hunt was deeply touched by what happened to Bruce Travers. He had become close to Bruce. Bruce had a wide-eyed enthusiasm; he was not a cynical, hard man who was a product of the streets like many with years in law enforcement. He was a gentleman, though a particularly tough, resilient individual.

The doctors told Jim and all his colleagues that Bruce was still in danger, and that he could still die. If he survived, he would have to undergo many operations, the doctors said, to regain a face similar to the one he had once had.

Many in Group 33 went to church and lit candles and prayed for their colleague, prayed for their friend. Bruce was liked by everybody. Just how truly heroic he was would not be made clear for some months, for the pain and the discomfort was just beginning. He still had 14 major operations ahead. When police ballistic experts recreated the shooting using triangulations of trajectory, they came to learn that the shooter had been crouched down and when he fired the .357 magnum the bullet had gone up into Bruce's lower jaw and burst out of his face, just beneath his eye.

As it happened, the assassin in the closet had been paid to do exactly what he did. His job was to shoot and kill anyone who tried to impede the selling of the cocaine. He, Jim knew, all the agents knew, was from another culture, another mindset. From where he hailed, the place he came, life was cheap; life was worth nothing. What struck them all as odd, though, was that he had known Bruce and all the rest of them were cops. They were yelling, 'Cops! Cops! Policia! Policia!' over and over.

Yet still he pulled the trigger, without a second thought.

PIZZA TWO

The Perfect Storm was out hunting again. Jim Hunt and Tommy Geisel were about infiltration, surveillance and arrests. Guised as street thugs, they were ideal partners. At any given time, Tommy and Jim were juggling numerous cases, different bad guys, different scenarios involving various drugs and ethnic groups. Any of these cases could be deadly, and they took necessary precautions – the best of which was to strike first. Neither Jim nor Tommy would allow a bad guy to get the drop on them. However, they were not about confrontation, not about being quick-draw cowboys. They were consummate con artists; they could talk the stripes off a running zebra. They, the Perfect Storm, were about gaining trust and getting bad guys to believe that they all came from the same place, were all outlaws.

Interestingly, most bad guys who dealt with Jim and Tom took a shine to them. They never bullied anyone, never called anyone names. They were always professional and polite and would go out of their way to do what they could. They knew, in the long run, they would create a network of individuals much more inclined to help them. It wasn't so much that Jim and Tom were nice guys; they were interested in developing informers and people who would 'assist rather than resist', as Jim put it.

One of the largest, most important cases the DEA ever had was created as a result of Jim Hunt smiling and being pleasant. This case was called the 'Pizza Two'. It involved the importation of heroin by Sicilians into America. It was called the Pizza Two because some of the players were the same individuals involved in the original Pizza Connection Case.

Jim and Tommy's involvement in the case was spurred by one Vinnie DeMarco. Vinnie was a maitre'd at the Embassy Terrace catering hall in Brooklyn, a place where mafiosi tearfully married off their sons and daughters. He was 55 years old, though appeared older, the skin on his face loose and sagging.

Vinnie DeMarco's son Benny had been fronted four ounces of pure heroin by one of these Sicilians. His name was Salvatore Canavo. He was a cold-blooded mafioso cut from the hard stone of Sicily, and a big heroin dealer. Canavo hung out on Bensonhurst, Brooklyn's 18th Avenue; he was one of the individuals who supplied heroin to the Gambino family. Benny was not a professional dealer; he was not a hardcore bad guy, and when he tried to sell the heroin, make a few bucks on the side, he was ripped off. He now owed some $75,000 to Canavo.

In sheer desperation, Benny turned to his father for help. Though his father was basically a working stiff, he still knew the way of the street. He loved his son dearly, knew his son had fucked up, and was intent on getting him out of trouble. He told Benny he would go to Canavo and tell him that he'd pay it off a little at a time, maybe $2,000 a month. Grateful, his son cried and held his father. With that, Vinnie DeMarco went and saw Canavo. He pleaded his case, said he would pay off his son's debt, swore on his dead parents' graves that he would make sure the money was paid. Canavo – cold, aloof, reptilian – said, 'Oh yeah? How about this . . . you owe me the money now. Your son's off the hook, but you – I want the money from you.'

Boxed into a corner, Vinnie DeMarco agreed to pay him off as soon as possible. Little by little, every week DeMarco brought Canavo money. Canavo kept a ledger book and every dime he got from DeMarco he'd deduct from the original amount. Problem was that DeMarco earned so little working at Embassy Terrace that Canavo became impatient. To help expedite paying off the debt, Canavo suggested to Vinnie DeMarco that he sell drugs. Reluctantly, DeMarco agreed. The sooner he got Canavo off his back, the better.

Canavo fronted DeMarco several ounces of heroin. Not knowing anything about the business, not knowing who wanted heroin, not knowing that the DEA had plants all over the New York tri-state area, DeMarco ended up selling the drugs to a DEA informer. Before he knew it, DeMarco was under arrest. He'd never been in trouble in his entire life. He was shocked and distraught and aged ten years. He cried uncontrollably in front of Jim Hunt and Tommy Geisel. When they checked his record, they realised he was a civilian, that he was a hard-working man. When they heard his story of woe, how his son had got him into this, how he had tried to protect Benny from Sicilian vipers, they felt bad for him. They offered him a deal.

Jim said, 'All right, look, we know you aren't a bad guy. We are going to give you the opportunity to help yourself. We want you to set up Canavo. Keep buying drugs from him. We'll provide you with the money. Record him, and whatever you do to help us, we'll help you in a big way.'

This was a golden opportunity for Vinnie DeMarco. He went about the business of setting up Sicilian heroin dealer Salvatore Canavo with enthusiasm. Canavo, in turn, said he would have someone who worked for him, Paulo Rizzuto, contact him and that he would provide all the heroin Vinnie needed. With that, Vinnie called Jim Hunt and Tom Geisel and told them what had happened, told them about Paulo. This is what Hunt and Geisel were always looking to do: parlay one person against another, and another, and another, working their way up the food chain.

Paulo came to the Embassy Terrace to meet with DeMarco. He had a heavy Italian accent, was a 'grease ball', as DeMarco would later refer to him. Without preamble or hesitation, Paulo assured DeMarco he could get all the heroin he wanted. That same week Jim arranged for DeMarco, Canavo and Paulo to meet at the My Way Lounge in Brooklyn. Jim wanted to see who this Paulo character was. Jim managed to have DEA photographers take clandestine photographs of both Paulo and Canavo. Now, for the first time, they realised who Paulo Rizzuto was: he was one of the original Pizza Connection participants who had managed to get away. This added a whole new element and sense of importance to what DeMarco had initiated.

Now Paulo began to supply DeMarco with pure heroin that DEA labs told them was high-grade Sicilian dope. It seemed Paulo had an unlimited supply. One night, Paulo showed up at the restaurant with still another Sicilian, a guy named Manny. Again, DEA photographers captured his likeness and within two days they knew his real name and identity and criminal background. They were shocked to learn that this was none other than Emmanuel Adamita. He, too, had been a major player in the Pizza One case. He had been arrested in both the United States and Sicily, and had miraculously escaped from both a Sicilian prison and an immigration prison hospital in Florida. This was a big fish, a great white shark. This, also, was a perfect example of how the DEA fought the war on drugs. They went from small fry to a great white shark.

Interestingly, Manny Adamita was directly related to Carlo Gambino's family, cousins of brothers John, Joseph and Rosario Gambino. Adamita had also once been a driver and bodyguard for Carlo Gambino. Now, suddenly, the DEA again had a major player in their sights. Rather than jump on him, collar him and haul him off to jail, it was decided that they'd keep working him and see where he led them.

Vinnie DeMarco continued to buy heroin from Paulo and Manny, and the case became more solid with every purchase, more solid with every day. DEA surveillance photographed Manny going into the Garage Sale café in Brooklyn, which was owned by Tony Spuvento, a member of the Calabrian Mafia known as 'Ndrangheta. Here, Manny said that the Gambinos were looking to buy large amounts of marijuana and they had people, 'good people', all over the country looking to cop. Vinnie immediately saw an opportunity to further ingratiate himself with the DEA, with the government.

'I've got friends who've got all the grass you want,' said Vinnie. 'They bring it up from Florida and the Carolinas.'

Manny was interested, and Vinnie said he would set it up. When Vinnie told Jim and Tom about this latest development, they were all ready with a plan that would further ensnarl Manny and company. The well-lubricated workings of the DEA kicked in and DeMarco was told by Jim and Tom to arrange for Manny to be brought to a hotel in Hilton Head, South Carolina, where he, Tommy and a third DEA agent by the name of George Ellin – the head of the DEA in Charleston at the time – would be waiting for them guised as major players in the pot business.

George Ellin was a tough-looking government agent with dark hair. He was a specialist, and his speciality was endearing himself to drug dealers. He knew the walk, the talk, the culture. He was often brought in to cases in different parts of the country to convince bad guys that they could deal with him and ultimately they would end up being brought down and sent to prison. If the DEA had a Sir Laurence Olivier, George Ellin was he.

The DEA always has 'props' ready for just such a case. They would use a confiscated speedboat that could go up to 110 miles an hour on the water and would have cost half a million dollars. They would use a warehouse filled with 20,000 pounds of high-grade marijuana. These were props that could convince the most cynical of drug dealers that Tom and Jim and George were major players, the real thing – trustworthy.

Manny readily agreed to go to South Carolina. They checked in to the Intercontinental Hotel. The room had a large terrace, where they had drinks. Both Jim and Tom were lounging around the pool, drinking and making it seem as though they were having fun, flirting with women at the pool. They took on the demeanour of carefree, wealthy pot dealers. Up on the terrace, George Ellin began his shtick, first talking about sports, the weather, fishing; it was good, he knew, to slowly work his way to the reason why everyone was there. While he was building a rapport with the Sicilian, he suddenly noticed – all an act – Jim and Tom down by the pool.

'Hey,' he called to them before turning to Vinnie. 'There's my nephew Tom and his pal, Jim. Good guys, really good guys. Come on, let's go down and have a drink with them.' Before Vinnie and Manny knew it, they were being shepherded downstairs by Ellin and were by the pool having drinks.

Between Jim, Tom and George Ellin, Manny didn't have a chance. It would be just a matter of time. But the game had to be played out until the last inning, at which point the DEA would hit a home run and the fugitive Manny Adamita and his cohorts would never see the light of day again. At the pool they drank, cracked jokes, talked about women and sports, how nice the hotel was, ogling women around the pool. Later that night they had dinner together. Of course, they took Manny and Vinny to the finest restaurant in the area. Manny drank so much he got sick. The following morning they talked about going fishing, but Manny had a horrific hangover. Still, he wanted to take a look at their boat. He was very impressed by it. He reluctantly agreed to go fishing. This boat was certainly not cut out for fishing, but it would be a way for the agents to get Manny to drop his guard further, for them to become closer to him. There were fishing poles, bait and lures and, in fact, they did catch fish that day. George Ellin offhandedly mentioned that they used this boat not for fishing but to transport marijuana from the outer islands to the Florida and Carolina coast.

Manny was, again, impressed. Jim, Tom and George Ellin were so convincing that he bought what they were laying down hook, line and sinker. Later that night, at dinner, the conversation turned towards marijuana. Manny said he needed a taste. They told him that would be no problem, that they understood. The following day, Manny and Vinnie headed back to New York. The trap was set and now they just had to place bait inside.

Back in New York, Vinnie continued to buy heroin from Manny, as Manny sent queries to his counterparts throughout the country about marijuana. He was now assuring his colleagues that he could get everybody all the high-grade marijuana they wanted. Tom, Jim and George wound up again meeting with Manny and DeMarco in New York. Now Manny wined and dined them in a restaurant in Little Italy and ultimately he said that he'd like Paulo to check out the grass. The agents had been expecting this; they were waiting for it. The Italians were taking the bait.

Several days later, in fact, Paulo came down to Tampa, Florida, and was met by Jim and Tom and taken to the secret stash house. However, before they took him there, they blindfolded him, to which he readily agreed.

'I understand,' he said. 'No problem.'

Inside the warehouse, which reeked with the sweet, pungent odour of sensimilla, Paulo's eyes grew wide at the sight of so much high-grade marijuana in one place. He was impressed; it was hard not to be. The screw was tightening. They talked about samples being delivered to New York. Jim readily agreed that they'd get him all the samples he needed. They shook hands, hugged and kissed, as is the Italian way. Paulo was again blindfolded and soon was on his way back to New York, where he assured Manny that these guys were on the up-and-up.

Now it was time for the government agents to get a sample to New York. Jim spoke to his boss Ken Feldman, who petitioned the upper echelons of the DEA to give Jim permission, because of an ongoing investigation, to bring 50 pounds of the marijuana, a bale of it, up to New York. Two first-class seats were arranged for Jim and the 50-pound bale on a commercial airline. With the necessary papers in hand, Jim approached the plane, asked for the captain and told him what was up. The captain looked at the papers and welcomed him and the marijuana aboard. Jim placed the bale in the seat next to him. So it wouldn't be bouncing all over, he strapped it in, and then strapped himself in. Passengers' eyes widened at the sight of him sitting there next to this huge bale of high-grade marijuana. People seemed to notice it because of the smell; it filled the first-class cabin. The plane landed without a mishap. Tommy met him at the airport, and soon Sicilians and Calabrians were smoking and sampling the marijuana. It was the best pot available and everybody wanted some.

Everything was going smoothly. Jim and Tommy had their sights on a bull's eye. Then, out of nowhere, there was a conference call in Miami between the FBI and the higher-ups in the DEA and it was decided that they were going to rush the closure of the case, shut the operation down in two weeks. Manny Adamita was far too important; they were afraid he'd get away. They felt that at this juncture, if he did disappear, it wouldn't bode well for anyone. They already had plenty on him and they wanted him brought down now.

Jim was not happy about this. He knew this decision was politically motivated – that the FBI was more concerned with gold stars and good press than seeing the case through to its natural ending. Jim and Tom felt that Manny would be able to bring them still bigger, more dangerous fish if they'd just give it some time; if they just let it play out.

Be that as it may, the order was irreversible, and both the FBI and DEA mechanised as swiftly as they could to bring down as many bad guys as possible. They were ready to pounce, all coiled muscle. There were numerous wiretaps up because of Vinnie DeMarco bringing Manny Adamita to Jim and Tom's attention and the potential for a substantial number of arrests was great if they played their cards right.

It was decided they should get as much bang for their buck as possible and Jim passed word to Manny via Vinnie that Jim and

Tommy wanted to buy a kilo of heroin. At this point, Manny was so at ease with Tom and Jim that he readily came to meet them with the kilo of nearly pure heroin. Jim and Tom had checked into a fancy suite at the Parker Meridien Hotel in midtown Manhattan. Manny was all hugs and kisses. He kept kissing them over and over again, as is the Sicilian way, told them it was great that they had met, that it was great to have friends you could trust, that the world was a rotten place and that they could all make money without worry. He kissed them again and again, often using the word paisan.

'So,' Jim said after a drink and too many kisses, 'do you have a package for us?'

'Sure, sure, yeah, I do. I got it in the car.'

'Well, you want to bring it up?'

'Sure, yeah,' Manny said and left to go get the package from the car, having no idea that he was about to walk into a lion's den. Agents followed him to his car and watched him get a package from his trunk then re-enter the hotel, get in the elevator and make his way to Jim and Tom's room, where he knocked on the door.

Jim opened the door and Manny walked in.

'Like I promised!'

Jim opened the package to make sure it was heroin and then came the moment when reality hit Manny Adamita like a lightning bolt. Jim Hunt turned to him, suddenly dour, and said, stern and strong and deadly serious, 'Manny, we're DEA agents. You're under arrest.'

Manny went from his original ruddy, dark colour to chalk white. Inside, his stomach twisted into a knot. His hands trembled.

'You're . . . kidding,' he barely managed to say in a weak voice.

'No . . . we aren't kidding,' Jim replied.

Over the next several days, 200 men were arrested both in the United States and across the globe – all because Vinnie DeMarco agreed to help Jim Hunt and Tommy Geisel.

STREET MONKEY

Because of the excellent work of Vinnie DeMarco in helping with the arrests of Manny Adamita, Paulo Rizzuto and a trainload of drug dealers stateside and abroad, he was allowed to plead guilty, and received probation – got a sweetheart deal. He had become very fond of Jim Hunt and Tom Geisel. He thought of them more as trusted friends and confidants than as cops. Therefore, it wasn't surprising that, several months later, when a friend of DeMarco's needed help, he reached out to Jim and Tommy and asked for a meeting, only this time it involved one of the most infamous murderers La Cosa Nostra had ever produced, opening a door into a Mafia cemetery the likes of which the world had never known

They arranged to meet in a luncheonette in Brooklyn. Vinnie DeMarco told them a friend of his was in 'real bad' trouble. 'I wouldn't come to you guys, bother you with this, but he's a good kid,' said DeMarco. 'He's gotten into something bad over his head. He's gotten involved in . . . with a real bad dude. He's scared shitless. He owes him money for some drugs. This guy not only kills people for the Bonannos but he kills for other families as well. He enjoys killing. He cuts them up. He's known as Whack-o.'

They looked at one another. There was a heavy silence. What DeMarco was saying, both Jim and Tommy felt, had the ring of truth. There was a fear and apprehension about his face and in his eyes, in his every gesture. They had come to know him well through working on the Pizza Two case. What Vinny was trying to do here was use Jim and Tommy to protect his friend, not only from 'Whack-o' but also from himself.

'How can we help?' Jim asked.

'Well, it's a touchy situation. I don't want to see the kid get killed. See . . . see the problem is – the kid wants to take out the guy before he strikes. He wants to hire a killer. What I'm saying is the kid needs help. He's looking for . . . well, to be honest with you, he wants to kill this killer before the killer kills him, ha ha. I know it sounds nuts, but it's what's happening,' he said.

'Does he have money?' Jim asked.

'I don't think so much.'

'Who's this guy? Who's this killer you're talking about?'

'Tommy Pitera,' Vinnie said. 'He's got a bar over on Avenue S and he's big into drugs. He's with the Bonannos.'

'Is he made?' Tommy asked.

'I'm pretty sure he is,' DeMarco said, his voice taking on a serious tone, like that of a doctor bringing bad news.

This was interesting to the two agents. An observant onlooker would have seen a hint of excitement in both their eyes. Jim Hunt asked, 'What's your friend's name?'

'Angelo Favara.'

Jim and Tom were thinking this might lead to something big. They knew for a fact that the Bonannos were heavy into drugs; they knew for a fact that the Bonannos were responsible for more heroin and cocaine being brought into the United States than all of the other five families put together. They were the go-to guys for drugs. The fact that DeMarco said this Pitera guy was with the Bonannos was what further piqued both Jim's and Tommy's interest. Maybe, Jim reasoned, the door could slowly be opening on another very large case. Even after the French Connection Case and after the Pizza Connection Case, Jim knew damn well that the Italians were still bringing huge amounts of drugs into the country, that the Italians were beginning to work with other ethnic groups – particularly Colombians. The Colombians, he also knew, had raised the level of their business acumen to such a high degree that the Italians saw them as viable business partners, not out-of-control cowboys like the Dominicans, the Mexicans.

Vinnie now sheepishly explained to Jim and Tom why he had said that they were hit men. Some months earlier, Vinnie DeMarco's son had been in jail for murder and was released because a witness backed out of testifying. Vinnie – wanting to keep Angelo Favara out of trouble, to protect him from himself – had lied to Angelo and told him Tom and Jim were hit men for hire. To bolster this line of bullshit, he also told Angelo that Jim and Tommy had killed a witness against his son in the murder rap.

'OK, set up a meet,' Jim told Vinnie, looking forward to where this would lead, though wary and on guard.

Rota's was on East Tremont and Castle Hill Avenue in Parkchester, Bronx. It was a nondescript bar with a thirsty blue-collar/middle-class clientele. The lights were low. There was a mirror behind the bar.

When Jim and Tommy arrived, they were in disguise, dressed in faded jeans, beat-up boots, their hair long and raggedy. They wore beards. These two had an uncanny ability to alter their appearance. They spotted Angelo Favara at the bar. He was in his late 30s, slovenly, ill-kempt, pale with dark circles under his eyes. He had messy black hair. He was five-seven. He looked like something that the cat had dragged in. He was what Jim called a 'street monkey'. Drinks were ordered. Tommy and Jim had beers. Angelo drank hard alcohol. Angelo was tense and uptight. He was a worried man. His eyes moved back and forth like two small, nervous fish. During Jim's professional career, he had met dozens of men like this. They had the world on their shoulders, were about to make a life change, were about to put their lives in the hands of others. There was no doubt in his mind that Angelo Favara was a scared man. After making some small talk, Angelo got right down to it. He had a lot on his mind and was anxious to express it.

'You guys come highly recommended. I trust DeMarco. He knows what he's talking about. I got myself in bad trouble. I'm the first to admit I've made mistakes. There's this guy in Brooklyn named Tommy Karate. He's a killer. I mean a stone-cold killer. He *likes* to kill people. For him, it's not a job, it's a pleasure. Everybody in Brooklyn knows it. He not only kills people, but he cuts them up as well.'

Here, Angelo looked for Tom and Jim's reaction. He saw nothing. He waited for a response.

'And what do you want from us?' Tom asked.

'I don't want to die. I want this guy dead; I want him killed. I'll pay, I can pay.'

Chuckling, Jim leaned forward as though he was afraid of being recorded and said, 'Look, we don't know you and you don't know us. We are very good at what we do. We are professionals. We don't come cheap. You got money to pay us?'

'Well, um,' Angelo began, unsure of himself. 'No, I don't have the money right now, but I'll get it.'

'How much do you owe him?' Jim asked.

'Oh, about eight thousand.'

'That's not much,' Jim said.

'No, it's not, but when you don't have it, it's a lot.'

'Well, what the fuck do you want from us?' Jim said bluntly.

Angelo said, 'Well, I thought because of your relationship with Vinnie, you might do this for free.'

Both Jim and Tommy laughed at Angelo's audacity. He obviously wasn't the brightest bulb in the box, they both knew. That was irrelevant. What was relevant was that he could bring them to something bigger.

'Why don't you work it off? It's not that much. Get some stuff

from him, off it, do it a couple of times and you'll be free of him,'
Jim said.

Angelo looked at them. 'The problem with that is it's easier said
than done. I get the coke and I end up doing it and then I end up
owing them more money. I swear I have every intention of giving him
what's due but then one thing happens and another thing happens
. . . I lost a child, I don't know why I'm talking about this now, but I
lost the child because of SIDS. It's a hard thing to get over, but when
I do coke, I don't feel anything. I feel numb.'

This, of course, is the age-old problem of drug abusers – they
cannot control what they do and how much they do it. An addict
puts not only his or her life on the line but also the lives of his or her
children, spouses, parents, and on and on. It was for these reasons
that, for the most part, the DEA stayed away from addicts. Here,
now, what Jim and Tom were looking at was a drug-using lowlife who
had got himself in trouble and was trying to weasel his way out of it.

Jim said, 'We're always looking for something good, good dope.
If this guy has good stuff, we'll take some off his hands. We'll buy it
directly from you.'

'Really?' Angelo said, brightening up.

'Sure. We'll take all you can get.'

'OK,' he said. 'I can do that. No problem.'

As Angelo talked, they drank. He finished a drink and had another.
The more alcohol he consumed, the looser he became with his
tongue. He kept going back to Pitera. He kept talking about what a
dangerous, bad, stone-cold killer he was. Nearly every other word out
of his mouth was 'killer'. He described him as a martial arts expert
who loved to murder people. 'He's pale, like a vampire,' he said.

Ultimately, arrangements were made for Jim and Tommy to meet
with Angelo in Brooklyn. They would meet a woman named Judy
Haimowitz, who, according to Angelo, was one of Pitera's main
dealers.

16

THE VAMPIRE OF AVENUE S

After Jim Hunt and Tommy Geisel had finished with Angelo, they discussed what they had heard on their way back home. They believed they were on to something. Both Jim and Tommy, however, were naturally sceptical. Often street people embellished and exaggerated to such a degree that they were living in a fantasyland. But there was something about what this Angelo character said about Pitera that not only had the ring of truth but also had an innate sense of dread, a sense of foreboding about it. Whether or not that was all in his own head or was reality, they'd soon find out.

The following day, Jim and Tommy reported to DEA headquarters on 57th Street. They repeated what they had learned to their boss Ken Feldman and their colleagues in Group 33. Everyone agreed it was certainly worth pursuing, and pursuing in a serious way. They ran a search for Pitera's file and checked his record. Interestingly, he had no police record, but they found out he was a highly trained black belt in karate who had studied martial arts in Japan for some two and a half years. He was also known to hang out with members of the Bonanno crime family.

When Tommy and Jim next went to meet Angelo in Brooklyn's Gravesend, they were not alone. They had back-up with them. Excited by the prospect, by the potential enormity of this case, they made their way to Brooklyn via its Belt Parkway. They went under the grand expanse of the Verrazano Bridge, the Narrows Straits on their right, Bensonhurst on their left. They got off at the Cropsey Avenue/Coney Island exit, took a left and made their way towards Gravesend. There were two vehicles: the one that Tommy and Jim were in and a van with four other agents. They were each heavily armed. Never knowing what they would face, they were on guard. Even if a small part of what Angelo said about Pitera were true, this could very well turn into a dangerous situation. They all realised you never knew what you were walking into. What seemed like an innocuous situation could turn deadly at a moment's notice.

More than anything else, Pitera's association with the Bonannos caught and held their interest in a huge way. This could very well be the chink in the armour of the Bonanno family they, the DEA, had been looking for; this might very well bring down the whole family if they could get the goods on Pitera, if they could turn Pitera and make him spill the beans . . . tell all he knew. It stood to reason that if Bonanno underlings were selling drugs, everyone in the family from the boss on down not only knew about it but also had given their blessings, their advice, their protection. In other words, it was not one or two or even three members of the Bonanno crime family hustling drugs. What was happening here, the reality of what was going on, was that the whole family was a well-lubricated machine whose by-product was a huge amount of heroin and cocaine. Jim and Tom well knew the pipeline that Carmine Galante had constructed at the behest of Joseph Bonanno in the 1950s was still running.

They met Angelo in the basement of his house on West 8th Street. It was unkempt, dirty – a mess. It didn't take long for Judy Haimowitz to show up. She was short and overweight and had a full head of curly hair that went every which way at once. Angelo introduced her to the agents. She was nervous. It was immediately apparent to Jim and Tom that she was not a professional, hardcore dealer as such, that, more than likely, she was somebody who got caught up in drugs because of her abuse of drugs, the world of drugs . . . the milieu of drug abuse. Without speaking to one another, Jim and Tom knew that their job would be to relax her and set her up, use her to get bigger fish. They sat down. Pleasantries were exchanged.

'I've got the stuff,' Judy offered before going to her handbag. She rifled through her bag and as she fumbled for the heroin, a gun suddenly fell out of her bag. The gun hit the ground. It was a .25 automatic. Tommy and Jim and Angelo looked at one another. This was more comical than dangerous, the agents thought.

'Oh, I'm so sorry!' Judy said before picking up the auto and putting it back in her bag.

'Don't worry,' Angelo put in. 'She's good people. Frank Gangi is her boyfriend. Real stand-up guy.'

Glad the gun was away, they all laughed somewhat nervously. She handed the heroin to Jim. He looked at it with great intensity, as though he was an expert geologist studying an uncut diamond.

'Looks real good,' he said. Judy Haimowitz was paid. Though she was a small player in a life-and-death game, because of agents Hunt and Geisel, she would, ultimately, play a significant role in the story of Tommy Pitera.

They discussed Jim and Tommy meeting Pitera; it was Pitera they wanted. Angelo explained to them that Pitera was paranoid, suspicious, very wary of meeting strangers. He was very fond of saying – Angelo said – 'If I don't know the cunt they came out of, I don't want to know them.' Still, Angelo said, he'd do what he could to facilitate a meeting between Pitera and Jim and Tom.

The deed done, Jim and Tommy made for the sidewalk, walking along a driveway that separated Angelo's place from the house next door. It was quiet, the night clear, stars shining in the black sky. The smell of Italian cooking, tomato sauce and basil and garlic, wafted seductively through the air. As they reached the sidewalk, they ran into a tall, dark-haired, attractive woman.

'Is Judy inside?' she asked the agents.

'Yeah, she is,' Jim said.

She thanked them, smiled and walked towards the house. She had, Jim was sure, a Canadian accent.

One way or another, Jim and Tom thought, they would manage to get the goods on Pitera – if possible, get him holding drugs. At that point, they had no idea just how cagey and cunning, treacherous, Pitera was. They headed back to DEA headquarters where they handed in the dope they had bought, which would be tested for content and purity. As it happened, it was particularly good heroin. There was about a 20 per cent cut on it.

They already had Judy Haimowitz. She had sold them both drugs. They had each seen her carrying a gun. However, rather than bust her now, they would diligently and slowly work her.

The game was afoot.

Later that evening, Judy Haimowitz went to the Just Us Lounge, where she found Frank Gangi. Gangi was a tall, thin, muscular man with particularly broad shoulders. His hair was thick and jet-black. Judy told him about the sale and the two guys from the Bronx she had met. She then told Gangi that Angelo had used his name, said his name to these two guys – that he, Gangi, was a stand-up guy.

This was bad form, Gangi knew. You don't go throwing around people's names. He immediately called Angelo and told him to come to the bar. When Angelo arrived there, Gangi berated him for using his name and suddenly gave him a hard smack across the face.

'Don't ever fucking use my fucking name, you understand, you little fuck?'

Angelo was not only hurt by the slap but also angered and incensed and embarrassed. He was soon heard telling people that he was going to go get a bat and break Frank Gangi's head open. Angelo Favara was all about bluster and hot air; he was not a tough guy. He was a drug abuser who got caught up in the world of drugs. They, Jim and Tom, would use him, make him a stepping stone.

17

SURVEILLANCE

It didn't take long for Jim and Tommy Geisel to cop again from Judy Haimowitz. Angelo was with them. Angelo, again, could not set up a meeting with Pitera. Still, Jim and Tommy felt that what they were doing was now slowly, methodically building a case that would ultimately end in the arrest of not only Pitera but also the people he worked with, his minions, and the people he worked for, his bosses. This time Judy Haimowitz was more relaxed. She readily handed over the drugs. She asked them if they'd like to do a toot. They declined. Here, now, was a very slippery road. Dealers liked to see their customers get high in front of them. Cops, for the most part, would not use drugs. Jim and Tommy had been in this position before. They had a pat answer, viable and ready.

'We got serious business later and can't party right now,' Jim said.

'OK, next time,' Judy said.

With that Jim and Angelo and Tommy were soon back outside. Angelo promised he would arrange for them to meet Pitera. He seemed sincere, though his words did not ring true to the seasoned agents.

Jim and Tommy and back-up agents from Group 33 began surveillance of Tommy Karate Pitera's bar, the Just Us Lounge. They quickly noticed that it wasn't a crowded, loud place. It was a quiet neighbourhood bar on a residential street in the heart of Gravesend, Brooklyn, more like a social club than a public bar. Curious, wanting to know themselves what was going on inside the Just Us Lounge, Jim and Tom made it their business to learn as much about the bar and Tommy Pitera as possible.

What Pitera had done, somewhat comically, when a civilian came into the bar, was charge an exorbitant price for a drink or beer. Pitera really meant this place was *just for them*, thus his calling the bar Just Us. What the bar was all about was creating a hangout for Pitera and his crew, his customer base – anybody in La Cosa Nostra. It was the squares, the 'civvies', as they called them, they wanted to keep out. The patrons who did enter the bar were rough and talked like they were right out of central casting for a mob movie.

Interestingly, it wasn't only men who hung out there. So-called 'guidos' – Cadillac-driving, pinkie-ring and gold-chain-with-medallion-wearing, blow dryer-using, Sergio Tacchini sweatsuit-clad men – hung out here. But there were also women who came into the bar, women who belonged, women who were part of the culture of Bensonhurst and Gravesend: guidettes. These women spoke the same vernacular as the men. For them, made men were very appealing. They had money and were oversexed. The women unapologetically teased their hair and wore five-inch heels with pants so tight it looked as though the seams would burst at any moment. Their make-up was overt and in your face, their eyeliner caked on, their lip-liner mismatched to their lipstick. Their nails were fake, airbrushed and ridiculously long. For these women to date or even marry a made man, a lieutenant, a captain, was a goal in life. No matter how you cut it, mob guys, mafiosi, had money to burn. One of the things they most liked to spend money on was women, lavishly and without reservation.

As Jim and Tommy observed the bar, learned about its rhythm and pace, they saw these women, heard them talk, and were . . . amused. They appreciated them for who they were. They didn't necessarily judge them or make fun of them, but they thought they were comical and harmless, which, for the most part, was true. However, tragedy, sudden and amazingly violent, could strike these women at any time. By becoming involved with mafiosi, they were entering a world where, at a moment's notice, they, their boyfriend or husband could be murdered.

Murder was as intricate a part of that life as were silk socks and diamond pinky rings. If any woman was in the wrong place at the wrong time, she could get killed. If they did something excessively disrespectful, they could get killed. For the most part, the mob did not kill women. But still, when tempers flared and bullets flew, anyone could die.

One weekday evening while Jim and Tom were observing the Just Us Lounge from a car across the street, Pitera walked into the bar. Jim and Tommy had seen photos of him and he was very easy to discern. His face was white like chalk, stern and stoic. He had receding straight black hair. Even in the dim light of Avenue S, they could see his eyes, a piercing blue. They stood out on his face like headlights. It was obvious he was an athletic man, wide-shouldered and muscular, well coordinated and comfortable in his own skin.

Tommy and Jim viewed Pitera only as part of something larger. It was the something larger they were after: the heads of not only the Bonanno crime family but the other heads as well. They knew, for instance, that all the captains in the Gambino family were moving drugs. They knew, too, that John Gotti's brother Gene was a drug dealer. They knew that Gambino captain Eddie Lino was a drug dealer. They knew that they all worked together, hand in hand; that they were all part of a large, tightly woven cabal; that the Bonannos sold drugs to the Gambinos and the other crime families. What Tom and Jim were after, the reason they were sitting there, was to gather irrefutable evidence that would hold up in a court of law against the blistering scrutiny of mean-spirited defence attorneys.

They, Jim and Tom, were consummate professionals. They were not in a hurry. They would put in as much time as necessary, unlike in most law-enforcement outfits, where everyone was in a hurry, everyone was looking for headlines, everyone was looking for the positive publicity that goes along with a big bust. Crime-fighting was political. The more accolades any given agency received, the more funding they were given, the more respect they received. The DEA, however, was more about working cases patiently and professionally until they came to a true fruition. Not only did this work well as a matter of policy, but also when they did move, when they did make arrests, the arrests stuck. Bad guys went to jail. That's what they were after: getting bad guys off the street once and for all.

Both Jim and Tommy could sense in their bones that something substantial was happening here. Yet, still, they had no idea just how diabolical and dangerous, just what a menace Tommy Pitera really was.

Pitera and a few other men exited the bar and hung out in front of it. They smoked cigarettes, talked quietly amongst themselves. At one point, Pitera seemed to stare across the street, stare at the Cadillac in which Jim and Tommy were sitting. It was as though he knew cops were in the car, though he did not know if it was the FBI, NYPD organised crime unit or the DEA. Whoever they were, he wanted to defy them, treat them as though he knew who they were and why they were there and almost dare them to do something.

18

PHYLLIS

Tommy Pitera had married his childhood sweetheart Carol Boguski. Carol was somewhat typical of a Bensonhurst/ Gravesend girl. She had the walk, talk, dress. When Tommy first met her, he was a far different person than he was now. As often happens with couples, one of the pair, for a host of reasons, outgrows the other. Tommy considered himself now more sophisticated, worldly, a man of respect. Though Tommy and Carol were not living together any more, did not see one another much, Tommy did everything he should for her and his son, provided what they needed in every way he could. He paid their rent, bought clothes, food, whatever else they required. Generally speaking, Tommy showed tremendous deference towards women.

Now it was the mid-'80s, and he was presently deeply involved with a Brooklyn girl named Celeste LiPari. Celeste was attractive. She had a triangular-shaped face, pronounced cheekbones, a narrow, delicate chin and a high, broad forehead. She had large dark eyes, full lips, a perfect figure – small waist, curved hips, full breasts. As attractive as she was, Celeste sounded like a rough, tough truck driver when she talked. She, perhaps more than even Tommy, wanted to be a gangster, comported herself like a gangster. Her Brooklyn accent was excessive. She talked out of the side of her pretty mouth.

For Tommy Pitera, Celeste was perfect. He worshipped the ground she walked on. Everything about her was right for him except one thing: her drug use. She was not an occasional, weekend user; she was one of those people who had 'an addictive personality' and she regularly used both cocaine and heroin. It got so that the two of them fought over her drug abuse. He swore he would leave her; she promised she'd stop. It went on like this for month after month. Now he was getting fed up; now he was getting desperate. The difficulty for him was that he loved the woman, and that was a big problem. It went beyond their relationship. He was a made man. He was a bona fide member of the Bonanno family. Having a girl like her, going around snorting cocaine and partying, undermined his credibility as a man. *If you can't control your woman, you can't control your business.*

He sat her down. He looked her in the eyes and explained the situation. He grabbed her by the shoulders and implored her to stop. She promised she would. The next week it would be the same thing. Unless she toed the line, he was afraid that sooner or later this could end in tragedy. He was careful to keep his business away from her, but she knew things about what he did, about who he was, and she was becoming a liability.

He came to realise that one of the problems was – Phyllis Burdi.

Phyllis was a Brooklyn girl, raised on its mean streets, and she too was a drug abuser who, like Celeste, used cocaine and heroin excessively. Phyllis came from a family of five who lived on Bay 35th Street in Bensonhurst. They were a large, loud clan and most people on the block shunned them. Phyllis, by far, was the prettiest one. Like Celeste, she was strikingly attractive. She looked very much like a young Cindy Crawford, though a Cindy Crawford who had been up for a couple of nights on a drug binge. There were circles under her eyes, her skin was mealy and her hair, for the most part, looked like she had just crawled out of bed. The most striking feature Phyllis had was her smile. It was a particularly beautiful smile that went from ear to ear and exposed large, square white teeth. Her lower lip was full and curved into a natural pout. Phyllis had an abundance of street smarts and knew her way around Brooklyn as well as she knew her way around her small, dingy one-bedroom apartment on West 5th Street. Some say that Phyllis was a prostitute, that she sold sex for clothes and for money and for drugs. There are people who say she prostituted herself on Coney Island when on a drug binge – a place where the disenfranchised of society go to party, for sex and drugs. Here, blue-collars let their hair down.

Phyllis was not a prostitute. What she was about was doing what needed to be done to make ends meet, whatever it was. She liked wise guys, and wise guys liked her right back. She had relationships, intimate, intense sexual relationships, with a long list of important mafiosi. One of her lovers was none other than Eddie Lino, the feared Gambino war captain – cousin of Frankie Lino, Tommy Pitera's boss.

It was no secret that Eddie Lino was deeply immersed in drugs. Phyllis told people that he gave her whatever she wanted, ounces at a time. Eddie Lino was only one of a dozen seriously connected men with whom Phyllis was having sex. She was that attractive. When goodfellas were around Phyllis, it was like bees around spring flowers. When she was dressed and well put together, she looked like a striking model who had just stepped off the pages of the latest *Vogue*. Everything about her worked. Her small, perfectly round breasts, the perfect bubble that was her derriere.

It didn't take long for Tommy Pitera to learn that Phyllis was providing drugs to his beloved Celeste. When he first heard this, he knew he had to be careful. He was aware that Phyllis knew a lot of powerful men; he, like everyone else, knew she was having an affair with Eddie Lino. Eddie Lino and Pitera were close. Pitera knew that if he went to Eddie and asked for his help in this matter, he'd get it, but it was a very delicate situation. This was about Pitera keeping his own house clean. He didn't want to hang his dirty laundry out for public consumption. Plus he had endless respect for Eddie Lino. He viewed Eddie as *the* dark prince of dark princes. He aspired to be like Eddie.

Taking that into consideration, Pitera wondered how he could go to Eddie and ask for his help in this matter. He would, he decided, be diplomatic, judicial. Pitera looked for Phyllis for several days and then finally ran into her at an after-hours club. By now, all throughout Mafiadom, Pitera was known as a killer; it was also known that he was butchering people, cutting them up after murdering them. He was notorious in the world of the notorious. Though Phyllis knew she had friends in high places, she also knew she had to take Pitera very seriously.

He took her outside and, leaning against a red-brick wall, speaking in his high-pitched voice, he said, 'Phyllis, I have a problem and I need your help. Celeste is out of control. I don't want her using drugs. But I – listen to me – I'm not blaming you for anything; I'm not saying you did anything. What I'm saying is that she can't control herself and I'd really appreciate it if you made sure not to give her any drugs – ever. She has a couple of toots, she starts drinking and next she's using heroin. I'd really appreciate this.'

Phyllis was somewhat surprised that Pitera was being so nice. That was the only word to describe his tone and pitch.

'I've never given her any drugs; we've gotten high together, but I'll be sure and never give her any,' she replied.

He stared at her. Having Tommy Pitera stare at you with those ice-blue eyes of his was unsettling, to say the least. He nodded. They shook hands. With that handshake and with his eyes, he warned her that it could become dangerous; that he absolutely, positively did not want Celeste using drugs, did NOT want Phyllis to give her any drugs!

19

THREE-TIME LOSER

Frank Gangi was six-foot-three, thin and wiry. When he walked around Brooklyn, he looked like a scarecrow that had stepped off his pedestal and was moving about. He had a large, oval-shaped face. He was a chain smoker, and when he laughed, phlegm readily bubbled in his lungs and he coughed. He did not have the demeanour, the features or the carriage of a predatory animal. When you looked at Gangi, you thought more of a cook working in a busy kitchen, a friendly grocery store clerk or, perhaps, the local pizza man, not a killer, certainly not a Mafia associate.

However, Frank Gangi was a dedicated drug dealer, had been charged with murder, though was acquitted. He was associated with the Bonanno crime family and he came from a culture of mafiosi. His father, uncles and cousins were associates in the Bonanno and Genovese families. His uncle was Angelo Prezzanzano, a respected capo in the Bonanno family. His father, Frank Gangi Sr, was also an associate of the Bonanno family and had dealt in drugs. His cousin, Rosario 'Ross' Gangi, was a highly respected captain in the Genovese family.

Frank Gangi was one of those individuals who existed on the

periphery of Mafiadom. He was the proverbial three-time loser. Whether it was a combination of bad luck, bad timing, being ill-informed or abusing drugs was up for debate. Suffice it to say, Frank Gangi would become one of the most important players in the life and times and crimes of Tommy Karate Pitera. Certainly a large part of Frank's difficulties in life stemmed from the fact that his father had spent three years in prison, from when Frank was five until he was eight. Without his father, the boy's feeling of isolation from his family and from society at large was amplified. His mother, Margaret, had a male child from a previous marriage and she openly and without question preferred her first boy to Frank. To further muddy the waters that were his turbulent life, Frank's father was murdered when Frank was nine years old. He was killed in a mob-related incident that involved Sicilian hit men being brought down from Canada to kill Frankie Tuminaro and the senior Gangi. With the loss of his father, Frank Gangi withdrew further and further into himself. Whatever problems the young boy had were magnified. He was destined for trouble with the law, society and especially those of his own kind. He would become a pariah from not only the Mafia but his own family as well. He would become a man with no country.

Though Frank Gangi was an average-looking man, women were drawn to him in a big way. He was tall and well put-together. He had the golden gift of the gab and was easy to warm to. He was not threatening. He seemed sincere and would readily offer to help if he could. Unlike many of the connected men that came from Bensonhurst and Gravesend, Frank Gangi was not a natural born killer; it seemed that he was born in the wrong place at the wrong time.

When he was in his early 20s, Gangi had a pot business. With his two partners, Billy Bright and Arthur Guvenaro, he sold hundreds of pounds of pot every week, happily filling the need for marijuana in Brooklyn and the tri-state area. Arthur Guvenaro was a freebase head and began stealing from Bright and Gangi. They realised what he was doing and made up their minds to kill him. The night of the murder, 27 April 1985, Bright and Gangi lured Guvenaro to their stash house near Stillwell Avenue in Gravesend and began freebasing with him. When Bright and Gangi finally pulled out guns, they were so stoned, they were inefficient, and their minds so fogged by the drugs that they bumbled the murder. Still, the two aimed and shot Guvenaro. After Guvenaro was shot several times, he dived through a large bay window, rolled onto the street and, miraculously, took off with incredible speed, bullets lodged in his upper back, as well as the back of his head. When he reached the corner, he dropped. A police car rolled up to him. His dying words were, 'Frank Gangi and Billy Bright did this to me.'

Gangi and Billy Bright were quickly arrested.

Shockingly, when the case went to trial, they were acquitted. Their lawyer convinced the jury that Guvenaro was the bad guy, that he had pulled out a gun and started shooting at them, and they were just defending themselves. Because there was no one to contradict them on the stand, the jury found them not guilty. They were, however, found guilty of possession of a gun. For the gun charge, they were each sentenced to a year in prison.

In the spring of 1986, Frank Gangi emerged from jail. He had little money, few resources and was looking for something to do. He was a friend of Judy Haimowitz's and she suggested he go see Tommy Pitera. She said that Pitera had a lot going on and could, perhaps, help set him up.

When Frank Gangi met Tommy Pitera in the Just Us bar in 1986, Gangi was taken aback by Pitera's voice. Those who knew Pitera knew the sound his voice made coming out of his mouth and readily accepted it. However, Frank Gangi was hearing it for the first time and couldn't help but think of Mickey Mouse or, worse yet, Minnie Mouse. Here was this ruthless killer, with a reputation that far preceded him, talking like a cartoon character. The comedy of it was not lost on Gangi. In that Gangi had this outgoing, gregarious personality, it was easy for him to get Tommy to like him, warm to him. After the two of them had talked a while, Tommy said, 'What can I do for you? What are you here for?'

In a vague sense, Gangi talked about borrowing money.

'Hold on a second. I'm not a shylock. That's not what I do,' Pitera said.

'I'm sorry. I thought maybe you could help me tide things over until I can get something going.'

'No,' Pitera said. 'I don't loan money. But maybe there are other things we can do together.'

Pitera already knew who Frank Gangi was. He knew his family was all mobbed up; that Frank had previously sold large amounts of marijuana; that he had murdered Arthur Guvenaro with Billy Bright. These were the best credentials Gangi could have had. Pitera knew he was an amiable guy who had come up the hard way, who came from the nearby streets, and he immediately viewed Gangi as a potential member of his world. Likewise, Frank Gangi had heard all about Pitera and was open to becoming involved with him and working with him. Pitera arranged for Gangi to be fronted weight in cocaine and heroin and even marijuana. With his reputation and former connections and outgoing personality, Gangi was able to quickly make money for not only himself but also Tommy Pitera. Like this, little by little, over the weeks and months, Frank Gangi became a trusted confidant of Tommy Pitera.

Pitera also hooked Gangi up with an Israeli coke dealer who was one of several sources Pitera had outside the Bonanno family. His name was Shlomo Mendelsohn. A rough-around-the-edges, military-trained Israeli, Shlomo was part of a drug-dealing cartel that comprised just Israelis. They were arrogant, tough, independent and well connected. Because Pitera liked to stay as far away from the drugs as possible, it was not unusual for him to have underlings meet people, pick up the drugs and distribute them appropriately. Knowing that Gangi was working for Pitera, Shlomo pretty much gave him whatever he asked for on consignment. Suddenly, Gangi was no longer a Mafia wannabe. Thanks to Pitera, he was up and running and in the game again, though Frank Gangi still had a problem that would come back and shake the very foundation of the Bonanno crime family.

20

GROUP 33

With Pitera's bar under surveillance and the DEA aware of his links to the Bonannos, Jim Hunt's boss Ken Feldman saw the potential for a big bust that would get some serious bad guys off the street. This, combined with Hunt's impeccable reputation, pretty much guaranteed Hunt would get whatever he asked for. One of the first things he requested was a nimble, quick-moving strike force made up of agents from Group 33 to bring down Pitera. His boss gave him the green light and soon he was using rotating shifts divided between nine sharp, highly experienced agents who would eventually monitor all of Pitera's moves, and who was going in and out of the Just Us bar. The strike force also managed to get warrants to listen in on Pitera's phone conversations. The team of DEA agents, each of whom Hunt had given nicknames, comprised Tom 'El Gordo' Geisel, Bruce 'Spike' Travers, Mike 'Nunzio' Agrifolio, John 'Big John' McKenna, Mike 'Big Mike' Rubowski, John 'Little John' Welch, John 'Jethro' Wilson and Violet Szelecky. They quickly noticed Frank Gangi show up on the scene. Frank was hard not to notice: at six-three, with his long beak of a nose and black fedora, he was easy to spot in the crowd.

Always suspicious and paranoid, Pitera was indeed a hard man to pin something on. As it turned out, he very rarely talked on the phone, let alone said anything incriminating. He drove many different cars so, at that point, it would have been exceedingly difficult to install a listening device.

In that Pitera had been born and raised in Gravesend, he knew its streets, avenues and alleyways, lots and dead ends like the back of his hand. Pitera, as most made guys, could smell a cop a mile away. He noted the DEA agents, but he didn't know who exactly they were – FBI, NYPD organised crime, DEA or ATF. To continue going about his business, Pitera again took to donning disguises. He was a natural born actor and could bend and twist his body any which way he wanted to. Like this, he often managed to slip away from his pursuers. On several occasions, while agents were sitting in front of his house, he'd leave the building dressed in his Hasidic disguise, moving slowly, bent over like a pretzel, and they did not know it was him. He also dressed as a woman and, disguised as a female, would boldly strut out of his house, take a left or right and soon disappear. At this juncture, Pitera was not under surveillance 24/7, though as the case unfolded, as facts and names and details became known to the government, they would become like white on rice to Tommy Pitera. Because Group 33 was the most active, aggressive of all DEA groups in the entire country, they were all always very busy, were working numerous cases with different ethnic groups at any given time. Cases at different stages of development had to be nurtured; witnesses and snitches, new evidence and new leads would fall out of the sky and have to be tended to immediately. For Jim Hunt, however, the Pitera case was important.

THE GUVENAROS

There were four Guvenaro brothers: Vinnie 'Mook', Louie 'Bopp', Frankie and Arthur. It seemed, for all intents and purposes, that the murder of Arthur Guvenaro was a thing of the past, over and done with. That might very well have been the case had Arthur Guvenaro not had a brother named Louie Bopp. Louie was a tough street-smart guy who was born and raised on Bath Avenue. As a youth, he had hung out with a group called the Bath Avenue Boys, all stand-up, two-fisted Italian-Americans. Louie Bopp was a naturally well-endowed athlete. Anything he tried in terms of athletics he did very well. He was a particularly adept street fighter. He had unusually large hands and was amazingly fast, and had knocked out most of his opponents before they even threw a punch. Coincidentally, sadly, Louie's older brother Vinnie Mook was murdered by Gambino capo Nino Gaggi, with the help of the notorious Roy DeMeo, for whistling at Gaggi's sister-in-law on 86th Street as she came out of the Hytulip Jewish Deli.

Louie Bopp made his living on the outside of the law. Though he was not a made man, he was most definitely connected. He had been born and raised in the Mafia culture, was a part of it, was thought well of – a rough-and-ready guy who often had a smile on his face.

Arthur Guvenaro was Louie's youngest brother. Louie had always watched over Arthur. He knew Arthur was troublesome, that he was using drugs excessively, and he had warned his kid brother, but Arthur, like all the brothers, was strong-willed and stubborn, headstrong, tough, and he wouldn't listen to his older – wiser – brother. Inevitably, inexorably, Arthur's freebasing caused problems that resulted in his murder. When Louie Bopp heard about his brother's killing, he was angry beyond words, distraught, and wanted revenge. Revenge in that neighbourhood was the norm, as much a part of it as the 86th Street elevated train. The fact that Frank Gangi and Billy Bright only received a year after murdering Arthur compounded Louie Bopp's anger and frustration many times over. When Louie Bopp learned that Gangi and Billy Bright were out of jail, he decided to kill them; he decided to take a contract out on their lives. Gangi and Bright had been childhood friends, two rogues cut from the same cloth. Bright had been doing business with Pitera before he went to jail, and now that he was out of jail their business relationship resumed.

It didn't take long for Gangi and Billy Bright to hear about the contract Louie Bopp had taken out on their lives and they ran to Tommy Pitera. Pitera was ideally suited to act as an intermediary on behalf of Gangi and Bright. He knew Mafia protocol exceedingly well. He knew its rules and regulations as well as the street on which he was born. Since both Frank Gangi and Billy Bright were working for him now, it was his responsibility to step up for them. Diplomatically, he suggested to Frank that he go to his cousin, Ross Gangi, a highly respected Genovese captain, and that he, Pitera, would speak up for Billy Bright.

'This way,' Pitera said, 'you'll have two families speaking up for you. Your position will be much stronger.'

Pitera was, of course, absolutely right.

* * *

A sit-down is a classic way the Mafia developed to iron out problems. It was easy to have a beef with anyone over a hundred different things, grab a gun and put a bullet in someone's head. Though a bullet to the head certainly ended arguments, finalised all debates, there was a better way to settle disputes, differences of opinions, the divvying up of various multi-family schemes without spilling blood. Unbeknownst to the police and, by extension, the public, the Mafia often had meetings to resolve disputes without rancour, yelling or cursing, or pointing of fingers. Again, this was a custom that was brought over from Sicily but refined and perfected by the American Cosa Nostra.

In a sense, sit-downs had become an art form. The modulation of voice had to be just so; the motions of hands had to be subdued; even the look from eyes had to be neutral, not filled with fire, hatred. Because the Bonanno crime family was deeply involved in this problem, Anthony Spero, the underboss, a highly respected individual in the family, agreed to 'host' the sit-down. He would be the final arbitrator. Whatever he decided would be law – indisputable. The meeting was held in a quiet restaurant in Bensonhurst. The attendees were Louie Bopp, Billy Bright, Frank Gangi, Gangi's cousin Ross, Tommy Pitera and Anthony Spero.

Louie Bopp was seething with anger. Regardless of how neutral he tried to appear, the anger boiled over and came from his eyes, his every movement, though he was respectful, shook hands and kissed. Louie first laid out his case, said that his brother had been murdered by Gangi and Bright and he wanted revenge, was entitled to revenge. Conversely, Billy Bright told how Arthur had been stealing from them, that Arthur was an out-of-control drug addict, that he 'brought it all on himself'.

Everyone there that day, sitting at the table, knew exactly what Arthur Guvenaro had been doing: he had been ripping off corner dealers. One day he was rich and driving fancy cars and the next day he was broke because of illogical, bad behaviour.

Spero listened calmly to both sides and weighed the options. Gangi and Bright were both earners for the Bonanno family. As if that wasn't enough, Gangi had his cousin in his corner, while Bright had Pitera speaking for him. Spero ruled that the matter was to be forgotten, that no one was going to be killed.

'It's over and done,' he said in little more than a whisper.

And it was over and done. Had Louie Bopp done anything more, tried to get his revenge, killed Gangi and Bright, he would have quickly and summarily been shot to death, no questions asked, no quarter given.

THE GRAVEDIGGER

On 11 February 1987, Pitera managed to lose the DEA, murder on his mind. He was headed to a desolate warehouse out in Queens for the purpose of filling a revenge contract. This was a particularly important killing for Pitera because he had been tapped by Joe Massino himself. Joe Massino was a rotund, particularly tough, though dapper, mafioso. He was a close friend of John Gotti. The two came up the ranks together. They socialised with one another. They were made from the same mould. Joe's nickname could very well have been Joe 'The Gentleman' for he was fastidious about his appearance and was always well groomed. He had a beautiful wife whom he loved very much.

Through guile, brutality, street acumen, shooting first and accurately, Joe Massino made himself the head of the Bonanno crime family. Philip Rastelli, the acting head of the family, had neither the balls nor the street smarts to go up against Massino. Whoever challenged Massino's rule was quickly eliminated.

One such person was Cesare Bonventre. He had been present the day Carmine Galante was shot to death. He had participated in the murder. A tall, hulking blond man who wore his hair slicked back and his shirts open, he was a mercurial mafioso who seemed to be bipolar. One minute he could be sitting there laughing and the next he was tearing your throat out. As per Joe Massino's order, Bonanno family members Sal Vitale and Louie 'HaHa' Attanasio picked up Bonventre to take him to a meeting with acting Bonanno boss Philip Rastelli. As is the way of made men, treachery virtuosos all, Bonventre was shot numerous times and killed on the way to the meeting. Specific orders had been given to make sure Bonventre was 'buried deep'. This task was given to Gabe Infante. Massino did not ever want Bonventre found.

Apparently, however, Massino's orders were not heeded – Bonventre was not only not buried deep but he was placed in a 50-gallon oil drum and left in New Jersey. When Bonventre was found, law enforcement immediately came snooping around Massino's camp. Plus, it was obvious to everyone in Mafiadom that Massino had ordered this killing. With that, Massino, not surprisingly, decided to kill Gabe Infante. Again, this was typical Mafia protocol. When the boss gives an order, it must be followed to the letter. In their world, in the world of crime, in the fiery netherworld of La Cosa Nostra, death can come from the smallest of infractions. Theirs is a constant life-and-death opera.

Lie . . . you're dead.

Steal from your boss . . . you're dead.

Covet another made man's wife . . . you're dead.

Not come when you are called . . . you're dead.

Not give the boss his due . . . you're dead.

Openly deal drugs . . . you're dead.

Practise homosexual activities . . . you're dead.

Break the vow of omerta . . . you're dead.

Don't bury a body deep enough . . . you're dead.

For Tommy Pitera, the reason for this killing was irrelevant. All that mattered was that Massino wanted this individual dead. Tommy would do it – no questions asked. He would do it well. He would, via this murder, garner the respect of Massino and earn brownie points with him as well.

Sal Vitale brought Gabe Infante to the warehouse under the guise of going to see a load of marijuana. When Pitera joined them, Infante was not frightened because Pitera was a known drug dealer. Because Frankie Lino was Pitera's immediate boss, he, too, was dispatched to the Queens warehouse. By the time he arrived at the warehouse, however, Gabe Infante was already dead. Pitera had shot him in the head several times with an automatic. Frankie Lino did not like dealing with Pitera. The fact is that he kept Pitera at arm's length. He didn't like being around him. He felt he was spooky – ghoulish. He had heard how Pitera adroitly butchered bodies.

The job done, few words were said. Pitera now did what he did best. They loaded Infante up in the trunk of his car and he and Vitale drove to the Arthur Kills Landfill on Staten Island. Here, quickly, Infante was buried. Another notch in his belt, a favour done for Joe Massino, Pitera headed back to Brooklyn, again going over the majestic expanse of the Verrazano Bridge. On his right, as he went, he could see Bensonhurst and Gravesend just beyond, the place of his roots, the place that had spawned him.

THE ART OF WALK
AND TALKS

Jim Hunt and Tommy Geisel were still buying drugs from Judy Haimowitz, both heroin and cocaine. The heroin was pure and potent and the agents were able to have the DEA labs test it and determine from where it came. It was high-grade heroin from Turkey, no doubt brought to the United States via Sicily, Montreal and Brooklyn, New York. The agents constantly tried to get Angelo to arrange to have them meet Pitera.

'Tell him,' Hunt said, 'we want a kilo. Two kilos. Whatever he can provide.'

Angelo said, 'He's paranoid. He's crazy paranoid. He don't trust nobody. He says to me he don't do business with anyone he don't know.'

Jim Hunt and Tom Geisel came to believe that the case could only go so far with Angelo's help alone. The case had to be broadened with the help of surveillance, wiretaps and more informers. Still, both Jim and Tommy had grown fond of Angelo and his wife, Ethyl. Life had thrown the Favaras numerous curveballs and they were black and blue. Almost as a matter of course, the DEA was compelled to use people like Angelo Favara. Regardless of what his status was in life, in society, they'd make the best out of him. Everyone in the DEA had come to know that in order to catch a shifty rat, you needed cheese.

By the same token, they believed it was only a matter of time before they could nail Pitera to the proverbial cross. They were out for blood. They were not out to make an arrest that could be beat. They already knew that Pitera had access to the best criminal attorneys in New York. Though as days and weeks slipped by, the Pitera task force came to realise that getting the goods on Tommy Pitera would be difficult.

It was patently obvious that everyone around Pitera was deathly afraid of him. It was very hard to find somebody willing to cooperate in bringing him down. Using the tapped phones and Angelo, they searched for a weak link, an Achilles heel, some place they could exploit. Normally everyone has an Achilles heel, but they came to realise that Pitera was unusual – exceptional. They noticed, too, that people around him seemed to disappear. There'd be a guy at the Just Us bar on a regular basis and then suddenly he'd be gone – disappeared.

The Mother Cabrini Educational Center was located at 246 Avenue U. This was the social club for the all-powerful, all-seeing, all-knowing Bonanno capo Frank Lino. The club, as most of La Cosa Nostra's social clubs, was on the ground floor, its windows covered in thick curtains, and inside there were card tables along with the ubiquitous espresso maker. The walls were adorned with photos of Frank Sinatra and Joe DiMaggio. It was somewhat ironic that Lino would name a meeting place for the Bonanno crime family after Mother Cabrini. It showed that he not only had a sense of humour but also audacity. The mob guys quickly, instantly, noticed the agents in different coloured unmarked vans with tinted windows. Pitera would enter the club, come out a little while later with another mafioso and go for a 'walk and talk'.

Walk and talks were a uniquely clever invention of La Cosa Nostra. They had become so wary and paranoid of FBI monitors, taps, eavesdropping, that the only way they felt safe to talk to one another was to walk the streets in no particular direction, going left, right, stopping and turning around, figuring the FBI couldn't record their conversations. The New York Mafia created walk and talks and took them to such a degree that they became, in a sense, an art form. In that those who had the most to lose were the higher-ups, the most paranoid were the capos and bosses, it was they who most often went on these sojourns. They'd walk, usually two people, sometimes three, shoulder to shoulder, in stride, whispering as they went, trying to look natural – like they belonged. Often, one or both of them at the same time would cup their hands around their mouths as they spoke for fear of high-powered audio recording equipment.

The DEA agents' long-lensed, motorised Nikon cameras took pictures as Tommy Pitera went on walk and talks with a host of Bonanno people such as Frankie Lino and Anthony Spero. To the government, this was a revelation. It proved that they were on the right trail. It was no secret to any of them exactly who Anthony Spero was. On other days, they photographed Pitera walking with Frankie Lino. The Mother Cabrini Educational Center acted like a sweet beehive and all the different mafiosi from Brooklyn made their way there sooner or later. The DEA noted Eddie Lino come and go. They noted Gene Gotti, John Gotti's younger brother, come and go. They noted Anthony Gaspipe Casso arrive, go inside and then leave.

With the long-distance lens, and the determination and acumen of DEA photographers, little went unnoticed or unrecorded. They noted that day and night Tommy Pitera most often wore black, like he was in mourning. At any given moment he could go to a funeral and fit right in. With that pale skin of his and those ice blue eyes, he was a sight to behold walking up and down Avenue U with various mafiosi. Of all the mafiosi, it was obvious to the DEA that Pitera was the most paranoid, most wary of being recorded. He always had his hand over his mouth, as if he were taking the last bites of a Nathan's hot dog from nearby Coney Island.

The DEA also trailed Pitera to Anthony Spero's club on Bath Avenue at Bay 16th Street. It was called West End. Spero had large flocks of pigeons up on the roof and often his pigeons could be seen flying large circles over Bath Avenue. Here, too, Spero and Pitera would go for walks around the block, talking quietly, surreptitiously, as they made their way up and down quiet tree-lined streets.

In the year or so since Gangi had hooked up with Pitera, he had come to know intimately the remorseless killer Tommy Pitera truly was. Everyone in the Just Us bar, indeed throughout the underworld, was always talking about this person he killed or that person he killed and what a badass killer he was. Gangi, too, heard that he not only murdered people but also cut them up – butchered them with amazing acumen. At face value, Frank didn't think this particularly bad or ghoulish – he saw it more as part and parcel of what had to be done, a necessary part of the job. However, as time went by and he actually saw for himself what Pitera was capable of, he came to know that Pitera was a living, breathing monster; that he killed the way a werewolf would kill, that he killed the way a highly trained ninja warrior would kill.

Murder, for Pitera, was as easy as combing his thinning black hair.

By now, the summer of 1987 was just around the corner. One evening in early June, Gangi got up from a nap, showered, dressed and went to the Just Us bar. Now Gangi was making money. He was always on the prowl, always looking for women. He considered himself quite the ladies' man. Females liked Gangi. One of the many women he dated was Phyllis Burdi, the woman who hung out with Celeste LiPari, Pitera's girlfriend; the woman who Pitera thought was supplying Celeste with drugs.

Gangi knew that Celeste was a heavy drug user. Often she was at the Just Us bar when Pitera wasn't around, going to and from the ladies room, back and forth like the Energiser bunny. He well knew that Pitera really did not want her using drugs, but far be it from him to tell tales about anyone. He himself was a big drug user. He'd snort cocaine and snort cocaine, get all wired up and drink half a bottle of scotch to come down. Like this, quite stoned, he'd get in his car and drive about as though he were sober. Several times he had to pay off Brooklyn cops who pulled him over for drunk-driving when his car weaved all over the road. One time he hit a stop sign on Cropsey Avenue and Bay 34th Street. He had to pay $500 to get away with that one. The combination of excessive coke use and excessive alcohol consumption destined Gangi for trouble – big trouble.

When he was really stoned, for the most part Gangi stayed away from the Just Us and people in the life. What he would do was find a girl and take her home. He always had all the coke anybody could want and he'd party, with the girl and the coke, drinking heavily. Sometimes Frank Gangi woke up with such a headache he thought he'd been shot. It seemed, deep inside, he was trying to numb himself. It seemed as though he had some great pain that he couldn't deal with when sober. What he was doing was not partying; what he was doing was killing himself, little by little digging his own grave. For these reasons, his family, knowing of his drinking and drug problems, kept him at arm's length. They didn't trust him. They viewed him as what he was: an out-of-control addict, volatile and untrustworthy.

Since Tommy Pitera used drugs very sparingly, drank lightly, Gangi was rarely stoned around him. For Gangi, it wasn't a matter of getting high or buzzed. He would readily drink a bottle of Jack Daniel's and snort an eighth of coke in one evening. He knew if Pitera saw him that way, their days together would be numbered. Not only that but Gangi had come to believe that if Pitera thought he was a liability, he'd kill him; he'd kill him as easily as passing gas.

On this night, as Gangi took a left and entered the Just Us bar, he ran smack into Pitera. Pitera said, 'C'mon. Take a ride with me, Frankie.'

'Sure,' Gangi said, having no idea what was about to happen.

They went outside and got in the car. Pitera did his usual thing, made a U-turn, went a couple blocks, made another U-turn, drove into a shopping centre and went in a big circle to make sure they weren't being followed. Pitera was a hard man to tail. He knew the moves. He had carefully studied surveillance. He had carefully studied exactly what cops do to follow people and he readily managed to slip away from the government. He knew these streets far better than any of the DEA agents.

As was Pitera's habit, strategy, he turned on the radio. He purposely tuned in to an AM frequency with loud static. He purposely turned the volume up high enough so that the sound became hurtful to the ears. He leaned towards Gangi and whispered.

'This way no one can listen.'

'What's up?'

'We gotta go kill Talal.'

'You want me to do it?' Gangi asked, seeing an opportunity to get close to Pitera, to prove himself. Gangi didn't want to kill anybody, but he wanted to impress Pitera. He felt the closer he got to Pitera, the more Pitera trusted him, the more money he'd make.

'No, no, I'll take care of it. We're going over to Richie David's house. He's got a briefcase for us. You'll go in and get it.'

'OK,' Frank said, the static bothering him, stirring up his hangover from the night before. Pitera kept looking in the rear-view mirror as he drove, making sure they were alone.

They made their way to Richie David's house. Richie was expecting them. When Gangi got to the door, Richie handed him a briefcase. Gangi, with his long, stilted gait, walked back to the car and got in. Pitera opened the case. There were guns inside. He took out an automatic, cocked it and put a bullet in the breach. He then carefully screwed a custom-fitted silencer on the front of the gun. It was obvious that he knew guns exceedingly well. Seeing him handle a gun was like seeing a doctor handle a stethoscope. The gun was part of Pitera's stock in trade, and he had made it his business to make any gun he held, any weapon he held, a natural extension of his body. He put the gun back in the briefcase and closed it. He placed the case on the back seat. Pitera put the car in gear and they started out. He made his way to Coney Island Avenue and they took a right. The victim, Talal Siksik, was being held at his apartment, number 1A, at 2807 Kings Highway and East 28th Street. The mark was dying because Tommy had been told by one of his crew that he was an informer. Pitera hated rats with an obsessive fervour.

They had some difficulty parking. Kings Highway was a shopping mecca for all Brooklynites and finding a parking spot was difficult. When they finally parked, Pitera stuck the 9 mm auto in the nape of his back and they made their way to Siksik's home. When the door opened, they found Shlomo Mendelsohn, also known as Sammy, and Billy Bright there.

Talal Siksik was handcuffed. His mouth was taped shut. It was obvious he was scared beyond words, petrified to the core of his being, and his eyes nearly popped out of his head when he saw Tommy. It was obvious, too, that he had been severely beaten. Tommy was angry about him being not only beaten but tortured as well. He yelled at Shlomo and Billy. Billy sheepishly said it was a misunderstanding.

It was now that Pitera showed his true colours. Drawing the gun from his waistband, he quickly walked over to the distraught Siksik, raised the gun and shot him in the head twice, just above the ear. Frank Gangi was shocked by the quiet, lethal ferocity of Pitera's attack. He had never seen anybody kill with such ease, aplomb. It was like watching a professional fighter in his prime knock out a man with a left hook. Pitera was sure of himself, confident. Every step he took was filled with resolve and purpose. It was obvious that killing a human being meant nothing to Pitera. On the one hand, Gangi had to admire how lethal and deadly he was. On the other, he was appalled by how indifferently Pitera claimed the life of Talal Siksik.

Gangi hadn't seen anything yet.

It would get far worse.

Pitera turned to Gangi and said, in his high-pitched voice, 'Help me get him in the tub.' Both Pitera and Gangi were strong men and carrying Talal to the tub was easy. For the most part, Talal had stopped bleeding. They placed him in the tub face down. Pitera now produced the kind of hacksaw used for autopsies. He took it and turned to Gangi.

'I want you to get undressed, get in the tub with him and cut him into six pieces.'

Gangi felt like he'd been hit by a bat. Never in his life had he done such a thing. Never in his life had he even thought of such a thing. This was right out of a fucking horror movie, he thought. He looked to Billy Bright. Billy remained mute, emotionless – stone-like. Billy knew he had to accept what was happening, that if he wanted to work with Pitera he could show no emotion one way or the other.

'Go ahead,' Tommy prodded Frank, offering up the hacksaw.

'I can't. I don't do that. If I knew you would ask me to do that, I, I, I—'

'You what?' Pitera said.

Gangi just stared at him and shook his head. It was obvious to Pitera that Hell would have to freeze over before Gangi would get naked and cut up Talal. Pitera was asking him to do this, encouraging him to do it, because he wanted to test him, see what he was made of. If Gangi cut the body up as he was ordered, Pitera reasoned, he could be trusted. He was one of them, cut from the same bloodstained cloth. Now, rather than debate the pros and cons of Gangi's actions, Pitera did what he did best: he took the bull by the horns and took care of business. He walked to the bathroom, got undressed, neatly folding his clothes as he did so. Then, without a second thought, he got in the tub with the body. He now turned on the water so it ran in a steady flow, though not too strong. He did this so the blood would be washed away, washed down the drain. Gangi watched this through the door. He didn't quite believe his eyes.

Without hesitation, inhibition, Pitera proceeded to remove Talal's head, arms and legs. He did this with the expertise of a professional butcher. When the body was in six pieces, Shlomo brought the trunk into the bathroom and Tommy calmly proceeded to put what was left of Talal inside. The trunk was closed. With that, Pitera proceeded to turn up the force of the water, washing down the remnants of the blood. He then took a long, careful shower, got out of the bathtub and casually began to dry himself. He now turned the water hot and let it clean the last of the blood.

Freshly showered and dressed, they were ready to go. With some disdain in his odd voice, Pitera told Gangi and Sammy to go get the car. They left and made their way towards a liquor store on Kings Highway.

'I need a drink,' Frank said, and entered the store. He bought a bottle of scotch. Outside, he took long, slow pulls on the bottle. He handed it to Shlomo. He also took long gulps.

'My God,' Gangi said. 'Jesus H. Christ.'

They walked on. The warmth of the scotch spread from his stomach outward. Gangi had not eaten and the effect was strong. He immediately felt better. He took several more long slugs on the bottle. They returned to the apartment and double-parked in front, went back upstairs and inside. They were going to use Shlomo's car to transport the trunk, but Shlomo's registration was expired so they decided not to use it.

Tommy decided that the body would be put in his car. The men picked up the trunk and made their way downstairs. It just about fit in the trunk of the car. Shlomo went and got a shovel from his car and put it in Pitera's car. With that, they all got in the car, Gangi driving. Pitera told Frank to make his way over to the Belt Parkway. Gangi knew the neighbourhood well, drove to Bay Parkway, took a left, made his way to the Belt and headed towards the city. For the most part, they stayed quiet and solemn and did not talk about what had just happened. Tommy put on music. As they merged onto the Belt Parkway, Tommy said, 'Get on the bridge. We're going to Staten Island.'

Frank Gangi was certainly not the brightest guy in the world, but it didn't take long for him to realise that they were going to bury Talal Siksik on Staten Island somewhere. They crossed the Verrazano Bridge. Gangi quietly stared out the window and enjoyed the view of the Narrows and the grandeur of Manhattan beyond. After going through the toll, unstopped and unchecked, they made their way to the South Avenue exit, got off and headed towards the William T. Davis Wildlife Refuge. It was in a desolate place. There were no cars, houses or people about. It was as quiet as a long-forgotten crypt. Pitera told Gangi to take the car and come back in 45 minutes. He didn't want the car there, as it might draw police suspicion. Pitera and the other two got out of the car. They retrieved the trunk from the back. Using a flashlight, Pitera, Shlomo and Billy Bright made their way into the bird sanctuary. Here, there were trees and shrubs and walking was not difficult. Gangi slowly turned the car around and drove back over the bridge to Brooklyn. He pulled up in front of the Just Us, went inside and drank some more.

While Frank drank, Tommy and the others, using a flashlight, found a spot some 30 steps from the road that looked good. Here they began digging. There was a half-moon low in the sky and it laid an ominous silver light, as if cake frosting, on the still bird sanctuary. Planes on the approach to Kennedy Airport were low overhead and you could, intermittently, hear the roar of their powerful engines. The ground was soft. Digging was not difficult. They each took turns, there in the pale light of the moon. Soon they had dug a hole deep enough to accommodate the trunk. Pitera kicked the trunk into the hole. It landed with a meaty thud. With that, they filled the hole, stomped the dirt down, carefully covered it with leaves and brambles and walked back towards the road. As they made their way back to the desolate street, Gangi was just driving up. The air was stuffy, still. Shlomo and Billy and Tommy got in the car. Frank pulled away.

'You been drinking?' Tommy asked Frank accusingly.

'Yeah,' Gangi said. 'Just had a shot at the bar.'

Pitera had heard that Gangi had a drinking problem, that he had a drug problem, yet he was willing to accept him and make him part of his crew – mainly because Gangi came from a family filled with mafiosi – men of respect, both soldiers and capos. But what happened that night put a distance between the two, an irreversible chasm that would only continue to grow.

Later that night, after Pitera showered and dressed, he went to the Just Us. Gangi was still there, at the bar drinking scotch. Since he had arrived at the bar he had done a couple of lines of coke and he was coke-lucid and didn't seem drunk at all. Cocaine can make a drunk person seem sober. It removes the drunkenness – the slurs, the walking crooked. Droopy eyes are suddenly bright and alive and all-seeing. A friend of Tommy's came in and told him that he had seen Phyllis Burdi and his girlfriend Celeste at The Esplanade. This obviously pissed him off and he, with Gangi in tow, quickly went over there. He learned that Celeste *had* been at The Esplanade earlier. Tommy drove over to Phyllis's house, but nobody was home. He began looking for them in different bars and after-hours clubs scattered around Brooklyn, without luck. Several times he was told he had just missed them. Somehow, in Pitera's mind, all of this was because of Phyllis Burdi. If it weren't for Phyllis, his girlfriend wouldn't be using drugs, causing him grief, out and about.

Pitera was a true creature of the night; he disdained the day, people who worked nine-to-five, people who were forced to do everything in life but what they wanted to do. Because he slept most of the day, Pitera took on a grey-white pallor that was reminiscent of Bela Lugosi's countenance in the original *Dracula*.

The DEA task force assigned to following Pitera, assigned to bringing Pitera down, readily adapted to his hours. They, like Pitera, were not nine-to-five people. They would do whatever the job called for. Often, during surveillance, they were up 24 or even 48 hours, living on coffee and fast food, eating on the go. They were flexible, malleable, ready, willing and able to do the job at any hour. They well knew that bad guys worked at night. They well knew, more specifically, that mafiosi came out at eleven or twelve o'clock at night and did their business throughout the wee morning hours. This was coupled with the fact that many bad guys these days were using drugs – powerful stimulants that made it easy for them to stay up all night long.

Because Pitera was so difficult to get evidence on, the DEA expanded the programme to record him. They put bugs in his cars. The problem was that he never spoke in cars. When he did, he would put static on the radio or blast music. Everyone knew, both the good guys and the bad guys, that bugging cars had become very popular amongst law enforcement. The good guys had got Tony 'Ducks' Corallo, head of the Lucchese family, talking endlessly while in his Jaguar, being driven around Manhattan.

Making things more difficult was the fact that Pitera drove not only his own cars but those of his crew as well. Pitera would suddenly be at the Just Us, at this corner or that corner, the DEA having no idea how he got there. At times, it seemed like he had some kind of diabolical, supernatural powers and the task force started calling him 'the vampire'. They still did not know that Pitera donned disguises.

A weak link – they looked for the weak link. They didn't know when or where they'd find it, but they knew sooner or later they would. Whatever could be said about Pitera, it was obvious that he believed he was being tailed. It was obvious that he knew he was under some kind of police scrutiny, yet he was not going to stop. Still, the DEA bought drugs from Angelo Favara and Judy Haimowitz that were ultimately supplied by Pitera and, in a larger sense, the Bonanno crime family. Judy Haimowitz was an exceedingly small fish. They knew, sooner or later, they'd be able to turn her, but that time had not yet come. They wanted a stronger case with witnesses who would be far more harmful than Judy Haimowitz.

Hunt and Geisel and Group 33 became more and more motivated, more and more driven, more and more sure that something big was just over the horizon.

HAPPENSTANCE

Frank Gangi, tall, thin and broad-shouldered, was having nightmares. As he slept, the horror of what he'd seen Pitera do plagued him. While he was awake, during the day, in the early evening, before he went to sleep at night, he still thought about what he'd seen – the methodical, cold dismemberment of a human being. There was a diabolical, macabre finality to what not only Pitera did, but also how he did it. Gangi had heard, over and over again, that Pitera had killed a lot of people. He started asking questions and he came to believe that Pitera had murdered dozens of people. When he thought back and saw in his mind what Pitera had done, he readily thought that Pitera could have indeed killed a hundred people. Not only did he shoot Talal Siksik in the head in front of three people, but he had also had a burial ground all ready. He had a private cemetery. It was scary, unsettling. Who the hell could do such a thing, he wondered. What was he made of? He didn't seem – human. He wondered if he got some kind of sexual excitement out of it, some kind of diabolical, sadistic charge – a kick.

These were disconcerting questions he could not pose to anyone. He was supposed to be part of the ultimate machismo society – the

The building where the young Frank Gangi lived during his formative years,
Bay 50th, Bensonhurst, Brooklyn (2008). *Author's collection*

The Esplanade restaurant, La Cosa Nostra hangout, where Tommy
Pitera and Gangi often went (2008). *Author's collection*

The ground-floor apartment with the double window is where
Arthur Guvenaro was shot by Frank Gangi and Billy Bright.
Guvenaro dived through the front window to escape,
but fell dead a block away (2008). *Author's collection*

Pitera's bar, the Just Us, is now the IQ Learning Center, Avenue S, Gravesend, Brooklyn (2008). *Author's collection*

Once a popular after-hours club frequented by Phyllis Burdi, Celeste LiPari and people in the Pitera mob, Avenue T, Gravesend, Brooklyn (2008). *Author's collection*

Travel Occasions was once the Mother Cabrini Educational Center, former Bonanno social club and Pitera hangout, located on Avenue U, Gravesend, Brooklyn (2008). *Author's collection*

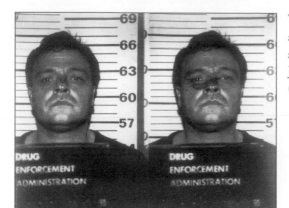

Tommy Pitera on the day of his arrest. Note the two black eyes, sustained during the arrest when Jim Hunt threw him to the ground (June 1990). *Courtesy of the DEA*

Pitera's pen gun, confiscated by the DEA from his Emmons Avenue apartment. *Courtesy of the DEA*

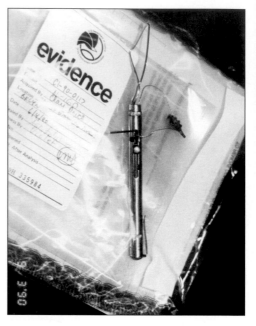

Enthusiastic cadaver dogs searching for bodies on the Pitera burial ground, to no avail (June 1990). *Courtesy of the DEA*

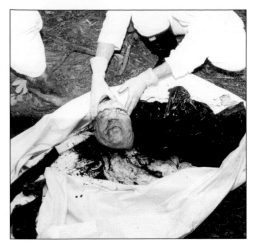

The head of torture victim Sol Stern, taken from a Pitera grave-site. Note that the cut was so high up that the neck is not part of the head (June 1990). *Courtesy of the DEA*

A human head pulled from the Pitera graveyard. Note the teeth in the bottom right of the photograph (June 1990). *Courtesy of the DEA*

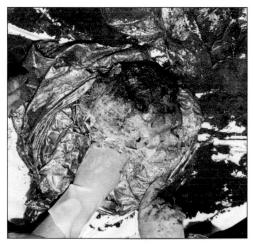

Remnants of an arm dug up at the William T. Davis Wildlife Refuge (June 1990). *Courtesy of the DEA*

The torso of one of Pitera's victims, removed from the William T. Davis Wildlife Refuge (June 1990). *Courtesy of the DEA*

Author Philip Carlo with Frank Gangi. *Author's collection*

Mafia. His father, cousins, uncles were stone-cold, dedicated mafiosi. The answer, for Frank Gangi, became more drinking and more drugs. He also chain-smoked and coughed incessantly. At the rate he was going, the way in which he treated himself, it didn't seem as if he had too much time left on the planet.

Be that as it may, Frank Gangi continued to work for and associate with Tommy Pitera. However, the fact that Gangi could not cut up the body, would not do what he was told, did not sit well with Pitera. He wanted submissive loyalty, given blindly and without question. What he asked of Gangi was unusual, he knew. However, with time, he hoped Gangi would come around and do what he was told when he was told.

Marek Kucharsky was a piece of work. He had been a professional boxer, was tough and irrationally fearless. He came from the mean streets of Poland, a place where might was always right. Because he was a boxer, because he was tough, he could knock out anyone who faced him, anyone who challenged him. Still, as tough as he was, as stand-up as he was, he was struggling to make ends meet. He was, essentially, another nobody wanting to be a somebody.

Kucharsky had managed to steal 60 valuable oriental rugs. The problem was he had no contacts for selling the rugs and turning them into cash. Marek knew Moussa Aliyan well. Moussa was an Israeli drug dealer, part of an Israeli cabal of dealers. He was a former lieutenant in the Israeli Army. He was fearless, highly motivated, arrogant to a fault, and lived in a large, spacious loft on West 38th Street in Manhattan. He and Pitera had a reasonably good working relationship. Pitera sold heroin to him; he provided Pitera with large quantities of high-grade cocaine. Moussa and Gangi sometimes hung out together. They got high together.

Marek did not know that Moussa was having sex with his girlfriend. Moussa had lots of coke and Marek's girlfriend was a coke whore. It seemed that in the '80s every other woman you met was a coke whore. If you had coke, regardless of how you looked, you got pussy. Moussa agreed to see what he could do with the rugs. Moussa was not really planning on paying for the rugs; he knew they were valuable, he knew that sooner or later they could very well be money in his pocket. Meanwhile, he'd stall Marek – and hopefully never pay him.

As Frank Gangi had become more and more friendly with Moussa as he sold more and more drugs for Pitera, Moussa ended up giving Gangi a dozen of the rugs. 'If you can sell them, sell them. If you want to keep them, keep them,' he said. Not knowing anything about Persian carpets, Frank took them back to Brooklyn. He put them on the floors of his house. He liked the way they looked. He had no idea they were worth so much money.

Subsequently, Marek kept showing up at Moussa's house looking for money, asking for money. Moussa stalled him, wouldn't answer the door. He figured sooner or later the Polish boxer would go away. Moussa had grown fond of the rugs. He wanted to keep them. He had already sent some back to Israel so his mother and father could enjoy them.

This all came to boil with a brutal murder. It was unplanned and happenstance. Pitera, Moussa and Gangi were at Moussa's apartment on the evening of 6 October 1987, drinking and talking. It was a warm night, though autumn was in the air. Both Moussa and Gangi were doing lines of coke. Pitera did not do coke like that. When he did coke, he did it in the privacy of his own moment and he did very little. He was fond of saying, 'I control it. It doesn't control me.'

Suddenly, Marek showed up. By now, he had become aggressive and mean. He wanted the rugs back or he wanted his money. He was yelling, pointing and being disrespectful. Inevitably, Pitera and he started arguing. Gangi got up and tried to throw him out. That was a mistake. Gangi was suddenly fighting with a professional boxer. He was big and strong and could hold his own, but not against a professional fighter. It was obvious that Gangi was not only losing the fight, but was also going to get his arse kicked. This was something

Pitera would never allow. Had he had a gun on him, he would have shot Kucharsky in the head. What he did have on him was a knife – a razor-sharp folding knife. He opened the knife and stabbed Marek in the side with tremendous force. The knife bit into the boxer like a rabid dog. Marek managed to get the knife out and close the blade on Tommy Pitera's finger. The cut was so deep his finger was almost severed. With that, the three of them got the boxer down onto the floor. Gangi got hold of the knife. Pitera demanded, yelled, that he cut the boxer's throat. Without hesitation, Frank Gangi drew the blade across Marek's throat. Blood squirted all over the place. He not only cut his throat but he also cut one of the major arteries. As Marek lay in the throes of death, Moussa, Gangi and Pitera stood over him. Pitera kicked the prostrate boxer several times – he was soon dead.

Immediately, Pitera started talking about dismembering the body.

Again, Frank Gangi was confronted with this scenario – being told to cut up a body. This time, he would not punk out. This time, he thought, he would show Pitera exactly what he was made of, that he was tough, that he had what it took. The bleeding from Pitera's cut had become so bad that he left to go and get it stitched. Moussa and Gangi carried the boxer to the hot tub. They undressed him. Moussa produced a hacksaw. Leaning over, in an odd position, Gangi proceeded to cut off one of Marek's legs. He had no knowledge of the joints, major muscles and tendons and it was very difficult. Not only that, but he just wasn't up to the task. He thought it barbaric and cannibalistic.

'It was disgusting,' he would later tell a confidant.

Moussa finished the job. It was obvious that Moussa had cut up bodies before. He did it quickly and efficiently with a savage vengeance that left Gangi somewhat speechless. Gangi wondered if he was a 'pussy'; Gangi wondered if he was weak. They finished and took what was left of the boxer and wrapped him in the rugs about which he had come. Not only did he not get the money for his rugs, but they also ended up becoming his death shroud.

Again, Frank Gangi found solace in scotch and whiskey. Whiskey and coke. They were the answer to all problems.

Pitera returned with a large white bandage on his hand. He also had Joey Balzano in tow. Joey was another Brooklyn guy, rough around the edges, loyal to Pitera, a wannabe mafioso. He had not been made. Without preamble, they took the carpets containing the remains of Marek and placed him in the trunk of the car that Marek had arrived in – his girlfriend's car. The four men returned to Brooklyn and went to Joey's house, where he grabbed shovels. They then proceeded to go back to the Belt Parkway and over the Verrazano Bridge. Gangi could not help but marvel at the efficient, ghastly ingenuity of Pitera's little burying ritual. You had a body to get rid of – no problem.

They quickly arrived at the bird sanctuary. Tommy told Moussa and Gangi to bury the suitcases. They followed him to the spot where he wanted Marek placed. Leaving them with two flashlights, he returned to Marek's girlfriend's car and left. He wanted Gangi to be part and parcel of all that was done. Pitera felt that if Gangi buried the body, he would always be as culpable and responsible as he was himself.

The bird sanctuary at night was shockingly quiet. There were no sounds. They began to dig the hole. Moussa, then Gangi would dig. They made some ghoulish jokes. When they had gone down about three feet, they kicked and pushed the remains of Marek, the Polish boxer, into the hole. They closed the hole with excess dirt. They made a half-assed effort to cover the hole. They both knew, however, no one would find his body. No one would find this place. Though it was smack dab in the middle of New York, this sanctuary on Staten Island was a dark, secretive place with no human beings anywhere in sight.

'How many bodies you think he has buried here?' Gangi asked Moussa.

'A lot,' he responded, raising his eyebrows.

Within several minutes, Pitera pulled up, as if on cue.

25

PARTY GIRL

One would think, considering how quickly Pitera killed, that he was invincible; that all his troubles could be solved with murder. Murder was like a coat of armour that Pitera constantly wore.

Surely, nothing could hurt him.

If Pitera had a weakness, it was Celeste LiPari. No matter how many times he confronted her, she continued to do drugs. No matter how many fights they had, she did drugs. He did not believe in hitting women. She caused him pain. She caused him turmoil. He felt, sooner or later, that her drug use would cause her to get involved with other men, other women, scenarios that would embarrass him. After all, he had an image, a profile to maintain. He was a man of respect. What kind of man of respect had a girlfriend who was abusing drugs in after-hours clubs and being put-upon and hit on by every coked-up, horny Tom, Dick and Harry, every guido in Brooklyn? He knew for a fact that Phyllis Burdi was a loose woman – a whore. He knew she was having sexual relations with half the New York Mafia. He knew, too, that one of her lovers was Eddie Lino. Eddie and Tommy were friends. They genuinely liked each other. They did business together. And here was Phyllis Burdi, the biggest puttana in all of Brooklyn, hanging out with his beloved Celeste.

By way of Frank Gangi, Tommy sent word to Phyllis over and over: stay away from Celeste; stop hanging out with Celeste; stop getting high with Celeste! It did no good. He kept hearing that the two were seen here, there and everywhere.

Murder . . . Pitera's remedy for all problems became a possible solution. Pitera had a meeting with Gangi in the Just Us bar.

'Look,' Pitera said, 'you have to try to understand this situation. I do not – do *not* – want Phyllis hanging out with Celeste. It's bad. I'm hearing things. Everyone knows.' He shook his head from side to side, dismayed.

Frank wanted to tell Pitera he should be talking to Celeste, not him. It was Celeste who was doing the drugs. It was Celeste, he knew, who often asked him if he had some coke on him. He'd run into her at different bars and after-hours clubs and the first thing out of Celeste's mouth was, 'You got any blow?' Gangi knew that Phyllis Burdi was promiscuous, but she was also a coke whore. She not only did coke but heroin, too. What Gangi would have liked to say to Pitera and what he did say were two radically different things. He had come to believe that Pitera was an out-of-control psychopath. The last thing he wanted to do was insult him, to get him angry.

'I'll find her,' Frank said. 'I'll talk to her again.'

With that, Gangi called Phyllis and met her at a bar near her house. They sat on stools at the bar and ordered drinks.

'Phyllis, how do I say this? I've said this so many times to you already. You have to stop hanging out with Celeste. Tommy knows. He's got people all over Brooklyn telling him things. He's got spies everywhere.'

Phyllis raised her eyes. She had heard this before.

'Look,' she said, 'I don't force Celeste to do anything. She calls me, she wants to come by, she wants to go out. She's my girlfriend.

What am I supposed to do? Say, "I can't hang out with you because your boyfriend doesn't like me"? She knows a lot of guys. They give her drugs.'

Gangi shook his head back and forth. He saw no good coming from this. He tried another tactic. 'Look, Pitera is a very dangerous man. You get this guy mad at you – it'll be very bad. There's no telling what he'll do. I'm talking to you as a friend now. I care about you. I don't want to see you get hurt.'

'Get hurt for what? I haven't done anything. Celeste is a strong-willed woman. Nobody can make this girl do anything.' She laughed. 'If he can't make her stop getting high, how am I supposed to stop her from getting high? The problem is with her. It's not with me,' she said.

Gangi knew she was right but that didn't necessarily matter. If Pitera got it in his head that she was corrupting the woman he loved, it would be catastrophic for her. This he knew. This everyone in Brooklyn knew.

Brooklyn, as large a borough as it was, was really a cluster of small communities – neighbourhoods – in which everyone knew one another. People from different 'hoods, most of whom were La Cosa Nostra associated, were mobile and travelled to clubs all across the borough. Not only legitimate clubs but after-hours ones as well. All the after-hours clubs were mob-run. The cops knew about them. The cops were paid off to look the other way. In all the after-hours clubs, the use of cocaine and other drugs was the norm, not the exception. After all, who would be up at four or five in the morning, dancing and partying up a storm, except for those on various stimulants? There were after-hours clubs in Coney Island, Bensonhurst, South Brooklyn, Flatbush, Gravesend, and they were all frequented by La Cosa Nostra.

After several drinks that night, Gangi and Phyllis did a few lines of cocaine, went back to his apartment and had sex. In some strange way, in the back of his mind, Gangi felt guilty for being intimate with her. He felt in his bones, somewhere deep inside, that something horrible could happen; something he, if he knew better, could stop. He saw the writing on the wall. He saw the dark skies. He remembered Pitera's burial grounds, the macabre solitude, the crypt-like silence, the eerie stillness of the sanctuary in the middle of the night. No matter how hard he tried to forget about it, he couldn't. Unlike Pitera, Frank Gangi was not made of stone.

26

SPEED BALLS

Whatever demons were plaguing Celeste LiPari inside could not be frightened off even by Tommy Pitera. Celeste knew what Pitera was capable of. She heard the rumours. She saw blood on his clothes. She heard the things that came out of his mouth which told her, in no uncertain terms, that he would kill with ease and indifference. Celeste also saw the genuine fear that lived in people's faces when Pitera walked into a room, a restaurant or a bar. Even made men, she knew, averted their gaze when Pitera arrived at a wedding, a funeral parlour. She knew, too, that he had gone to Japan to learn how to fight, to learn how to kill, and that he read voraciously about violence, war, killing, dismemberment and anarchy. Knowing all this, Celeste continued to use drugs. Celeste continued to party indiscreetly. True, Phyllis Burdi could not make Celeste use drugs, but Phyllis was surely a negative influence. The two of them, in a sense, were like two peas in a pod. They were attractive, sexual and addicted to drugs.

On 10 September 1987, Phyllis and Celeste, all dressed up, make-up on their faces, their nails painted bright red, five-inch heels on their shoes, went out to have a good time. They went from club to club, to people's homes, then back to club-hopping. They ended up at an after-hours joint called The Wrong Number on Avenue T. They repelled the entreaties of various men. They snorted coke in the bathroom. Fearful that Tommy might show up there, the two women left and went back to Phyllis's house at 20–22 West 5th Street. They were not alone. Several men and two more women came with them. They would have a party. What would fuel the party would be high-grade cocaine and heroin.

Oddly enough, heroin had become popular again. Wired cokeheads all over the country were using it to come down, to calm themselves. It was also popular to mix heroin and cocaine together and shoot them up at the same time. This was known as a 'speedball'. John Belushi and a long list of others died by shooting speedballs. Both Phyllis and Celeste mainlined heroin. Of the three ways to use heroin – snort it, skin-pop it and mainline it – mainlining it is the most dangerous. The drug is injected directly into a main artery and quickly, with the bat of an eye, moves throughout the body. Phyllis's apartment was small and unkempt – a mess. Because she was often up all night and all day, she had its dirty windows covered with shades and dust-laden curtains. The curtains drawn and the shades down, one could barely discern night from day. When on drugs, one's perception of time is completely turned upside-down, so Phyllis and her friends had no idea what time it was and didn't give a flying fuck. Fuelled by the cocaine, they rapidly discussed nonsense. There was a couple there and they began to have sex. Celeste wanted to come down and would do that with heroin.

At any given time, it is difficult to discern the purity of heroin on the street. It could be as high as 85 per cent or as low as 5 per cent. Heroin that was 85 per cent pure was – lethal. One could readily liken it to cyanide. Celeste had no idea of the exact purity of the heroin she was using that morning; all she knew was that she wanted to come down, and so she mainlined the drug.

She, like the others there, lay back, her eyes hung at half-mast. Her facial muscles became lax, her mouth slowly opened, spittle ran from her lower lip. She soon drifted off on a silky, opium-laden cloud. It was warm and soothing and took her away from all her problems. Whatever pains, whatever turmoil Celeste had suffered was soon forgotten – left behind. As Celeste drifted further and further into the fatal embrace of opium, her heart slowed, her breathing became shallow. Oblivious to those around her, to Brooklyn, to the world, Celeste soon stopped breathing. The weak beat of her heart became fainter and fainter and soon it stopped. Quickly, surprisingly so, her face took on a waxy, pale hue.

Those there that morning, all high on heroin, had no idea what had just happened, knew nothing of their friend's death. By the time it was discovered that Celeste had OD'd, that Celeste had died, that the grim reaper had stolen her away, it was hours later.

With friends throughout Gravesend and Bensonhurst and Coney Island – both within organised crime and within the police department – it didn't take long for Tommy Pitera to hear that Celeste had died. That Celeste had died at Phyllis Burdi's house.

He'd been home sleeping when there was a knock on the door. Frank Gangi and another Pitera associate, Joey Tekulve, known as 'Joey Pizza', were standing there, all gloom and doom, obviously something deeply troubling them both.

Earlier, when Phyllis had found Celeste, she had called up Judy Haimowitz in a panic, hysterical, wanting to know what to do. Joey had been at Judy Haimowitz's house and advised her to call the cops. Joey then called around, looking for Gangi, and found him at Moussa's apartment. When Gangi heard the news, he sped back to Brooklyn and picked up Joey Pizza at the Just Us. They both knew Pitera would take this very badly. They both knew that Celeste was probably the only person in the world Tommy loved. This would not be good. They didn't want to be the ones to tell Pitera about Celeste's death, but they knew if they didn't give him the information and he found out, he'd be fit to be tied.

171

Now, they were standing at Pitera's door and he was looking at them questioningly. Frank Gangi told him what they'd heard, that Celeste had died at Phyllis Burdi's house.

Tommy reacted to these words like he'd been hit by a bolt of electricity. He yelled, cursed 37 ways from Sunday. He quickly got dressed and they made their way over to Phyllis's apartment on Avenue T. When they arrived, there were police cars and an ambulance out front. Stoic and angry, seething, Tommy Pitera got out of the car and quickly walked inside. When they arrived at the apartment, the door was open. A rookie cop Pitera knew was there. Celeste's body hadn't been removed yet, and when Tommy saw it he broke down, began crying hysterically. It was an odd, unsettling sight to see a man like him, so cold, so indifferent, break down and cry like a baby. Phyllis came out of the bedroom. She looked worn and haggard, worried and frightened.

'I told you to stay the fuck away from her,' Tommy said, moving towards her quickly, looking as if he would kill her, take her neck in his hands and throttle her to death, take her head in his hands and break it off her shoulders, bend her over his knee and break her back. Surely, if the cop hadn't been there, he would have killed her on the spot. The pain and hurt he felt were replaced by a fiery anger that bordered on insanity. Pitera slapped her hard across the face. The rookie cop got between Phyllis and Tommy.

'Please, Tommy, you can't do that. You gotta leave. Tommy, please,' the cop said.

'I'm going to get you, I'm going to get you,' he told Phyllis as he made his way towards the door and was suddenly gone. His anger, his hatred, his words seemed to hang in the air behind him.

Already Celeste's body had begun to rot and the smell of her corpse filled the air. Downstairs, Gangi, Pitera and Joey Pizza walked around the block. Over and over again, Tommy said he wanted her dead. He wanted Frank to kill her. He knew Frank had a relationship with her and he felt Frank could get close to her and do the job. In a sense, it was a wonder that he didn't want to kill her himself, torture her; exact his own revenge in his own way. Be that as it may, he told Frank he wanted her dead and he wanted him to carry out the contract.

This was a dilemma for Frank Gangi. He wasn't the killer that Pitera was. He could never kill a woman. He certainly didn't want to kill Phyllis Burdi. She was his friend and she was his lover. Just the day before she had been over at his house along with Celeste and another woman named Michelle. They had cleaned his apartment and he had paid them with cocaine. Frank often had more cocaine than he had cash money. Now he was confronted with this life-altering, life-changing dilemma. Rather than debate this killing with Pitera now, knowing Pitera was upset beyond words, Frank said nothing. He listened to Tommy's pain. He listened to Tommy rant and rage about Phyllis Burdi.

27

SHOULDA, COULDA, WOULDA

For several days, Phyllis lay low, knowing there was danger in the air. Had she had more sense, if she hadn't been so attached to that neighbourhood, she might have left town, gone to Florida, perhaps out to the west coast, and let things cool down. Yes, Phyllis Burdi was street savvy, but because her whole life revolved around the mean streets of Brooklyn, she did not have the wherewithal, the worldliness, to go to another place and make a life for herself. She stayed in Gravesend, looking over her shoulder as she went; she still got high, but she was more on guard. More on guard but still there, still in the jungle – a jungle prowled by Pitera.

Over the coming days and weeks, Pitera badgered Gangi about Phyllis – 'When will she be dead?' Gangi did what he could to stall Pitera. He hoped that, with time, Pitera's anger would abate, but just the opposite happened. It seemed that every hour that went by Pitera became angrier and angrier. He was like some wrathful god who would not have peace, who would not rest, until he had revenge.

Still, Pitera was Frank's boss, and as much as it pained him to think about it, he knew he'd eventually have to do what Pitera said. In the meantime, he stayed away from Phyllis. Gangi figured if he didn't see her, Pitera couldn't get mad at him for not setting her up, killing her. He purposely avoided clubs she went to, bars she hung out in. In the back of his mind somewhere, he hoped Pitera would get caught up in something else, but that didn't occur and every time Pitera saw Gangi the first thing he asked was: 'What about Burdi?'

'I haven't seen her,' he said. 'I call her, she doesn't call me back.'

With that, Pitera stared at Gangi in the faint light of the Just Us bar. 'You lying to me?' Pitera asked Gangi.

'No, why would I lie to you? I know what Burdi is. She's a whore,' he said.

'Find her. Kill her,' Pitera whispered in that strange voice.

Then, when Gangi next saw Pitera at the Just Us, he gave him an ice pick. Gangi said he couldn't kill Phyllis that way. This didn't please Pitera, though he seemed to accept it. He took the ice pick back and, in turn, gave Gangi an automatic with a silencer.

'Use this,' he said. 'You understand?'

'I understand.'

By pure happenstance, Frank Gangi ran into Phyllis Burdi early that morning at an after-hours club. She told him how she missed him. She kissed him and hugged him. The familiar though foreign smell of her aroused him. She was one of the hottest women he'd ever known. She had taken sex to new heights for him. She had done things to him that he'd never heard of before. No doubt fuelled by cocaine, Phyllis Burdi knew much about the perverse, dark world of sex in its more macabre-kinky forms. Though she had an angelic face, she demanded and needed more than simple intercourse or oral sex. She liked to have sex with more than one man at a time. It was also rumoured that Celeste and Phyllis had been lovers.

As Frank looked at Phyllis that night, he had a heavy heart, for he knew her days were numbered, though he wouldn't be her killer. He just couldn't do it. He warned her, told her to leave town – to go away. He said he'd be willing to give her money to get out of town for a while. She didn't seem to be interested in any of that and before he knew it they were heading back to his place, kissing in the car as they went, groping each other, snorting coke. The thought of killing her, calling Tommy Pitera and giving her up, was as distant to him as the moon. Gangi could not, he decided, kill her or give her up. He'd get her out of town; he'd make sure she left. But, first, he wanted her; he had to have her.

At his apartment, they had hot, lustful sex. It was raw and nasty. On tables, the couch, the floor, in chairs, near the windows. Spurred on by the high-octane fuel that cocaine is to the human libido, it went on for hours.

Suddenly, the coke was gone. So was his erection. They both wanted more. It was five in the morning, slowly getting light outside. Gangi began making phone calls, looking to cop. After several attempts, he got lucky and Moussa Aliyan said that he had coke and they could come over.

Yes!

With speed and alacrity, they got dressed, donned sunglasses, were quickly out the door and speeding towards Manhattan on Brooklyn's Belt Parkway. There was little traffic. As they made their way through the Wall Street area, they watched the stiffs in suits heading to work. They were like two creatures from another planet – cocaine aliens; the Bonnie and Clyde of the after-hours set, up all night on drugs and hurrying for a new supply. They arrived at the desolate West Side street. The sun was still low in the sky. Long shadows skulked along the quiet cobblestone street. Like two fugitives, they got out of the car and quickly made their way up to the loft building, rang the bell and were let in.

Cocaine – the devil's dandruff – to people who have been up all night on the drug and suddenly run out of it is like food to a starving man; water to someone who is dying of thirst.

Quickly, Gangi copped an eight ball (3.5 grams). It was high-grade cocaine, a glistening, pink/pearly white colour commonly known as bubblegum. Using a bank card, Gangi crushed up one of the rocks. He took a long, satisfying toot. He passed it to Phyllis and she, in turn, took an even longer line of the pearly pinkish powder.

Aaaahhhh: the nervous anxiety they both felt from the sudden coming down was quickly replaced by a euphoric warmth. They took more and more and still more. They stayed up that whole day snorting coke and intermittently having sex. Finally, with the help of alcohol and heroin, sleep enveloped them and took them to another place.

Back in Gravesend, Brooklyn, Tommy Pitera was up and about – prowling. As was widely known, Pitera only used cocaine on occasion, very little. His motto was, 'I use the drug; the drug does not use me.' He never binged for days on end on cocaine. He took a toot here and there and that was it. Pitera was very concerned with staying physically fit and he worked out every day without fail. He did not smoke cigarettes. His biceps were well defined; his shoulders were round and the size of two perfectly symmetrical grapefruits. His hands, from many years of hitting heavy bags, were like two steel sledgehammers. His trapezoid muscles were overly developed. He had honed himself into a well-lubricated killing machine.

Often, as Pitera plied the Gravesend streets, he thought of Phyllis Burdi. His reptilian blue eyes would see girls walking the street and he'd pull over, ready to grab Phyllis, but it wasn't her. When, he wondered, would he get his hands on her? Have his revenge?

He tried to find Frank Gangi that night, left a message for him, but didn't hear back.

Then, coincidentally, he called Moussa. Gangi answered the phone, as Moussa had gone out on a run. 'What's up? Where you been?' asked Pitera, angry, almost seeming to know the answer, Gangi thought.

Paranoid that he knew he'd been with Phyllis, that he'd been seen leaving the club with Phyllis, Gangi told the truth. 'I'm with Phyllis. She's here,' he said.

'You are with Phyllis?'

'Yeah.'

'Where is she?'

'Inside, sleeping.'

'Why didn't you call me?'

'I was going to call you, I swear!'

'No matter what, you keep her there. You understand? Keep, her, there!'

Before heading to the city, Pitera went back home and grabbed his dismembering kit. It was carefully wrapped up in a shammy. There were scalpels, razor-sharp knives, small two-finger saws for cutting joints, bone and tough sinew. He then picked up Vincent 'Kojak' Giattino and Richie David and two oversized, cheap suitcases. Pitera calmly drove into the city, alongside the Narrows that separates Brooklyn from Staten Island, under the Verrazano Bridge. The sun reflected off the fast-moving water, making it appear like a sea of glistening silver coins.

Silent, his mind playing over and over what he'd do, Pitera made his way to lower Manhattan via the Brooklyn Battery Tunnel and went straight to the drug dealer's loft. He rang the bell. The buzzer sounded. He quickly made his way upstairs. He fitted a silencer on a 9 mm automatic. The elevator opened directly into the apartment. Pitera walked in, carrying the gun. Ominously, Kojak was carrying two suitcases.

Wanting to get on Pitera's good side, Gangi was standing there at attention, eager to please. He seemed older, paler, his face more lined. There were puffy circles the colour of eggplants under each eye. He knew what was about to happen, was saddened by its realities. He knew, too, that he had no say in the matter. He wanted to sit down with Pitera, explain that it wasn't Phyllis's fault . . . that Celeste took the drugs all on her own, that Celeste wanted the drugs, that Celeste craved the drugs. The problem, he wanted to say, was not Phyllis but Celeste. It was a bona fide argument, but one Gangi would never make; one Pitera would never hear.

'Where is she?' Pitera growled.

Gangi pointed to the bedroom. 'She's there,' he said.

'She sleeping?'

'Yeah,' Gangi answered.

Pitera crossed the room, his steps quiet like the turning of a page. With a practised hand, he chambered a bullet and opened the door. Naked, Phyllis Burdi lay there, as vulnerable as the day she was born. With no hesitation or reservation, Pitera raised the gun and fired – once, twice, three times. Without ever knowing it, Phyllis Burdi was suddenly dead. There was no pain. There was no surprise.

Pitera ordered Kojak and David to pick up the lifeless Phyllis Burdi by her ankles and wrists and carry her to the bathroom. He told them to place her in the oversized jacuzzi tub. He turned on both the hot and cold faucets and let the water run just so. When it was the right temperature, the right amount coming out of the faucet, he went back outside and retrieved his dismembering kit. Without preamble, Pitera slowly, methodically, completely undressed himself. When he was shockingly naked, he stepped into the tub with her, both of them naked now. He began making deep, expert cuts on her shoulder blades, at the top of her spine, where her hip joints met the pelvic bone, just to the left and the right of her pubic hairline. As the body bled, he used a razor-sharp serrated hunting knife and he expertly severed her head, knowing exactly where to cut the spine, trachea and neck muscles. He picked up the severed head and put it on the edge of the tub. It faced the entrance. He then went to work on removing her left and right arms. Within minutes, her arms and her head were detached from her body. At this point, Frank Gangi walked to the threshold of the bathroom.

'Come in. Come in, here,' Pitera demanded.

Appalled, Gangi slowly walked into the bathroom. The smell of blood and death filled the air. His stomach turned at the sight of Phyllis's head at the edge of the tub, facing him. One eye was half-closed and the other eye, wide open, looked off to the left. He'd just been making love to her. She had just been giving him oral sex. Now her lifeless head was just there like some errant piece of soap. He remained speechless, mute, as quiet as stone. What could he say? Wanting to show Gangi the effect Glaser rounds had on the body, Pitera shot Phyllis in the chest three more times and explained how the many pellets encased in the heads caused massive damage.

Pitera now grabbed Phyllis by the legs, wrapped his hands around her Achilles tendon, pushed the leg forward and, using the hunting knife, cut the large muscles that connect the legs to the torso and soon made his way through the socket joints that hold the hips and legs together, expertly severing one, then the other. He told Gangi to bring him the plastic bags. Deftly, indifferently, he placed the legs, torso and arms in three different bags, knowing the weight of the torso would not rip through the bag. He put her head in a separate bag. When he was finished, four black plastic bags were neatly lined up in the bathroom, holding the remains of Phyllis Burdi.

He had Kojak put the bags into the two cheap suitcases. Carefully and scrupulously Pitera washed the tub, then meticulously washed himself, moving slowly, as though he had just come back from a workout. When he was sure he was thoroughly clean, he dried himself, got dressed and ordered Kojak and Richie to take the remains out to the bird sanctuary and bury Phyllis Burdi there. They left and headed out to Staten Island. Distraught, Gangi went back to Gravesend, Brooklyn in his car. Tommy Pitera took Phyllis Burdi's head home. There, people in the know say, he did something unspeakable with it. Satisfied, he placed the head in the freezer of his apartment. It would remain there until Pitera decided to get rid of it by dumping it in the nearby Atlantic Ocean, where crabs and fish would eat the brain flesh.

28

NO REMORSE,
NO CONSCIENCE,
NO SCRUPLES

Killing Phyllis Burdi did not bring Pitera much solace. He had loved Celeste. He had loved her more than he had loved anyone in his entire life. They were soulmates. He had shared things with her he had never told anyone. She had got to know him deep inside and she loved what she had seen and come to know. The two of them were very much alike. If ever there was a female gangster, it was Celeste LiPari. Pitera wished he could kill Phyllis over and over again.

Be that as it may, it didn't take long for word to slowly spread throughout Bensonhurst and Gravesend and Coney Island and Dyker Heights – Mafiadom – that Tommy Pitera was burying people – killing them at will, chopping them up and burying them as though he had some kind of state-issued permit. At first, these things had been said in guarded whispers. Now they were part of normal conversation in that world. His reputation as a killer extraordinaire, as a killer out of control, as a killer unchecked, grew and grew and grew still more.

The people he worked for, his bosses Anthony Spero and Frankie Lino, the upper echelon of the Bonanno family, had heard what was happening, but they did nothing to rein him in. It was also no secret that he had killed Phyllis Burdi. They, too, knew exactly the kind of woman she had been. They, too, knew that she'd been warned away from Celeste many times over. As far as all of them were concerned, she was where she belonged.

Yet the murder of Phyllis, the concept of a mafioso having his own burial ground, his own Boot Hill, as it were, was unsettling. It was unsettling to not only civilians but also people in the life.

29

FIRE-BREATHING DRAGON

More than ever, the DEA was working the Pitera case. Little by little, they heard things through the grapevine that they had set up all throughout Brooklyn. They now had both the Just Us and the Cypress Bar and Grill bugged, as well as a nightclub Pitera owned called Overstreets. They knew Pitera personally spent little time in the Cypress bar, but still they hoped to garner something they could use against him. He had bought Overstreets with the proceeds from his drug-dealing enterprises, showing good business acumen. Overstreets was a hot discotheque on the second floor of a building on 86th Street and 4th Avenue. Cash in hand, young people lined up there every night to party. It was popular, a moneymaker. Drugs were also sold at the club. By now, the government also had listening devices in Pitera's car and in his associates' cars. The government had now come to know, however, that Pitera was wily in the extreme. When he said something incriminating in any of the cars, he always had, as a matter of course, either static on the radio or the radio was so loud his words were lost. Rather than being disappointed, the task force was more motivated – more driven. They felt he was challenging them, daring them.

When they had him under surveillance and he met with different members of the Bonanno crime family, they constantly saw him covering his mouth as he talked. Mind you, this is in the street, with cars and cabs and buses passing by, but still there was Tommy Pitera concerned about surveillance, concerned about being bugged, concerned about having his words pulled out of thin air. There was equipment that could do that, but not on the large scale that Pitera seemed to think possible. The more the DEA watched him, the surer they became of everything they'd heard about him.

Conversely, Pitera sensed the presence of the cops. There were approximately nine people from Group 33 observing him, and it didn't take long for a street-savvy mafioso like Pitera to know which way the wind was blowing. He still didn't, however, know specifically what branch of law enforcement was sniffing, but he knew he was being observed, watched and scrutinised. Whoever they were, it really didn't matter to him – they all wanted one thing and that was to put him away, to garner large headlines in the papers. That's what they were after – press, not justice, he believed. Whenever there was a Mafia bust, it was always front-page news, the lead-off story on all the news channels. The government waved around mafiosi as though they were flags. It helped bolster their careers, everyone knew, and it helped bolster their budgets when it came time to divvy up money in Washington. They were, Pitera believed, selfish and self-serving, dictatorial and one-sided. It was not about the rule of law, Pitera believed, it was about headlines; it was about hanging the scalps of mafiosi out in the light of day for all to see and know and smell.

Contrary to what Pitera believed, for Jim Hunt and Tommy Geisel it *was* all about the rule of law. It was about protecting society from career criminals; it was about getting killers off the streets; it was about keeping chaos at bay and the streets safe.

Back to basics – Jim and Tommy continued to cop cocaine and heroin from Angelo Favara. Angelo sometimes bought the coke from

Judy Haimowitz and sometimes bought the drugs directly from Pitera. Thus, little by little, as though putting together a complicated puzzle, they were building a case against Judy Haimowitz – and against Pitera. The government knew that Judy would readily turn when confronted with serious jail time. However, she was not the kind of witness who could make or break the case against Pitera. They needed substantially more. Pitera had never been there when they'd bought drugs from Judy or Angelo, nor had he personally sold them drugs.

They encouraged Angelo Favara to arrange a large buy with Pitera, but Pitera had come to view Angelo as trouble. He kept Angelo at bay, at arm's length; didn't trust him. When Pitera looked at him, he saw a weasel or, worse still, a rat. Still, the DEA agents encouraged Angelo to talk to Tommy about arranging a big buy if not from Tommy, then from any of the people who worked for Tommy. If Angelo managed, as he did, ultimately, to cop drugs from people who worked for Pitera, conspiracy laws would kick in and they'd have Pitera by the proverbial balls. Any angle the DEA could exploit, they would. If Jim Hunt had learned anything over the years, if Jim Hunt had garnered any insights from being the son of the revered *Jim Hurt*, it was to work as many venues, leads and opportunities as possible; not to discount anything. The more hot pokers you had in the fire, the better.

One of the people who worked for Pitera was Andrew Miciotta. Andrew was an intricate part of the drug-dealing constellation that Pitera had created. Jim Hunt and Tommy Geisel managed to, initially, buy heroin from Andrew via Angelo. Eventually Andrew, a short, stocky, balding man, agreed to meet with the two agents and sell them heroin directly. They, as such, were not interested in Andrew – they wanted his boss. They wanted Pitera.

For Jim Hunt, bringing down Pitera was not about press or promotion or a feather in his cap. He genuinely hated bad guys – especially drug-dealing mafiosi.

He felt Pitera was contributing to the downfall of the community in which he lived; he felt that all the Piteras of the world were about chaos and disorder and the breaking of the rules and regulations that governed a well-run, civilised society. The fact that Pitera was definitely connected to the Bonanno crime family amplified their efforts a hundred-fold. This was not some renegade tough guy willing to take chances and sell drugs. This was a member of an organised, mechanised international underground society that would rape and pillage, steal and rob, suck the lifeblood from everything it got its hands on. This was a fire-breathing dragon and Jim Hunt was intent upon lopping its head off.

30

THE LOSS OF A TENTACLE

Tommy Pitera was open to doing business with any ethnic group that could help him prosper. He knew that to have only one source of product was not good. He readily dealt with Russian mafiosi and Israeli gangs. The Israelis in particular were tough, extremely well-trained men – all of them had been in the Israeli military – and they were remorseless killers. Pound for pound they were by far the toughest of all the gangs in New York City. They took what the Israeli armed forces taught them about killing and used it on the street. They were like a paramilitary group. They knew how to use explosives, all types of firearms, poisons, etc. They had an overt arrogance about them, as though they felt they were better than anyone else, as though they were above the laws of the United States, as though they had an absolute right to break the law, to sell drugs, to steal and kill whenever they wished.

Pitera and Frank Gangi had done a lot of business with the Israelis – in particular with Moussa Aliyan, who'd long been a member of an Israeli gang in good standing. But all that changed on New Year's Eve 1987. What occurred exactly to bring their wrath down upon

Moussa's head has never been established. Suffice it to say that on this particular blustery, cold night, when he arrived home after partying at the nearby Nirvana Club, he was met by not only the cold winds whipping off the Hudson River but also a fuselage of bullets fired by guns in the hands of his former gang members, led by one Johnny Attias. He went down and died on the street in front of his apartment building. It was as though this was some kind of payback for what had happened to Phyllis Burdi in his home, a supernatural retribution: revenge had occurred.

Some five hours after Moussa's body was picked up and taken to the morgue by the New York City medical examiner's office at 30th Street and 1st Avenue; his body was on an autopsy table. He, like Phyllis, was soon cut up into pieces. Later, when Frank Gangi found out about Moussa's murder, he was certain that Pitera had had something to do with it. When Gangi asked Pitera about this, he vehemently denied it.

31

THE BODY IN THE ALLEY

J oey Balzano was a very good-looking Italian-American with black hair and blue eyes. People in Bensonhurst often compared him to John Travolta. He had big white teeth and an ingratiating, sexy smile that warmed pretty much any woman with whom he came into contact. He was a ladies' man, not so much because he put tremendous effort into courting women, into bedding them, but because he was so naturally attractive that women courted *him*. He was also a member of the constellation of characters that rotated around Pitera.

Unlike most of the characters in Pitera's circle, Joey was not dour or introverted. He was extremely outgoing. His regular girlfriend was Renee Lombardozzi. She was the stepdaughter of Carmine Lombardozzi, who was an old-school mafioso. He was one of the attendees of the famous Apalachin Conference in 1957. Many in the know liken Carmine to Meyer Lansky – that is to say, he was brilliant with numbers. He single-handedly ran all the Gambino's shylocking operations and their multifaceted, insidious infiltration of Wall Street. Carmine could very well have been a professor of economics at a prestigious prep school. Renee was brought up in the world of La Cosa Nostra. She knew the walk and the talk. She was an intricate part of its culture. As the stepdaughter of Carmine Lombardozzi, she attended all the Mafia weddings, Mafia birthday parties, Mafia deaths and celebrations. Renee was streetwise.

Joey Balzano and Renee Lombardozzi lived in a nice one-bedroom apartment at Cropsey Avenue and Bay 50th Street. The apartment had a terrace and was furnished well. There was an expensive Japanese silk partition that divided the living room and a view of the Gravesend Bay from their terrace. Beyond the Gravesend Bay could be seen the horizon of Coney Island – the Parachute and the Wonder Wheel seeming to grow out of the ground.

Although Joey Balzano was gifted by nature with good looks, he was also cursed by nature, for he was a bona fide drug addict. Whatever successes his looks and charms would have got him went up in a puff of smoke as readily as crack from a freebase pipe. Joey was addicted to 'the pipe'. When freebasing, he – like all freebase heads – would go through an astronomical amount of cocaine in a 24-hour period. When Joey first started working for Pitera, he moved large quantities of drugs without problem or mishap. He was a moneymaker. All that inevitably changed when instead of giving Pitera money due on drugs taken he gave excuses. He didn't give the right amounts. He was short.

Pitera had no patience for people who did not keep their word: slackers. He warned Joey. 'You've gotta give me what's due when it's due, not when it's convenient for you,' he said.

'Of course, sure, I understand. No problem,' Joey said. 'I just, I fronted a bunch of people and they're stalling me.'

'Stalling you?' Pitera repeated. 'Stop them from stalling and get the money,' his blue eyes menacing and reptilian.

Frank Gangi had met Joey Balzano through Pitera. He immediately took a liking to him. Joey, Gangi would later say, was a very easy guy to like. Apparently, Gangi liked Joey so much that he fronted him more drugs than he should have. Without Pitera knowing it, Gangi had fronted him a quarter pound of cocaine, cocaine that was quickly cooked up in Joey and Renee's house and smoked.

Not surprisingly to Gangi, Pitera began badmouthing Joey. He said he didn't trust him; he said he was an out-of-control cokehead. 'Don't front him any more. Until he gets caught up, no more!' Pitera said.

'OK,' Gangi said, seeing the wisdom in Pitera's words.

Three days later, Pitera called Gangi and told him to meet him at the bar. That's what Pitera's phone conversations were all about: meet me here, meet me there. He never said anything incriminating. When Gangi arrived at the bar, Pitera was there.

'This fucking Joey . . . I hear he's telling people about burying bodies. I hear he's talking about people being cut up and buried. Has he gotten straight with you?'

'No,' Gangi replied.

'Like I've been saying, I don't trust this guy. He's gotta go,' Pitera said, looking for Gangi's reaction. Pitera – to a degree – was a good judge of human nature. He well knew that Gangi and Joey were friends. This, in Pitera's mind, was another way to test Gangi – test his loyalty, his moxie.

'Whatever you think is right,' Gangi said.

Since Gangi had seen Pitera kill Phyllis, cut her up, cut her head off, get naked and into the tub with her, he'd viewed Pitera in a far different way. He came to think of Pitera as an insidious creature from another planet – a creature from another dimension. He knew well that if Pitera was talking about killing Joey Balzano, Joey's days were numbered. Gangi had not forgotten the murder of Phyllis Burdi, he had not been the same person since her murder. He was drinking excessively. He was using far more cocaine than he should. He was smoking four to five packs of cigarettes a day. Now his voice was rough and scratchy. When he laughed, he'd inevitably break out into a coughing fit, his eyes tearing, his face bunching up.

Unlike Pitera, Gangi was not about to kill someone over money.

That evening Gangi went to visit Joey at his home on Bay 50th. They talked, in whispers, about the money Joey owed Gangi and, more importantly, Pitera.

'Joey, Tommy is a real, real serious guy. You can't fuck with him in any way. He has no sense of humour.'

'Can you fix it?' Joey said. 'I just need a little time. I can get caught up.'

'Joey,' Gangi said, 'it's not a matter of getting caught up. He heard you've been saying things about people getting buried. His mind's made up.'

'You can't fix it?' Joey asked, hopeful, his eyes wide, pleading.

'Look, Joey, listen to me, I'm not that close to him. No one is that close to him. I think the person who was the closest to him was Celeste. Take my advice, as a friend: get out of town. Go make a life somewhere else.'

'Where?' Joey asked. 'Where am I going to go?'

'Wherever you go, you'll live. If you stay here, you're dead,' Gangi whispered.

All this Gangi had said in a very low voice, not wanting Renee to know. One way or another, he didn't trust Renee. He felt that if something happened to Joey, sooner or later, she'd turn on him. Joey now looked at Gangi beseechingly.

'I don't know what to do . . . tell me what to do. Tell me the best way to deal with him.'

Gangi heard Renee move about behind the partition. Rather than say anything with her in close earshot, he wet his finger, leaned over and wrote on the black lacquer table: *LEAVE*.

A few days later, Gangi called Joey and said that Tommy was willing to talk. Joey was pleased to hear this, but he was wary – on guard. By the same token, he was hopeful that, with Gangi's help, he could regain his honour. Still, when he left the house, he told Renee, 'If I don't come back, Frankie and Tommy killed me.'

When Joey got outside, he only had to wait a few minutes before Gangi pulled up in one of Pitera's many cars. Gangi had given Joey every chance to leave, save himself. What was happening now was his own doing. They drove over to the Just Us to pick up Pitera. Gangi knew that Pitera's intentions were not good. Gangi knew, too, that Pitera had come to view Joey as a slacker and a rat – a liability. Regardless of what was going to happen, Gangi could do nothing to stop it. His association with Pitera had put him in a position whereby he had to toe the line, he had to listen to Pitera or he was dead. It was that simple. Yes, he had uncles in high places, but nobody could help him with Pitera. They were dealing drugs, which was a no-no. Gangi was not made, and Pitera was. What Gangi had in his head was to make enough money and take off, start another life in another place, maybe Florida or California, somewhere warm.

When they pulled up in front of the Just Us, Pitera saw them through the window and came outside. Respectfully, Joey got out of the car and offered the front seat to Pitera.

'No, you take it. I'll get in the back,' Pitera said, sliding onto the leather seats.

Gangi had no idea how this would happen. He did have an ice pick with him in the inside pocket of his jacket, as Pitera had ordered. Being from the street, knowing they might be observed by the police, Gangi took U-turns, lefts and rights, more U-turns and parked in a parking lot to make sure they weren't being followed. Joey, being a drug dealer, understood the modus operandi. Often he himself had done such things. Tommy talked about a good restaurant, the Top of the Sixes, said that there were a lot of girls there. When they were out with Joey, he was what they called a 'cunt magnet'. This, however, was all a ruse, a way to relax Joey, get him to drop his guard. There would be no fancy dinner at Top of the Sixes that evening.

They next headed to the Green Lantern Bar on New Utrecht Avenue and 71st Street. Pitera said he had to pick something up. He got out of the car, went inside the bar and came out a few minutes later. He had met Richie David inside and got a gun from him. Back in the car, he said to Gangi, 'Go to the corner and take a left.'

Pitera knew what he would do and where he would do it; he had mapped it all out in his head. It was a dance of death, the steps of which he knew well. Without warning, he raised the handgun, put it to the back of Joey Balzano's head and pulled the trigger twice. The gun was fitted with a silencer and the noise was minimal. The damage done to Joey Balzano, however, was not minimal. The bullets had ripped through his hair, skin and skull with ease and made grey pudding out of his brain. This wasn't enough for Pitera. He took out a six-inch hunting knife, razor-sharp and shiny, and drew it quickly across Joey Balzano's throat. He cut not only the throat but also both the carotid arteries. Pitera now told Gangi to stick him with the ice pick, wanting to make Gangi part of the murder. Obeying, Gangi took out the ice pick and rammed it into Joey's chest, though at this point it was a lifeless one containing a heart that had stopped beating.

The job done, Joey Balzano dead, Pitera directed Gangi to drive to an abandoned alleyway close to New Utrecht Avenue. As they arrived there, the B train came barrelling down the elevated tracks. It made a lot of noise and sparks fell from the two-storey-high tracks. They pulled Joey from the car and placed him on the ground. Joey Balzano was fond of nice jewellery and diamonds, and they took his Rolex watch and gold chain. He had a huge diamond pinky ring on. Try as they might, they couldn't pull the ring off. Tommy used his hunting knife to cut the finger off, grabbed the ring and put it in his pocket.

Gangi, unsettled by the whole event, unsettled by leaving the body there like that, kept saying, 'We gotta go! We gotta go!' Pitera remained as cold as ice. A more appropriate nickname for Tommy Pitera, rather than Tommy Karate, would have been the Ice Man.

They got in the car and pulled away. This, the taking of a victim's jewellery, was an interesting, telling phenomenon. It is classically what conventional serial killers do – take belongings and body parts from their victims; these are known as totems. Whenever Tommy Pitera had the opportunity, he took a victim's jewellery. Later, a treasure trove of his victims' jewellery would be found in his safe. Conventionally, a mafioso would never take the belongings of a victim. This directly ties the murder to the person holding the victim's belongings. It was a good way to link the murder with the killer. It is obvious that Tommy Pitera knew this, yet he still took their jewellery. Those in the know say Pitera took the jewellery not for its monetary worth but to prove his – prowess, to prove that he killed when and where and how he wanted to; his omnipotence. It was tangible evidence that could hold up in any court anywhere in the world. Somehow, it seemed that Pitera was thinking with a warped, perverse aspect of his ego rather than with the street sense that he was so well endowed with . . . he believed.

32

THE CLEANER

At any given time, Pitera was driving between six and ten different cars. Some of these cars he owned, others he borrowed from capo Frankie Lino, who had an executive car service in Brooklyn. Lino readily made cars available to Pitera, making it very difficult for the DEA to bug any of these many different rotating vehicles. For Pitera, cars were as interchangeable as underwear. More often than not, he used them in crimes and so they had to be cleaned up or got rid of. To that end, Pitera tapped into La Cosa Nostra networking. Again, the five New York Mafia families all cooperated with one another, bound together through customs, mean streets and avenues, tunnels and bridges. Through contacts Pitera had in La Cosa Nostra he was able to take the car in which they had killed Joey Balzano to a body shop on Flatlands Avenue where Manny Maya worked. Maya was a Jewish-Cuban man with dark hair who did a lot of work at this shop. Maya also dealt drugs on the side for the Bonanno family.

The car Pitera brought in that day was heavily stained with blood, looked like something out of a horror movie. Pitera told Maya to clean the car up. Maya tore out the entire interior of the car, hot-steam cleaned it thoroughly, let it dry and reupholstered it. When he was finished, it had a brand new interior and not a trace of blood anywhere; a seasoned bloodhound couldn't find blood in that car. The old interior was summarily burned in a 50-gallon drum. When Tommy picked up the car, it was as though it was brand new and he could drive it without concern.

Though Manny Maya was associated with the Bonanno family, he would readily provide his unique cleaning service to any of the other four families – Genovese, Gambino, Lucchese and Colombo. They all brought bloodstained cars to Manny Maya. Pitera readily gave his blessings to Manny and put no restrictions on him.

Pitera was also particularly close to feared Gambino war capo Eddie Lino. Lino was John Gotti's right-hand man, assassin extraordinaire for the Gambino family. He had also once been Phyllis Burdi's lover. Lino had heard about Pitera killing Phyllis; he accepted it as one would the changing of the seasons. He knew that Phyllis had been warned over and over again; he knew that she had ignored the warnings. He himself had warned her to stay away from Celeste. He knew no good would come of their association. When Phyllis was murdered, cut up, disposed of, Lino did not come around looking for any type of revenge.

Tommy Pitera's reputation as a competent assassin, as a man who kept his mouth shut, had grown to such proportions that he was a kind of 'Billy the Kid' of La Cosa Nostra. As further proof of the intricate links binding the five families together, when John Gotti wanted a certain rat murdered, he gave the contract to Eddie Lino, who, in turn, gave the contract to none other than Tommy Pitera.

After numerous purchases of narcotics from Judy Haimowitz and Angelo Favara, the case around Pitera building inexorably, Jim Hunt and Group 33 applied for a court order to wiretap Judy Haimowitz's home phone. The wiretap of Judy's house proved to be an interesting – bizarre – source of information. The DEA rented an apartment in Bensonhurst and from this apartment they began to monitor the phones of all the players in Pitera's circle. They would have gladly, indeed gleefully, tapped Pitera's phones, but Pitera did not have a phone in any of the places in which he lived: 3030 Emmons Avenue, Apt 5A; 2355 East 12th Street, Apt 4T, or the brownstone he owned at 342 Ovington Avenue in Bay Ridge. He believed phones were nothing but potential problems, that the police could easily tap phones, and so he refused to have one in his home.

When a phone is tapped by the DEA, it is electronically monitored 24 hours a day. Late at night, as Judy Haimowitz's phone was listened to, they realised she had an obsessive – addictive – penchant for dialling sex lines, no doubt spurred on by cocaine. She preferred the most salacious of sex lines imaginable, with the most perverse, base words spoken, involving bondage, rape, anal manipulations of all kinds, interracial scenarios, etc. That is to say, she had a choice of what type of sexuality she could listen to and what she chose was kinky and bizarre and off the beaten path, as it were. As she listened to the words, she masturbated loudly, without concern for who might be listening. Indeed, all of Group 33 heard her, heard her moan and groan – with abandon – as she orgasmed and the phone suddenly went dead. Judy Haimowitz became the butt of a whole host of jokes by not only the male agents but also all the agents involved in the case. What Judy Haimowitz was about – who she was – was, relatively speaking, comical . . . not diabolical.

It was Pitera who was diabolical.

It was Pitera they wanted.

Still, Judy Haimowitz spoke freely about the selling of drugs on her phone and gave the government a whole treasure trove of information involving drug sales – who was buying them, when and where, and the amounts involved. What further strengthened the case against Pitera was that Angelo Favara had sold large amounts of heroin to Hunt and Geisel that he had obtained directly from Pitera, which they had quickly handed over to the government.

33

'YOU'RE NOT MY BOSS'

Some people feel comfortable handling guns, some don't. Blind-folded, some can take apart a gun and put it back together again. Without blindfolds, some can't begin to take apart a gun.

Frank Gangi was one of those people who didn't like guns, had no affinity for them. Though he knew them as an intricate part of his trade, a necessary tool, he did not handle them well; he wasn't a good shot, though he coveted the power a gun had, how readily and rapidly it could steal away a human life. Though he didn't like them, he admired them from afar. Trying to overcome this impediment he had, he often held a gun while lounging around his house, watching television. Someone had told him, actually Tommy had told him, that the gun should be an extension of his body. 'You should be as comfortable with your gun, handling it, as you should be comfortable with your own dick, handling it.'

The problem was that while doing this impromptu exercise one day at the house of one of his girlfriends, a tough, talking-out-of-the-side-of-her-mouth guidette named Patty Scifo, known as 'Patty Girl', Frank accidentally pulled the trigger of his pistol and inadvertently shot himself in the leg. He stood up and jumped around the room, bleeding. He called a friend by the name of Andy Jakakis, then called the Just Us and asked Pitera to come over.

Andy Jakakis was an old-school tough guy who wasn't really tough at all. He was grey and balding, thin-shouldered, though he walked with a defiant swagger, as if he were six-foot-five and the baddest badass in the jungle. Gangi had first met Andy while doing time for the shooting he and Billy Bright were involved in, the murder of Arthur Guvenaro. Because Andy was in his late 50s and Frank in his mid-20s, Andy kind of became a father figure to the young Gangi. He watched over Gangi, he advised him as to the different protocols mandated in jail; they became friends. Gangi grew so fond of Andy that when he had an opportunity to help him by making a witness in the case against Jakakis change his testimony, Gangi pulled some Mafia strings and made it so the witness never showed up in court. Upon Andy's release, he started hanging around Gangi, stayed at his house and became a kind of gopher-confidant. Andy was under the impression that Gangi was a big-time mafioso: he knew who Gangi's relatives were; he knew, too, that Gangi was now hooked up with Tommy Pitera. Andy felt an unusual, somewhat unhealthy closeness to Gangi. He did not like Pitera. He was fond of saying: 'God put me on this Earth to protect Frank Gangi.'

So, the day Frank shot himself, Andy showed up all concerned, all worried, his brow knitted together. Gangi made up a story of being shot at by people who owed him money. With that, Pitera knocked on the door. Being an expert on wounds and injuries, Pitera looked at the bullet hole with a cold, clinical eye. He then called a gynecologist, the brother of a friend named Gerald Marino, who came over. Mafia members were often in contact with doctors who would tend to gunshot wounds and not report them as mandated by hospitals and the law. Doctor Marino said the bullet had not struck bone. The doctor, a small, nerdy, blond-haired man, cleaned and dressed the wound, collected some money and left.

Andy, disturbed by the incident, dismayed by the fact that someone would shoot his idol, was walking back and forth, threatening, cursing to himself. He got on Pitera's nerves; this was an easy thing to do. Pitera didn't like people and most everyone annoyed him. He turned to Andy and said, 'Calm down. Be quiet. You're getting on my nerves. Sit down.' He pointed to a chair.

Defiance about his eyes, defiance in his body English, Andy said, 'Hey, I don't have to listen to you, you're not my boss. I don't take orders from you. You understand? I only listen to Frank – understand?'

This galled Pitera no end. He demanded respect and, for the most part, people complied and kowtowed to him. Waiters fawned over him. Other wise guys gave him a wide berth, and here was this Andy guy defiantly pointing his unmanicured finger at him.

As hard as this might be to believe for a civilian, for a layperson, Andy had just killed himself. There was no way that he, Pitera, would allow Andy Jakakis to speak to him like that in front of other people. Over the coming days, Tommy Pitera talked, somewhat insistently, about killing Andy Jakakis. He told Gangi that he had to go; he told Gangi that he wouldn't rest until he was dead.

'I'm not only going to kill him,' he said in his Minnie Mouse voice, 'I'm going to torture him on the dance floor of Overstreets.'

This literally nauseated Gangi. He was fond of Andy; he was like a surrogate father to him. He knew Andy meant nothing by what he had said to Pitera, he was just a foolish old man who had said something out of line. There was no reason in the world for him to die, for him to be tortured!

Immediately, Gangi tried to talk Pitera out of the killing, but Pitera wouldn't hear it. He wouldn't rest until Andy was dead. Gangi thought of Pitera as an irrational, out-of-control, unhinged psychopath. He thought Pitera should be locked up in a mental institution. Be that as it may, Pitera was free and in charge and he wanted blood. He was like a vampire who had an insatiable need, an overwhelming desire, for blood.

This drew Frank Gangi further into the numbing world of alcohol and drug abuse. His mind, his soul, couldn't deal with the hardcore realities of what Tommy Pitera was all about – images of what he had done to Phyllis Burdi often filled the pink insides of his closed eyelids. The smell of her murder, the blood, the torn flesh came to him whether he wanted it to or not. He was haunted by what he had seen. When the images became too much, he turned to a bottle of scotch, long, glistening lines of cocaine, the magical mystery tour of numbed oblivion that is freebasing.

Bubble, bubble, toil and trouble . . .

loomed large and real on the near horizon.

Frank Gangi was stuck between a rock and a hard place. The way he saw it through his stoned eyes was like this: either he killed Pitera or he killed Andy Jakakis. Killing Pitera, he knew, would be no small task. Pitera seemed to see all things at once at a 180-degree angle. He was as quick as a rattlesnake. Gangi believed he had a supernatural sixth sense that would make it not hard to kill him, but near impossible. He didn't drink, Gangi knew. Gangi never saw him high; never saw him vulnerable. As he thought about killing him, he realised that Pitera always sat with his back to the wall, that when in the car he sat in the back seat; that he never let anybody sit behind him. It was as though he was expecting someone to try and kill him and he had built an invincible wall around himself. Just the thought of trying to bring a gun up to Pitera's head gave Gangi the willies. His hands shook, his mouth got dry, his stomach turned to knots. The only way he could escape this conundrum was more drink, scotch, coke. Frank Gangi was no longer getting high to have fun, to socialise, to party; he was getting high to escape the realities of life as he knew it.

Andy's gotta die, he thought. When he accepted that reality, when he bought into the steps killing Andy involved, it devastated him. He never wanted to hurt Andy. He'd kill himself before he let Andy be tortured. He resolved in his heart, in his mind and in his soul, for what he felt were the right reasons, to kill Andy, to kill his surrogate father – to kill one of the few friends he had ever had.

It was now mid-June 1988. The weather that June was unseasonably warm and humid. Though Gravesend was close to Coney Island, little breeze came from the ocean and the air was thick and hot and unpleasant. A former boyfriend of Judy Haimowitz, Toby Profetto, a close friend of Gangi, accompanied Frank this night.

Gangi had told Toby about his predicament. Toby agreed to help Frank with this most difficult of tasks. Toby was a medium-sized, muscular dude with curly hair, a typical Brooklyn wannabe. His idea of success in life was to be inducted into one of the five families. Toby was also a killer. He was one of those rare people who could take a human life as readily as step on an ant. That night Profetto and Gangi went out on a mission, a mission that had little reward, a mission that would only result in the death of an old man who couldn't really hurt a fly.

'OK,' Gangi said. 'When the right time comes, I'll turn up the music real loud and we'll do it.'

'OK,' came the answer, cold and detached, as though it came from the mouth of a dummy on a ventriloquist's lap.

This dynamic duo picked up Andy Jakakis at a popular pizzeria called Spumoni Gardens on 86th Street. Gangi was driving. Andy sat in the passenger seat. Toby was sitting directly behind him. Gangi took a right onto West 11th Street. This was a quiet, desolate street. On the right were homes and on the left were train tracks. A song by the Rolling Stones came on: 'Start Me Up'.

'I like this song,' Frank said, turning up the volume louder and louder, and louder still. Moving to the beat, Andy Jakakis had no idea the grim reaper was in the back seat. Without hesitation, Toby put the gun against Andy's head and fired. The bullet tore through his skull, hit his forehead, bounced back and zigzagged around his brain. Gangi pulled over to the kerb. He could see a massive wound on Andy's forehead. Blood came from it, but the bullet did not burst out of his flesh. This was the middle of the day but there were few people about. Gangi took a right, a left and made his way over to an empty lot on Bay 50th Street. This part of Bay 50th hadn't been fully developed yet and Gangi got it in his head to leave the body right there in a lot in broad daylight. In his panic, in his adrenaline rush, he didn't realise that capo Todo Marable lived just opposite this lot. Todo was a feared captain in the Bonanno family. As they hurried the body out of the car and into high grass in the lot, one of Andy's shoes came off and fell down by the passenger seat. When they got back to the car, Gangi saw the shoe and pushed it out onto the kerb.

No matter how you cut it, this would not sit well with Todo. This was a personal offence. It was like taking a dump on his front door. No mafioso anywhere in the world would stand for such a thing. His wife lived here. His children lived here.

Trouble was in the air.

In the stifling heat of that summer, it didn't take long for the body to emit a horrific odour that was soon noticed and the body was discovered. The police were summoned. Big crowds gathered around the lot, pointing, staring, wondering, speculating.

Who the hell would do such a thing?

When Todo Marable found out a body had been left across the street from his home, that a shoe belonging to the body had been left on the kerb, he wondered what it meant. Surely it was some kind of message.

But a message of what? Who, he and all members of his borgata wondered, would do such a thing?

Why would they do such a thing?

What did the shoe mean, they all wondered.

Immediately the jungle drums of the Mafia started resounding and the question was: who left a body with one shoe near Todo's house? When Pitera got the news that Andy was dead, he was pleased. He felt that, for the first time, Gangi had acted like a man, that he had stepped up to the bat and done what he was supposed to do. Inadvertently, this murder brought Pitera closer to Gangi. He felt a warmth towards Gangi he hadn't felt for him before.

34

THE DYNAMIC DUO

It was one of those pleasant summer nights, when people sit on stoops in beach chairs in front of their houses all over Brooklyn, just before night falls, during those 15 or so minutes called dusk, an abundance of ladybirds filling the air. It was such a lovely evening that the patrons of the Just Us came outside and were sitting on car fenders in front of the bar. There was Tommy Pitera, the fierce war captain Eddie Lino and Frank 'Ruby' Rubino. Frank Rubino was a burly, squat, tough Italian. He drove a brand new grey Jaguar. Up until that date, he had had a good relationship with Eddie Lino; they were partners in the heroin business. Now the good days were gone. As is often the way of the Mafia, when they are about to kill someone, they are all smiling and friendly and warm, offering drinks and sumptuous dinners.

Between Tommy Pitera and Eddie Lino, you'd be hard-pressed to find a meaner pair in all of La Cosa Nostra, either in the United States or in Sicily. Though they were from two different families, they often worked together, were good personal friends, had respect for one another. Eddie Lino was the go-to guy for heroin for the Gambino crime family. But, interestingly, all of what Eddie Lino did was, of course, off the record, off the books. His drug-dealing was so blatant, so amazingly profitable, that for the longest time he could not get made – officially inducted into the Gambino family. Paul Castellano refused outright to have him made because of his immersion in the selling of heroin. It was only after John Gotti had Castellano murdered in front of Sparks Steak House that Eddie Lino was finally made and, soon thereafter, given his own borgata. Eddie Lino and John Gotti were close. They were more like brothers than friends.

Though John Gotti never had anything to do with the actual selling of drugs, never touched drugs, never saw drugs, he well knew what Lino was doing, what Lino was about, and he gave his blessings. Gotti, like everyone else in La Cosa Nostra, quietly pocketed a fortune as he silently, discreetly, looked the other way, north and south and east and west, as Lino went about the business of wholesaling large amounts of heroin. Lino and John Gotti's bond was so great that when, a little way down the road, Anthony Gaspipe Casso was given the assignment of killing John Gotti for murdering Paul Castellano without the killing being sanctioned, the first person he took out was Eddie Lino. On 6 November 1990, Anthony Casso sent crooked NYPD detectives Stephen Caracappa and Louis Eppolito to do the job. Lino was so feared, such an adept killer himself, that Casso used cops to take him out.

Apparently, Lino had got wind that Frank Rubino had turned bad. Lino wanted him dead and he asked his pal Tommy to do the job. At this point, Tommy had garnered a reputation within La Cosa Nostra as an amazingly adept, efficient killer. His reputation had grown to such a degree that people were calling him – behind his back – 'the wacko'. This had less to do with his outward appearance than with how readily he killed and the fact that he, just as readily, cut people up and buried them; that he had private burial grounds on Long Island and Staten Island.

Tall and gangly, buzzed on coke, Frank Gangi now turned the corner and began walking towards Lino, Pitera and Rubino. Outgoing and gregarious, Gangi was about to approach them when Pitera waved him away with a curt movement of his icy blue-grey eyes. NIX IT-SCRAM, Pitera silently said with his eyes. Gangi got the message. He walked into the bar, ignoring the three. Gangi did not know what was happening but, considering that Rubino was standing between Pitera and Lino, a very mean pair of bookends, it didn't look good for Ruby.

Soon, Lino, Pitera and Rubino got into Rubino's grey Jaguar and drove away. Rubino was driving. Lino was sitting in the passenger seat. They were some four blocks away from the bar when Lino told Rubino to pull over, which he readily did. The moment he put the car in neutral, Pitera pulled out an automatic with a silencer on it and shot Rubino in the back of the head, killing him. Even though this was Gravesend, Brooklyn, ground zero for the Mafia, what Pitera had just done was amazingly audacious. The fledgling dragon that had once been inside Pitera had grown to monstrous proportions, now had long scales . . . was fire-breathing. In that Pitera obsessively collected jewellery from his victims, he ripped a gold necklace with a fish medallion off Rubino and he and Lino got out of the car and left Rubino there like that for all to see, know and be horrified by.

This type of killing, so brazen and so public, would inevitably come back to haunt La Cosa Nostra. It caused intense police scrutiny and brought media attention, and horrified an innocent public. It was one of those times when it seemed as though these two men, Lino and Pitera, felt that they had a holy mandate to kill whomever they wanted, whenever they wanted, and blatantly leave bodies wherever the hell they pleased. As a mafioso recently said, it was 'in bad taste'.

Murder, successfully killing people and breaking the law on a regular basis, as La Cosa Nostra does as a matter of course, has to do with luck. No matter how well planned, no matter how thoroughly thought out any given crime is, any given murder, without luck, can fail – and fail miserably. Considering how often the DEA was following Pitera, it's a wonder they didn't see him that night, hanging out in front of the bar, driving off and killing Frank Rubino. Luck, apparently, was with Pitera and Eddie Lino that night.

Interestingly, Pitera's luck slowly began to turn a short time later. He now had a new girlfriend. Her name was Barbara Lambrose. She bore a distinct resemblance to Celeste. She had a 14-year-old son. He was a good-looking, athletic teenager, but he was wired and destined for trouble. He didn't do well in school; he didn't listen to his mother; he was starting to use drugs. Pitera had taken a liking to the boy, whose name was Joey.

Today, Pitera was driving his Oldsmobile. The feds had recently managed to bug this car. Presumably because he had Joey in the car that day, neither the radio was on nor was there static. Apparently, Joey's behaviour was giving his mother grief and she had complained to Pitera, asked him to talk to her son.

'Joey, you know,' Pitera began, 'your mother's a very nice lady. She's had it hard. There's no reason for you to give her more grief. I'm from the street. I'm telling it like it is. You gotta shape up. You gotta be . . . you gotta stay away from drugs. Drugs will make you lose control. You never want to lose control. You see me? I never lose control. You have a mother who loves you and cares for you. You have to show her respect.'

And Pitera went on to lecture the boy on staying out of trouble, on not using drugs, on doing well in school. Then the boy said something that was inaudible to the agents and Pitera's response shocked and stunned the listening agents:

'If you kill somebody,' he said, 'you've got to cut the lungs and open the stomach. If you do that, the body can sink. If you don't do that, it will float and it will be found.'

Tommy Geisel and Jim Hunt looked at each other.

This would be helpful, they knew, in a court of law, but it was not definitive evidence as such. It would bolster the contentions, the allegations and the evidence they did have, but in reality he could have just been making this up. It wasn't proof in and of itself, though it sure cast Pitera in a bad light.

STICK SHIFT

Sharks. Pitera and his crew were like a bunch of reef sharks constantly looking for prey, constantly on the move, always hungry. Always ruthless, Pitera could be readily likened to a great white shark that dominated and frightened and controlled and even ate the reef sharks. Pitera, like a great white, was slow-moving and methodical, though deadly when he made a move. He had morphed from a dragon into one of the most feared, efficient killers the Mafia has ever known – a white shark, *Carcharodon carcharias*.

One of the reef sharks that was a member of Pitera's crew was Lloyd Modell, another Mafia wannabe. He had dark hair and dark eyes and a large hook nose. He had such a dire need to be in the Mafia – had fantasies about it most of his adult life, loved movies about gangsters – that he actually changed his name to Lorenzo Modica, an Italian name that he hoped would get him inducted into one of the five crime families, though that was not about to happen. It was a rare thing for non-Italians to fool their way into being made. For the most part, in order to be made people in La Cosa Nostra had to know you, your history – or, as Pitera put it, know the cunt you came out of.

Having said that, his not being Italian would not dissuade Lorenzo Modica from being a gangster. He was so intent upon proving his worth that he would kill quickly and readily, without remorse or conflict.

Lorenzo Modica knew a Colombian by the name of Luis Mena, also an associate of Pitera's, a coke dealer. Luis Mena said he could get them 'all the coke they wanted'. Mena said he knew Colombians who had heavy weight and that he'd be happy to set them up to be ripped off. The coke that the Colombians provided, swiftly and without difficulty, was top notch. Lorenzo went and spoke to Tommy about ripping them off. Tommy readily agreed. Lorenzo mentioned killing them. Pitera thought that a good idea. This was right up his alley.

In July 1988, Luis Mena called Lorenzo to tell him there was a load of coke in. The two soon met.

'How much you got?'

'Whatever you want,' Mena replied.

'We'll take 20 keys,' Lorenzo said.

'You got it,' Mena said, and arrangements were made for the deal to go down later that day.

Lorenzo tried to find Pitera but wasn't able to. He knew he couldn't pull this off by himself. He went and found Frankie 'Jupiter' Martini, another reef shark in Pitera's gang, to work with him and help him facilitate the rip-off.

Contrary to common belief, the Colombians were, for the most part, businessmen. They could be ruthless killers whose cruelty knew no bounds, but if you dealt with them straight, if you kept your word, they were good people with whom to do business. They were reliable, honest, on time and their product was always superior to all others. When you bought coke from Colombians, you were getting it directly from the source. They did not cut their product. On a regular basis, the coke the Colombians sold, when in weight – packaged in neat, hard bricks – was 98 per cent pure.

The two Colombian coke dealers Lorenzo and company would be

meeting were Carlos Acosta and Fernando Aguilera. Both of them were in their early 20s, dark-skinned and thin, innocuous, would blend into any crowd anywhere. They sported short hair. Not in a million years would anyone make them as coke dealers. This was no accident. The fact that they could blend in so well is exactly why they were chosen in Colombia to do what they did in Brooklyn. Unfortunately for them, they did not quite understand just how mean the mean streets of Brooklyn could truly be. They would soon learn a lesson that would be forever indelibly seared into their brains.

Carlos and Fernando showed up on time at the rendezvous, the shopping centre at Shore Parkway and Bay Parkway. It was a hot day, and they were both wearing T-shirts and shorts. They greeted Lorenzo, shook hands. Lorenzo assured them that he had the money. They assured him they had the drugs. He suggested they make the transfer in the garage of a nearby building. They agreed. Lorenzo got in the back seat. He had a revolver in his waistband, hidden by his shirt tails. Unobserved, not knowing what lay ahead, the Colombians dutifully followed Lorenzo's instructions to the garage in a new red-brick apartment building at 1445 Shore Parkway. Coincidentally, the building was only a block away from Pitera, Billy Bright and Frank Gangi's stash house, where hundreds of pounds of pot were stored, waiting to be sold.

The cocaine was in the trunk of the Colombians' car. Cocky, wanting desperately to prove himself, Frankie Jupiter walked up to their economy Ford. He was smiling. He was getting them, in his mind, to drop their guard. He said he wanted to see the coke. The Colombians said they wanted to see the money.

Lorenzo knew it was time to act. He'd been waiting for this moment for what seemed an eternity now. He had a clear view of the back of both the Colombians' heads. With confidence and surety, lethal, he whipped out the gun, put it just behind the driver's head and pulled the trigger; without hesitation, he moved right, took a bead and fired again. Before they knew it, both the Colombians were dead, their brains destroyed.

In the garage, the gunshots were like deafening cannons, loud and resonating. Lorenzo and Frankie Jupiter wanted to get the hell out of there quickly. Now Lorenzo realised for the first time that the car was a stick shift.

'Fuck – it's a fucking stick shift! I can't drive a fucking stick shift. Can you?' Lorenzo said.

'Fuck, no!' Frankie said.

They stood around the car with the two dead Colombians, wondering what to do, scratching their arses. If it weren't so sad, it would've been funny. Ultimately, they took the drugs from the car and hurried out as though they were two miscreants stealing food from a Korean grocery. They had planned to drive the car out of the garage and set it on fire, but now that wasn't possible, so there the Colombians stayed.

It didn't take long for a resident of the building to discover the bodies. The police were summoned. The garage was soon filled with forensic technicians, police photographers and hard-eyed, stone-faced Brooklyn detectives from the 62nd Precinct on Bath Avenue.

When Pitera heard about what had gone down, he was pissed off. He thought that what had happened was stupid and sloppy, amateurish, and he did not want his name or his reputation associated with it in any way. Angry, he and Gangi went looking for Lorenzo and found him at his apartment.

'What the fuck did you do?' Pitera wanted to know.

In a rush of words, Lorenzo told Pitera that they had had no idea the Colombians drove a stick shift; that neither he nor Frankie knew how to drive a shift.

'It was just one of those things. It all happened so quickly,' he said.

'Did you get the drugs?' Pitera asked.

'Yeah, yeah I did,' Lorenzo said, all proud, sure that this would get him to become an 'official' member of the Mafia – his dream come true. What he had done was show that he was a buffoon and would never get made, Pitera knew.

Rather than the 20 kilos of cocaine that had been ordered, there were 12 kilos. Still, it was a big score. Pitera, as punishment, took nearly half of what they had taken – five kilos of high-grade, pure cocaine. Sold in grams, eight-balls and ounces, these five kilos would be worth a fortune.

Satiated, Pitera, the great white shark of this particular part of the ocean, this reef, moved off and did what he had to do.

Ripping off drug dealers was to career criminals like taking sweets from a baby. The dealers had nowhere to turn to for justice – they could not go to the cops, they could not seek help through the conventional modes of protection set up to enforce the rule of law. They therefore set up their own means of protecting themselves, their interests, their drugs and their cash. Still, if the dealer was murdered the trail usually ended right there. As an example, after the murder of the two Colombians nobody came looking for Carlos Acosta and Fernando Aguilera. Their identities died when they were murdered.

Shortly after the rip-off of the two Colombians in the garage, Luis Mena went to Pitera with another set-up. He said he knew of a 'cash house' in Howard Beach in which vast sums of money were counted, packed and shipped off to Colombia. Two women worked there just about all day, every day counting money using professional counting equipment you would find in a bank and making sure the money was sent when it should be. Mena said, 'At any given time, there's a couple of million dollars cash there.'

Upon hearing this, Pitera's eyes lit up. He decided to put together a lean, mean crew to facilitate this rip-off. It would include himself, Luis Mena, Joe 'Dish' Senatore and Richie Leone, a stocky, brash man, dark-haired, about five-ten; a dedicated Pitera devotee who would do anything to turn a buck. Joe Dish was elderly, balding, grey-haired and looked more like a cop than most cops. He had one talent, and that was posing as a policeman to give access to bad guys wanting to rob houses. Joe Dish not only looked a lot like a cop but he also had the facial expressions, the voice and the physical demeanour down pat. He was proud of saying, 'There's no house I can't get somebody into.'

Initially the four men discussed the score at the Just Us bar, got in Pitera's car and drove over to Howard Beach to actually scope out the house. It was an unremarkable two-family house on a quiet block in a quiet neighbourhood. From the outside, you'd never be able to judge what was going on inside. Images of the house, the block and neighbourhood fresh in their minds, the crew drove back to the Just Us, sat down and started talking about the actual robbery. Here, now, Pitera threw something on the table that not only startled Mena and Joe Dish but also made them back off, at first slowly, then quickly. Pitera said that he did not want to leave any witnesses; that he wanted to kill the two women, cut them up in the tub and bury them.

Luis Mena said that he was all for robbing them, perhaps beating them over the head, but not killing them. Joe Dish parroted what Mena had said. This really pissed Pitera off. He felt, knew, he was doing the right thing – what was necessary. No matter how you cut it, he reasoned, if they were dead, it was over and done with there and then. Both Joe Dish and Luis Mena refused. This caused an immediate gap, an animus to form between Pitera, Dish and Mena. Pitera felt that they were punks; that they could not be trusted. Anyone, he knew, not willing to get blood on his hands did not deserve his respect, confidence. Pitera had worked with Joe Dish several times, with Dish posing as an NYPD detective to give Pitera and company access to rip off different drug dealers. These robberies had gone smoothly. No one had been murdered. All prospered. But that was then and this was now. The comfort Pitera had felt with Dish, with Mena, was now gone. He also felt that ripping off the cash house was no longer a good idea; that ultimately he'd make himself vulnerable; that people he didn't trust would know what had happened, which could boomerang and inevitably come back to haunt him.

36

WILLIE BOY

John Gotti was fit to be tied. One of his closest friends, compatriots, the man he trusted most, was a rat – a stinking, fetid, beady-eyed rat. The fellow's name was 'Willie Boy' Johnson. He was a large, unattractive man with a big stomach. He combed his thick head of black hair straight back. He was kind of a beat-up version of Jackie Gleason except that he had a broken nose that went off to the left, received in a fight he had in his teens. He walked with his shoulders back and his head high, with attitude. He was six feet tall and weighed over 300 pounds – a big, burly man. Willie Boy Johnson was a genuine, two-fisted, tough guy, half-Italian and half-American Indian. He had known John Gotti since they were both kids. Not only was he an adept street fighter, but he was also a brutal, lethal man who danced to his own rhythm. He was known as Willie Boy because he had been hanging out with older boys since he was a kid. In that he was not fully Italian, he could not be made, though when you looked at him, he looked Italian. When John Gotti found out that he was an FBI informant, that he had been wearing a wire, that information he'd garnered would be used against him . . . Gotti, he nearly blew a gasket. He yelled, screamed, cursed, broke furniture.

'Dead! I want him dead! Dead, dead, dead! You hear?' he told anybody who would listen. Oh, how John Gotti wished he could kill Willie Boy himself, take his throat in his hands and squeeze. But he knew that pleasure would not be his, that the first finger pointed would be at him. Gotti turned to his most trusted assassin: Eddie Lino.

It cannot be emphasised enough here what a truly dangerous man Lino was. He was sly, sneaky – lethal. There was never a murder contract he was given that wasn't fulfilled. He was feared throughout all of Mafiadom. This is no exaggeration. Eddie Lino's partner in the drug business was John Gotti's brother, Gene Gotti. In fact, the two were arrested at the same time, though they would be tried separately.

At this point, free on bail, Eddie Lino was John Gotti's grim reaper. Now, John Gotti told Lino that Willie Boy Johnson had to go. For Gotti, this was not only about business. This was personal. He had loved Willie Boy Johnson. When Gotti wanted to murder the man who had accidentally killed his son Frank, he sent Willie Boy Johnson and others to go grab the guy, torture him and kill him. For John Gotti, Willie Boy Johnson was . . . family. Sitting opposite Gotti, Lino, dark-eyed and dark-haired, with the countenance of a dangerous, poisonous snake, stared at him and listened to the order. Nothing else had to be said. Eddie Lino got up and left. Willie Boy Johnson's days were numbered.

As an indicator of just how highly Tommy Pitera was thought of in the underground society that the Mafia is, Eddie Lino turned to Tommy Pitera to help kill Willie Boy Johnson, according to US Attorney David Shapiro and DEA Agent Jim Hunt. Lino trusted very few people, but he trusted Pitera. Lino, a natural born killer, saw in Pitera the same traits, the same attitude he had; it was as though they had come from the same womb. This was, without question, one of the most important hits of modern times and here Eddie Lino was wholeheartedly involving Tommy Pitera, making him an intricate part of the hit team. That's what Eddie Lino was good at: not necessarily killing himself but arranging the details – where and how it happened.

Pleased, Pitera gleefully listened to Eddie giving him the job. For Pitera, this was like receiving an Oscar. John Gotti, after all, was the *capo di tutti capi*, the boss of bosses, one of the most famous mob bosses in history. He was on the cover of *Time* magazine; he was the Teflon Don; he was Superman in that world. If, Pitera knew, he did this well, it would help his career immeasurably. Everyone would look up to him, point at him. He would be an omnipotent presence in La Cosa Nostra.

'I'm honoured,' Pitera said, and went about the business at hand: killing Willie Boy Johnson, a seasoned killer himself. Before Pitera could do the job, however, he had to get permission from his boss, Bonanno capo Frankie Lino. Lino, in turn, went to the underboss of the family, Anthony Spero. Both gave permission for Pitera to fill the contract. This would bolster the relationship between the Bonannos and the Gambinos, they both knew. It was a good thing.

At 6 a.m. on the morning of 29 August 1988, Willie Boy Johnson nonchalantly left his house, took a right and began walking. He was wearing dungarees and a denim shirt. On his block, there was a house being built, a construction site. As he walked, he saw Tommy Pitera step out from behind a mound of sand. He immediately knew what was up. Seemingly out of nowhere, Pitera's trusted aide-de-camp, Kojak Giattino, and the premier assassin in the Gambino family, Eddie Lino, appeared with guns in hand. Seemingly as one, all three shot at the large, fleeing form of Willie Boy Johnson. Calmly, Pitera knelt down and positioned himself, cupped his left hand in his right, took careful aim and drilled Johnson with holes. Johnson went down, shot some ten times. Pitera had used a special bullet on him, a Glaser round, the one he had used on Phyllis Burdi. Each of the Glaser rounds did horrific damage to the inside of Johnson's body. As Johnson's blood pooled on the hot August street, Pitera and Kojak spread a link of spikes across the street and they all got in a stolen car and pulled away. The spikes would prevent anyone from following them and indicated the wide expanse of Pitera's killing acumen.

Thus, Willie Boy Johnson was killed and Tommy Pitera acquired a new 24-carat-gold stature within the tight fraternity of La Cosa Nostra – an Oscar for murder.

Later, when John Gotti learned that Willie Boy Johnson was dead, he was pleased. It would be just a matter of time before he rewarded Pitera handsomely.

It didn't take long for Jim Hunt and Tommy Geisel to hear, by way of the Brooklyn jungle drums, that Tommy Pitera had taken out Willie Boy Johnson, known on the street as 'the Indian'. A rumour, Hunt knew, was one thing . . . proof was another.

37

THE GARAGE

Group 33 was extremely busy and active 24/7, so inevitably Jim and Tommy were called away from Gravesend. They worked cases in the Bronx, Queens, Harlem and even Staten Island. Group 33 was, by its very nature, mobile and fluid, able to deal with the huge amount of drug dealing in a large metropolis such as New York City. They also managed to get more wiretaps on the phones of Frankie Martini, aka Frankie Jupiter and other people who worked for Pitera. They, Jim and Tommy and Group 33, were careful to make certain that Pitera didn't know that they had him under surveillance. They did everything they could to keep Pitera from making them. It was obvious that Pitera suspected police scrutiny, was wary of police surveillance, but they did everything they could not to substantiate his suspicions. They knew that once he realised he was being tailed he'd change his modus operandi, change the way he did business and make it that much harder to put together an airtight case against him. They were absolutely not interested in arresting him and having him beat the case. What they, especially Jim, wanted was for the case to be foolproof.

On occasion, Jim discussed important cases with his father. For the most part, the job had not changed – it had always been about carefully putting together cases, developing informants. Interestingly, Jim Hunt Jr was arresting the sons of bad guys his father had arrested, for the same reasons, under the same circumstances – the selling of drugs.

In February 1989, on a blistering cold day, Jim Hunt and his partner, sitting in Jim's black Cadillac with tinted windows, were parked near Pitera's house on East 12th Street. The skies were low and thick and churning with angry grey clouds. Strong winds off the nearby Atlantic Ocean whipped through Gravesend. Pitera left the house, got in a black 1998 Oldsmobile he owned, drove over to the Belt Parkway and headed east. The agents followed him from a distance. Pitera made his way to the garage where Manny Maya worked on Flatlands Avenue. He left his Oldsmobile there for some work to be done, took another car and headed back towards Gravesend. This was a very interesting turn of events for the government. They had stumbled on something important, Jim immediately knew. They put the car under surveillance, began copying the licence plates of cars entering and exiting the shop and soon realised the garage was a virtual mecca for La Cosa Nostra. They matched plate numbers to capos in different families. Over the next several days, the garage was under DEA scrutiny and the government agents watched car interiors being taken out, cleaned and reupholstered. They also watched cars put up on lifts and, apparently, checked for listening devices. *Very interesting.*

38

B & E

In Brooklyn, as anywhere in the world, there are always people on the lookout for 'scores'. Often the people involved are professional thieves, rip-off artists, cat burglars – or tradesmen who on a regular basis are welcomed inside people's homes by unsuspecting innocents. If a tradesman comes across something particularly valuable, he could very well pass the information on to a thief, to someone willing to do a rush break-in.

B&E crews are made up of toughs with guns willing to knock on a door and pose as any of a dozen different people to get the homeowner to open the door. Once the door is cracked a quarter of an inch, they hard-shoulder it and burst in, guns drawn, yelling, screaming, cursing. The object: to scare. These crews usually consist of two or three men, coarse, gruff, hard individuals. It is obvious they might confront women, mothers, grandmothers, young females, yet they are more than happy to break in. If there is a totem pole of crimes, B&E gangs of this nature are surely at the low end of it.

Workmen were restoring fancy kitchen cabinets in the home of wealthy Russians who lived on 104th Street in Canarsie, a nice, residential neighbourhood, solidly upper-middle class. The head of the household was a successful jewellery dealer. As well as selling jewellery on the up-and-up, he sold stolen jewellery, precious stones, all types of extremely expensive watches. One of the cabinetmakers was Larry Santoro, a larceny-hearted tradesman who would steal money from a blind man. Santoro went to Manny Maya who, in turn, went to Frank Gangi, and told him about the Russian jeweller. Gangi was always up for a score. Though this kind of work was not something he liked, something he did often, something he was particularly adept at, he'd still do it. No matter how much money Gangi made, it never seemed to be enough. That was, of course, due to the fact that he was abusing alcohol and cocaine to such a degree that money passed through his fingers like water; he was irresponsible. A man who had his act together might very well have passed on this opportunity, but Frank thought it was a good idea and in turn went to his old partner and friend, Billy Bright.

Since their time in prison together, Bright had become a born-again Christian, though he was a paradoxical born-again. He believed in God, the Ten Commandments, the many dictates of the Bible, but he was also willing to sell drugs, rob and steal. Bright had no reservations about robbing a woman in her home and readily agreed to do the job. The two of them soon sat down with Larry Santoro. Larry explained that he would leave the back door of the house open, that they should get there early in the morning, that at that point there should only be the jeweller's 'young wife' at home.

'It'll be a piece of cake,' Larry said.

After the meeting, Billy said that he would use one of Pitera's guns, as he was holding Pitera's stash of guns. This was an interesting anecdote. Pitera always had a cache of guns being held by someone else. These guns Billy Bright was holding for him were for killing. Pitera, in fact, had a permit for target-shooting. The gun he had the permit for he actually did carry around with him, though he never used it in any crimes, and never would. The fact that Pitera had a gun permit was an infamy, a miscarriage of justice, a wrong that would soon be righted by Jim Hunt.

By now it was late February 1989. Gangi and Billy Bright made their way to the Canarsie home of the Russian family, the Blumenkrants. The house was on a quiet residential street. The homes were set apart from one another. Frank and Billy parked their car down the block, got out and walked back to the house. They had guns in their waistbands. The sun shone. Birds chirped gaily in trees that lined the block. Self-absorbed, people were on their way to work. Though it was early, children were out playing on lawns. Unchallenged, unnoticed, Gangi and Bright made their way to the house. Calm on the outside, their faces relaxed, though nervous inside, they reached the home and, as though they owned it, walked to the backyard. As they had planned, they found the back door open. Without hesitation, they went in. Bright pulled out the gun. They had been expecting to find the wife of the jeweller but instead were confronted by an elderly lady, his mother.

'Be quiet,' Bright ordered. 'We don't want to hurt you. We just want the jewellery. We don't want to hurt you.'

Her eyes were nearly popping out of her head. Bright's words, however, did seem to soothe her. She calmed down somewhat. They demanded the jewellery. They wanted to know where the safe was. They threatened her. She apparently knew little English, as she kept answering them in Russian, saying over and over again, *I have a bad heart. I have a bad heart. I need my medicine*, in Russian. Not knowing what the hell she was saying, they threatened her, pointed guns at her, demanded 'the jewellery'. In Russian, she kept begging for her medicine, desperately pointing to her bag.

Bright finally retrieved the bag, found the medicine and gave it to her. She immediately took the pill. They now went and found Larry's cousin, the other cabinetmaker, handcuffed him and took him and the elderly woman to the finished basement. It was there that they found the trove of jewellery. Neither one of these two were particularly informed about the worth of jewellery, different stones. They took everything she had. With the jewellery in a bag, Billy Bright and Gangi left the house, walked back to the car and took off, overjoyed. Everything had gone as planned. They high-fived one another and slowly drove away, back to Gravesend.

Unbeknownst to Larry Santoro, Manny Maya, Billy Bright and Frank Gangi, the Russian jeweller was friends with a capo in the Gambino crime family, Joe 'Butch' Corrao. They could not have found a worse person to rip off. This capo was a particularly tough, jaded individual. He was not just a capo, he was a war capo. His wife had left a very expensive pair of diamond earrings with the Russian family. Joe Butch wanted the earrings back. He also wanted a part of what was taken. The Gambinos had heard that whoever did this had earned $250,000 from the rip-off.

As neither Gangi nor Bright were professional thieves, professional B&E people, they did not have fences readily available, though it didn't take them long to find fences willing to take the jewellery off their hands. Gangi split up his part and sold pieces to the owner of The Wrong Number, a Genovese captain named Salvatore Lombardi, aka Sally Dogs, and to a jewellery store on Fourth Avenue called Bianco Jewelers.

In reality, La Cosa Nostra is one big fraternity. Except during times of war, they intermingle as freely as stockbrokers on the New York Stock Exchange. Even members from different families regularly have coffee, lunch, dinner together. Part and parcel of why they're so successful is how they *network*. This custom is something that they brought over from Italy. In any town across Sicily, people walk and talk after dinner. Families, friends – it's a built-in custom. The Italians in La Cosa Nostra kept this custom very much alive and because they did not have nine-to-five jobs they were free to meet as they pleased, walk and talk to their hearts' content, until the cows came home. Because their business was crime, because crime was their primary concern, what they talked about all the time was different aspects of different crimes.

When Joe Butch Corrao said he wanted to find the thieves who took the jewellery, word quickly spread throughout Mafiadom, from block to block, neighbourhood to neighbourhood – all over Brooklyn. Capos heard it, lieutenants heard it, soldiers heard it. It didn't take long for the Bonanno family to hear what had happened. It didn't take long for Tommy Karate to hear. Since he was always interested in earning brownie points with the Gambinos, it didn't take long for him to find out that Billy Bright and Frank Gangi had been involved. This was a shocking revelation for Pitera. What they had done could very well have caused problems between the Gambinos and the Bonannos. Neither Bright nor Frank Gangi had come to Pitera and asked his permission to do this score. They were way out of line; Pitera was responsible for them, their actions.

As it happened, there had to be an official sit-down over this incident. Gangi's cousin Ross, a capo in the Genovese crime family, sat down with Joe Butch and Tommy. Joe Butch was bent out of shape. He not only wanted his wife's diamond earrings back, but he was also demanding half the score. Ross Gangi explained the reality of the relationship he had with his cousin.

'Frank's his own man,' he said. 'There's nothing I can do. I can't order him to do anything. He's been a problem all his life. He uses drugs, drinks too much. I'd do anything I can for you, Joe. You know that. But the kid's a wild card.'

By saying what he had just said, Ross Gangi was, essentially, giving Joe Butch the right to kill Frank Gangi. If it hadn't been for Pitera's intervention, for the respect and admiration the Gambinos had for Pitera, the meeting might very well have ended there with the deaths of Billy Bright and Frank Gangi. Pitera spoke up for them. He promised to get what jewellery he could back and give it to Joe Butch. Joe Butch seemed to accept that. The meeting broke up. They all went their separate ways.

Watching, waiting patiently, the DEA was building a case against Pitera: noting who came and left the Just Us, what was said on the tapes, the rumours spreading throughout the dangerous Mafia jungle known as Gravesend.

39

RATS

Rats . . . Pitera hated them with such fervour that he wouldn't allow anyone in his crew to wear a moustache, for moustaches resembled whiskers, and rats had whiskers. Richie Leone was a member of Pitera's crew; Sol Stern was on the fringes of the Bonanno family. Through sources he found reliable, Pitera came to believe, with his obsessive paranoia about rats, that Stern and Leone were informers, were talking to the FBI. He also believed that Richie Leone had stolen bearer bonds that should have gone to Pitera. For them, this was a death sentence, immediate and without appeal.

Pitera devised a plan to kidnap both Leone and Stern. Initially, Pitera was going to use Gangi as part of the kidnapping team, but he was still angry with Gangi over the jewellery robbery. He had come to believe that Gangi was irresponsible because of drug and alcohol abuse. During the sit-down with Joe Butch, Ross Gangi, Frank's cousin, had even told Pitera that Frank was 'out of control . . . unreliable'.

Pitera sent word to Leone and Stern that he had a sweet score he wanted to involve them in. It involved ripping off a large amount of marijuana from a couple of hippies. Unaware and unsuspecting, Leone and Stern showed up at Pitera's club, Overstreets, at the prescribed time on the morning of 15 March 1989. Billy Bright and Richie David were already there, as well as Pitera. Unwittingly, Leone and Stern had walked into a lion's den – a medieval house of torture.

For Pitera, this was not about questioning them, an inquisition, or finding the truth. This was about retribution. Revenge. Pain. Suffering. Murder. On the left as you came into the club was a long bar. In front of the bar was a wooden dance floor. On the far wall, there was a balcony with movie theatre seats. Club goers could sit there, smoke pot and discreetly take a snort of coke without being bothered. Because it was a mob-controlled club, people who went there felt safe. There were few fights. Known troublemakers were kept out. The bouncers were like attack-trained Dobermann pinschers. Pitera had an office there and next to the office was a bathroom where there was a jacuzzi bathtub. Soon, the jacuzzi tub would be used in a most unspeakable way.

Pitera was in a particularly bad mood that night. Since the loss of Celeste, he had changed. He had become quiet, more introspective and, in a word, meaner. He had little patience for anyone. He very rarely laughed. Both Stern and Leone were handcuffed to pipes on the ceiling. It was three o'clock in the morning. There was little traffic on the streets outside. The club's windows were tinted so people could not see in, though a viewer could look out. Pitera uncuffed Leone, shot him and demanded he dance across the floor. Leone had no choice. He danced the best he could, blood seeping through the dime-sized hole in his leg. Pitera shot him again and again and again. Leone lay on the floor, a heap of muscle, bone and flesh. Blood pooled around him.

'Please,' Leone begged. 'Please, just kill me. Just fucking kill me!'

Bright did not want to see him suffer like this. Though Bright was a killer, he did not have the black heart, the lack of conscience, the lack of feelings Pitera had. Bright moved closer to Leone and shot him in the head, killing him. Sol Stern was so horrified, so beside himself that he shat in his pants, stinking the club up.

Next Pitera turned his attention to a very distraught Sol Stern. He proceeded to shoot him numerous times. The man howled and screamed as though he'd been pierced with red-hot pokers.

When Pitera was finished with this sadistic game, he had them brought to the tub. He undressed, grabbed his dismembering kit, got into the tub and cut them each – one after the other – into six pieces. He, with Bright's help, then wrapped them in black plastic and stuffed them in large, cheap suitcases. Sol's valuable wedding ring was stuck on his sausage-thick finger. Pitera wanted it. He couldn't get it off. He used a knife and cut the finger off at the joint and stole the ring. This ring would later come back to haunt Pitera. Again, Pitera was taking totems from his victims, a typical serial-killer phenomenon.

Pitera then made sure the dance floor and club were cleaned thoroughly. Stern was very heavy and they had difficulty fitting him into the suitcases. They had to wrap the two heads separately. After showering thoroughly, Pitera slowly got dressed, and Bright and David grabbed the suitcases and headed towards Pitera's car, put the four cases and the heads in the trunk. They made their way to Staten Island, over the two-mile stretch of the Verrazano Bridge, Brooklyn on their left, the city on their right. They could see the Statue of Liberty and Ellis Island from the middle of the bridge. The water in the Narrows was calm. After going through the tollbooth, they made their way to the bird sanctuary, driving slowly, making certain to abide by all traffic laws. They reached the street, which abutted the bird sanctuary, parked the car, retrieved the suitcases and heads, and quickly made their way into the forest. They went about 30 steps, found a clearing and put down the bodies. It being March, the soil was somewhat firm. Digging was harder. They took turns trying to make a hole large enough to accommodate both suitcases. It was arduous work. When the hole was deep enough, they dumped the two suitcases in. Pitera wanted the heads buried separately, so he had a second hole dug some ten feet away and dumped the two heads there. They covered the holes up and left, a shy dawn slowly growing on the eastern sky, a chill wind blowing off the nearby Atlantic. Pitera felt good about what he had done. He felt justice had been served . . . street justice.

Billy Bright showed up at the pot stash house he, Gangi and Pitera kept. Gangi had slept there that night. He was with a girl he was seeing named Sophia. When Billy Bright arrived, he was covered in dirt and his face was long and sad. Gangi took one look at him and knew what was wrong: the dirt told the story.

'Would you like to talk?' Gangi offered.

Bright immediately told him everything that had occurred. Gangi listened sympathetically. He was glad Pitera had not chosen him to be a part of this.

'He's fucking out of control,' Gangi said, wanting to distance himself from Pitera, wanting to distance himself from it all. He was still plagued by what had happened to Phyllis Burdi. He couldn't get it out of his mind. He would later relate that this trauma caused him to drink and use drugs excessively: he was now consuming a full bottle of scotch every day, plus several grams of cocaine. If he hadn't been such a naturally strong, robust individual, no doubt he would have passed out one night and not woken up.

Trouble, he felt in his bones, loomed large and foreboding. His answer was to snort a long line of glistening cocaine.

PART 3

THE BEAT GOES ON

40

THE COP KILLER

It was now early July 1989. The temperature at noon that day was near 100 degrees. Jim Hunt was in an unmarked DEA car parked on Flatlands Avenue. He was watching the garage, body shop and mob hangout where Manny Maya worked. Jim was certain the body shop was a front for cleaning cars used in murders and the distribution of large amounts of narcotics.

The DEA investigation into Pitera and his crew was finally in full gear after the days, weeks and months since the Pitera case had begun. Through what they heard on wiretaps – there were now taps in the Just Us bar, Overstreets, the Cypress Bar and Grill, Judy Haimowitz's house and Frank Gangi's house, and there were bugs in whatever cars Pitera drove, too – the strike force had come to learn that Pitera was regularly selling large amounts of both heroin and cocaine – through a rotating, ever-changing network of different people who worked for him – as well as being an assassin not only for the Bonanno family but also the other families. They knew that he was responsible for killing Willie Boy Johnson, that Eddie Lino himself had made him part of the hit team that had brought down Johnson. Now the task at hand was finding tangible, viable evidence that could be used in a court of law that would hold up under blistering scrutiny from the best criminal attorneys in the country.

Today, Jim Hunt was alone, watching the garage. His partner Tommy Geisel had a wedding he needed to attend. Rather than lose a day, Jim had that itchy feeling in the nape of his neck and decided to keep an eye on the garage and Pitera hangout by himself. For Jim Hunt, a successful case often came about out of pure happenstance, good luck, being in the right place at the wrong time, or even the wrong place at the right time.

While he was sitting there sweating profusely, his beeper sounded. When he checked the number, he saw it was a DEA informant he'd been working with for several years who had successfully brought down major players in the cocaine and heroin business. Her name was Maria Polkowski. At this juncture, she had nothing to do with the Pitera case, though Jim thought she might very well get involved with the case down the road. She was an obese Brazilian woman who had larger balls than most men. She was amazingly adept at getting people to believe bold-faced lies. She not only spoke English and Portuguese but five other languages fluently as well. Maria was a stellar informer for the DEA, and they paid her well for the services she provided: not only was she an amazing actress, but she could also think on her feet, adapt to any situation quickly, had the courage to go up against dangerous men with big guns and bad attitudes. Sharp knives.

Jim called her. She said she was in Queens with one Hector Estrada and a 'very important Mafia guy', she said.

'Why do you think he's in the Mafia, Maria?' Jim asked.

'I know it. I'm sure he's in the Mafia. He's very connected.'

'Because he's Italian?'

'No, don't be silly. This guy's really mobbed up. Come quickly, James. I don't feel safe here.'

Hunt did not want to leave the stakeout. Had it not been Maria calling, he would not have left, but she had proved immensely reliable, well informed and had helped Jim make many cases. Reluctantly, he put his car in gear and sped over to Astoria Boulevard in Queens. Jim went to the Italian restaurant where Maria had said she was. Neither she nor the Mafia characters were inside. Perplexed, he got back in his car. As he drove around the block, he spotted Maria in her amazingly colourful garb walking with two men. One was a gruff, tough-looking dude, a South American with dark skin, no doubt Hector Estrada. The other was like a blond surfer. This surfer-looking dude soon separated from Maria and Hector, got in a small convertible and pulled away. Jim felt he could always find Maria and so he decided to follow the surfer.

He drove straight to a B-rated strip club on Astoria Boulevard. Jim sat outside wondering what to do. He decided to go in and see what was up. Inside, it was air-conditioned and the cool air was a much welcome change. The place was empty. The surfer was sitting at the bar near the door. Jim audaciously walked over, sat down right next to him and ordered a beer.

'How you doing?' the surfer said.

'Good, good. Yourself?' Jim said.

They began to talk about the weather. The surfer introduced himself as Giles and they shook hands. As Jim enjoyed the cold beer, the surfer ogled, somewhat excessively, the broken-down stripper up on stage. Out of the corner of his eye, Jim eyeballed the surfer; he was looking at a somewhat baby-faced, innocuous man who didn't seem capable of hurting a fly. Jim would soon find out that was a major misread. Jim finished his beer and left. In his gut, Jim felt for sure that something big was in the air. It was one of those things that you could not learn in school; it was a gritty, guttural sensation – some would call it a sixth sense, some would call it street sense. Jim wasn't sure where this would go, but he took it seriously. He called headquarters, told his boss what he had seen and asked for back-up. Within minutes, two teams of DEA agents, Jim's symbiotic brothers, were speeding towards Queens with their sirens on and red lights flashing. While Jim sat in the car waiting for his people, his beeper again sounded. It was Maria again. He called her right back.

'Hector called and said he wanted to meet me,' she said.

Jim knew Hector to be a Colombian coke dealer.

'I met him in the restaurant. He was with two guys. One of them was Mafia. I'm sure he's Mafia. His name was Vincenzo. The other one was this blond guy, Giles.'

'I met him,' Jim said, 'in a bar a couple of blocks away.'

'Well, this Giles guy, he's a fugitive, and a very dangerous man, and the thing of it is that he wants to buy cocaine. A lot of cocaine. They want, like, 200 kilos. The problem is that Hector can't get what they want right now so he lied, he lied and said he bought a lot of cocaine from me ten times. He lied and now he wants me to come up with cocaine. All 200 kilos. What should I do, James?'

'I want you to play them. You're very good at what you do. Don't worry. I'll make sure nothing happens to you. Tell them you'll get the drugs, no problem. You got it?'

'I got it,' Maria said in her peculiar Brazilian accent.

'I'll get back to you,' Jim said.

Jim's people drove up. He quickly ran down what was happening. As he talked, Giles the surfer left the club, got into his car and pulled away, not noticing the government. Jim and the other agents decided to follow him. He led them all the way to Secaucus, New Jersey, then went into a townhouse. They ran his plates. The car was a rental car registered out of Florida under the name Vincent Mancino. At that juncture, that meant nothing one way or another. They eyeballed the house for several hours. A woman in her 30s left, got in a car and drove away. Near midnight they decided to wrap it up and pick it up the next day.

As Jim made his way home, he had that feeling in his gut – something big, potentially dangerous, was afoot here. He'd work it indefatigably to its final outcome. In his business, fortuitous situations could fall from the sky and they had to be worked diligently. He did not like the idea of taking his attention away from the Pitera case and its cast of characters, but Jim was in the business of responding quickly, being malleable when potential situations arose, and fighting fires whenever and wherever they burned.

The day had been long, hot, arduous and somewhat nerve-wracking. When Jim's head hit the pillow, he had no trouble falling asleep.

The following day, Maria Polkowski, big and round and colourful, wearing far too much make-up, clown-like, showed up at the DEA's office on 57th Street. Jim and Tom sat her down at a desk and listened to her story. She first talked about Vincenzo. She described him as a good-looking man with dark hair, definitely in the Mafia, married to a Canadian woman. He was on the lam, she said, and lived in Canada. She said, too, that Hector was creating problems for her. She didn't have coke like that. She didn't want to be put into a position where she was asked for something she could not deliver. Jim calmed her down, told her she was the best they'd ever had.

'If anyone can pull this off, you can. I know you can,' he reassured her. 'I will make sure nothing happens to you, I promise,' he said.

She looked at him long and hard. She liked Jim, trusted him, had a bit of a crush on him. 'OK,' she said.

Jim told her to call him the moment she heard anything further, that he'd be at her beck and call 24 hours a day. Bolstered by his kind words, she left, a newfound spring in her heavy step. Jim proceeded to call an old contact and good friend of his, Mike Spataro, a retired NYPD detective out of the organised crime unit who was now working for the DEA. Nobody knew more about organised crime characters than Mike. He had a memory like a steel bear-trap. He had copious notes that included aliases, nicknames, tattoos etc. Jim asked him about this Vincenzo. He said he was good-looking, in his 40s, had dark hair and was married to a Canadian woman. Spataro told Jim that he'd see what he could find out and then get back to him.

* * *

With no new developments in the case Maria had just brought them, two days later Jim and Tommy were back in Brooklyn's Gravesend, continuing their surveillance of Tommy Pitera and the jaded constellation of bad guys that revolved around him. They were still working out of the house in Bensonhurst that monitored all the many taps they had on cars and homes relevant to the case. They had come to know that Pitera was far more devious than he seemed on the surface. Over and over again, Pitera had warned all his people about talking on phones or in their cars. The Pitera strike force noticed that Frank Gangi was a 'Pitera regular', as they started calling his people, and there seemed to be something . . . unhinged about Gangi. They already knew that Gangi was from a Mafia family; that he had uncles in the Mafia and his father had been immersed in that world. They knew, too, that he had been involved in a murder – the killing of Arthur Guvenaro.

Recorded conversations Judy Haimowitz had with porno lines still came in on a regular basis. They had become a running joke all throughout the DEA. Jim Hunt and Tom were still buying drugs from her, still building a case against her, which, ultimately, they hoped they would use as a hammer to nail Pitera.

Some five days after Maria first contacted Jim, she called him again.

'Oh my God!' she said. 'The Colombian guy called and they're coming to my house.'

'They know where you live?' Jim asked.

'Yes, I told them. You know that's how I get people's trust.'

Jim didn't like this. He shook his head. Rather than admonish her, he said he'd be right there. Jim and his boss Ken Feldman sped over to Queens. As they pulled up in front of the house, by pure happenstance, the yellow convertible pulled up and Giles walked into the house with a green duffel bag. This piqued the agents' interest in a big way. What, they wondered out loud, was in that duffel bag? Within minutes, Giles exited the house, got back into his yellow convertible and took off, unconcerned, seemingly unaware. With that, Jim got out of his car and went upstairs to see what was up. He knocked on Maria's door. She opened it. Her eyes were all wide.

'My God,' she said, 'look what he gave me!' She opened the bag and inside was $400,000 Canadian. Jim looked. He was as shocked as she was. Maria continued. 'He gave me this as a down payment for the 200 kilos.'

This, Jim knew, changed the complexion of the case. These were serious players. If they were willing to just drop off almost half-a-million dollars as a good-faith deposit, they were the real deal.

'What am I going to do? What am I going to do?' Maria asked.

'Just relax,' Jim said. 'I'll help you through it. I'll guide you through every step. You're the best. Just remember that.'

'OK, James, OK,' she said, seeming more relaxed.

Jim had an uncanny way of getting people in his business to like him, warm to him, trust him. He now took the bag from Maria. He would take it to the office, where it would be marked as evidence. As he made his way downstairs, shockingly, Giles the blond surfer was coming up. They passed one another. Giles was so wrapped up in thought he didn't notice Jim or his bag. Jim was shocked. Surely, he thought, he'd make him.

Outside, back in his car, Jim put the duffel bag in Ken's lap and said, 'You're not going to fucking believe this. He brought up the bag, gave her $400,000 Canadian as a deposit, good faith, and I took it, and as I'm walking down the stairs he walks right past me. We walked right past each other. We touched shoulders.'

'No,' Ken said.

'Yes,' Jim said.

'Four hundred thou?' Ken asked, opening the bag, his eyes wide.

'Four hundred thou.'

Jim immediately called Maria. He wanted to know what was up.

'Is everything OK?' he asked.

'Yes, there's no problem. Everything is OK. He came back to give me the phone number to call in Canada.'

'In Canada? Where in Canada?'

'Canada,' she said.

'Where in Canada?'

'Toronto, I think,' she said.

'You think? You don't know?'

'Toronto, I know.'

'Are you sure, Maria?'

'I'm sure . . . Toronto.'

As proficient as Maria was, Jim knew her to be, as he would later explain, 'crazy'. He explained it like this: 'She was somewhat spaced out. Out to lunch.'

'So, let me get this straight,' Jim said. 'He wants you to bring him the drugs in Canada . . . in Toronto . . . and call this number that he gave you when you get there.'

'Right.'

'OK, we can do this, we can make this work.'

'James, with your help, I'm sure we can,' she said.

Jim hung up. He turned to Ken.

'It looks like we're going to Canada,' he said.

'OK,' Ken replied.

Next, Jim called the Canadian authorities, the Royal Canadian Mounted Police. He got the head of the Mounties, Sergeant McDonald, on the phone and ran down the situation in quick cop-alese. That very day Maria, Tom and Jim boarded a plane for Toronto. The Pitera case, for now, was out of sight, but not out of mind. As Tom and Jim sped to Canada, DEA agents were circling Pitera, watching his minions, looking for that weak link – looking for his Achilles heel.

When Tom, Jim and Maria arrived in Toronto, they went straight to meet Sergeant McDonald at Mountie headquarters. Sergeant McDonald had a feeling he knew who they were talking about. The first thing the sergeant did when Jim, Tommy and Maria arrived at his office was show them a picture and ask, 'Do you know this guy?' as if he already knew the answer, his tone sombre and overtly serious.

Jim took one look. The man in the photograph had a thick head of dark hair and a beard, but it was obvious that it was Giles – the surfer.

'That's him,' Jim said, showing the picture to Maria. She took it. She agreed with Jim that it was the Giles character.

Sergeant McDonald shook his head as though he'd just been given some very bad news. 'Well, we have a serious problem here,' he said. 'This man is one of the most wanted men in Canada. His real name is Yves LeSalle and he is a cop killer. He killed a police officer during a robbery in Houston, Texas, and then three security guards during another robbery he committed after having escaped from a maximum-security prison here in Canada where he had been serving a life sentence.'

'Holy shit,' Jim said. 'I was so close to him I touched him.' Jim felt bad for not having cuffed him the day they first met. Jim hated cop killers. Both the good guys and the bad guys understood you don't kill a cop. To do so was an infamy. Not only had this Giles guy killed a cop, but he had also killed three other men in uniform. At the very top of the list of bad guys were cop killers.

Sergeant McDonald said, 'The problem is that if we see this guy, we've got to arrest him on sight. There's no way, I mean, think about it, that we can play out a sting with him.'

Both Jim and Tom knew his argument had merit. If Giles got away when they had an opportunity to arrest him, the Mounties' careers would be on the line. Jim and Tom decided not to make an argument of it right now; they would work the case to see how it played out. Sergeant McDonald explained that they believed Giles had connections to the Mafia, to the Bonanno crime family. This, of course, Jim and Tommy found endlessly interesting, having had no idea that this would all lead back to Brooklyn . . . to Tommy Pitera. Sergeant McDonald agreed to help them with the understanding that if Giles showed up, he was theirs.

Jim immediately turned on the charm. If anyone could convince Sergeant McDonald to cooperate with them, let them play this out, it was Jim. This all had to do with the fact that Jim was truly being sincere, wasn't playing anybody. He knew what he was doing, was a professional and would, one way or another, get the job done. Jim, in this case, wanted to have his cake and eat it, too.

When Jim, Tommy and Maria left Mountie headquarters, they checked into a nearby motel. Now Maria called the phone number that Vincenzo had given her. She said she was looking for Vincenzo. She was told he wasn't there, that she should call back in an hour. When, an hour later, she called back and asked for Vincenzo, a man with a very gruff, gravelly voice answered. He identified himself as Vincenzo. She said she had come to Canada as per their agreement, was in Toronto with 'the goods'.

'What? Toronto?' he said incredulously.

'Yes, Toronto.'

'What are you doing there?'

'He told me to come here, I'm here. That's what he said.'

'No, you were supposed to come to Montreal.'

'Nooo,' she said. 'He told me to come to Toronto. I know he told me to come to Toronto.'

'My God,' the man with the gruff voice said. 'Look, I'll call you back.' He hung up.

'This guy's crazy!' Maria said.

Jim, knowing that Maria was somewhat unhinged, knowing her perceptions were occasionally off base, asked, 'Maria, are you sure they said Toronto?' He immediately accepted that Maria had somehow made a mistake.

'Jim,' Maria said, 'they said to come to Toronto.'

Jim was not about to argue with her. 'Look, Maria, you've just got to convince them to come here. It will make everything a lot easier, OK?'

'OK,' she said.

Before she called the number again, Jim spoke to Sergeant McDonald. He explained that apparently the bad guys were in Montreal, not Toronto. Sergeant McDonald said that opened up a whole Pandora's box of more trouble. As per Jim's instructions, Maria called the number again. Vincenzo answered. She explained that she had done what was asked of her, that the goods were in Toronto. He explained that did no good for anyone.

'Well,' she said, 'my driver and I came up. The material's in the car. I had no idea I had to come here and now I have to go there. That changes everything. I don't want to go. You want it, you come here.'

'Look, Maria, I don't know who told you to go to Toronto, but that was a mistake. We're here, our operation is here,' he said in his gravelly voice.

'You need to come *here*,' she said.

Maria, Jim and Tom discussed their going to Montreal, the different ramifications of the trip. Since it was a mistake for them to be in Toronto to begin with, Jim decided they ought to push for it. With that Maria called back Vincenzo and said she'd drive the car to Montreal. He was grateful, said thank you and hung up. Jim next called Sergeant McDonald. Maria soon called Hector and yelled at him, saying that they had told her to go to Toronto and now they wanted her to go somewhere else. Hector denied that he had ever said Toronto. It went back and forth for quite a while. Ultimately, Hector said he was going to Montreal and would figure everything out for her. He said he would arrive on a 7 p.m. flight.

Sergeant McDonald put Jim and Tom in contact with high-ups in the narcotics division in Montreal. He explained, briefly, what was going down, and Jim, Tommy, Maria and two Toronto Mounties were soon on their way to Montreal. The Mounties were there to make sure Jim and Tom got what they needed, cooperation and help, and that the surveillance on Hector was carried out correctly. Jim and Tom had decided to follow Hector, see where he went. They were certain he was the key, that he would lead them to Vincenzo and Giles.

When they arrived at the airport, they hurried from the plane and were met by a dozen Mounties connected to the narcotics bureau. Each was dressed in plain clothes. Their boss was named Sergeant Martin. He was a tall, strong-looking man who had obviously been around the block several times. He was seasoned and well versed in the workings of the criminal mind. Jim and Tom took an immediate liking to him. The feeling was mutual. Sergeant Martin explained that four surveillance teams were set up outside, that they had guys dressed as hard hats and blue-collar workers and women pushing baby carriages. Jim liked what he saw and heard. They found the gate from which Hector would be disembarking. There was a somewhat crowded bar nearby. Sergeant Martin, Jim and Tom made their way up to the bar and ordered beers. Jim quickly brought Sergeant Martin up to speed. Sergeant Martin reiterated what Sergeant McDonald had said in Toronto: if they came upon Yves LeSalle, they had to arrest him. 'If we see him and we don't arrest him, Jim, we'll have to contend with that again. I couldn't handle that. He's a killer. He's proved this over and over.'

Jim nodded his head silently in agreement. He was able to see the gate from the bar. People were starting to disembark. Jim looked down the bar and quickly realised Yves was standing not three feet away from his elbow. Jim started motioning with his eyes to Sergeant Martin and Tom but neither one of them was picking up his cues. He moved his eyebrows and his eyes, but they weren't getting it. Finally, in little more than a whisper, he said, 'That's him. He's here. Right next to me. That's him!'

As incredulous and improbable as this was to believe, it was absolutely true. It was as if fate had picked up Yves LeSalle and put him down there. Jim wanted this to play out. He understood Sergeant Martin's sentiments, but he knew there was a lot at stake here; he

knew there were bigger fish to fry. Jim and Sergeant Martin moved
to the other side of a wide pillar. Jim reiterated his feelings. Sergeant
Martin took a long, deep breath. He had somehow known it would
come to this, but he had had no idea he would end up at a bar with
Yves. Suffice it to say, Jim and Tom and a team of seasoned Mounties
were given the green light to follow both Hector and Yves when they
left the airport. More agents were brought in; the Mounties were
taking this very seriously.

Yves spotted Hector and walked up to him. They embraced and
walked off together, having no idea how many eyes were intently
watching them, following them, clocking them, as flights were
announced, the world went about its business.

Outside, they got into Yves's yellow convertible and drove away.
A dozen different unmarked cars carefully followed them. Yves and
Hector seemed, to a degree, oblivious to the tail. Yves had become
cocky, so sure of himself that he had lost sight of the fact that he was
a much-wanted cop killer. Yves pulled into a Marriot hotel parking
lot. Hector checked in. The two of them made their way into the
hotel bar and began drinking in earnest. Unbeknownst to them,
they were surrounded by law enforcement, seasoned, hard cops who
knew the ropes. After an hour or so, Hector went upstairs by himself.
Meanwhile, Yves got in the car and drove to an apartment house in
downtown Montreal. Soon cop cars, staying at a discreet distance,
surrounded the building. Before they allowed Yves to get away again,
they'd kill him.

Early the next morning, there was an extensive debriefing at the
Montreal office of the Mounted Police. Succinctly, Jim ran down the
case. It was clear they knew what they had to do. The plan they put
together was that they would have Maria call the club and have the
bad guys meet her at a Holiday Inn near the airport. She would tell
them that she had the drugs secreted in her van. The police would
rent the two rooms on either side of Maria's. They would bug Maria's

room extensively. Anything that was said, they'd record. Anything that was done, they'd see.

As per instructions, Maria called the club. Vincenzo again answered. He was pleased Maria had seen reason and come to Montreal. She invited him to the hotel, as Jim had instructed her to do, where they could consummate the deal. Vincenzo readily agreed to come, having no idea of the razor-sharp trap that was patiently waiting for him. Sure enough, at the prescribed time, the bad guys showed up: Vincenzo, Yves and Hector. As the agents and Mounties watched on monitors to the left and right of Maria's room, they saw a calm, cool Maria greet her guests as though they were long-lost friends. The bad guys were all smiling and seemed happy. Maria was the perfect hostess. Vincenzo called room service and ordered a very good bottle of scotch. They made toasts to future business they would do together.

'Salud! Salud, salud!' they said, accompanied by the sound of clinking glasses. All chummy, all warm, they sat down . . . one big happy family.

Vincenzo explained that for him the coke business was new, that he had been in the heroin business previously. He said there was a lot of money to be made in heroin because the product could be cut so much. Doe-eyed, all innocent, Maria said she knew nothing about the heroin business, she had never even seen the drug; she asked questions about it of Vincenzo. It was obvious that he had been dealing in heroin for many years. He said that he and his 'uncle' had done very well with it.

'But,' Maria asked, 'how do you know if it's good?'

'Well, I have a hot box and I put it in and see if it melts. But you know what the real test is? When the nigger hits the floor,' he said, tapping the arteries in his arm with two fingers.

The men got a big laugh out of that. Maria didn't quite understand what he meant. She asked him to explain.

'When the dope is good, the nigger ODs. In other words, we find some niggers and we give them the drugs and we see what happens.'

'Oh, that's clever,' Maria said, subtly, encouragingly.

Now, changing the conversation, this Vincenzo character told Maria that he would like to take 20 keys of the cocaine now.

'Excuse me?' she asked.

'I want 20 kilos now and I'll take the rest in a couple of days.'

'That wasn't our agreement,' she said. 'Our agreement was that I'd bring the drugs here and get paid. That's it.'

'Look, Maria,' Vincenzo said, his eyebrows rising, getting angry, 'we gave you $400,000 already. When we get the drugs, we'll give you the rest of the money. There's no problem here.'

'That's not what the deal was,' she said.

This went back and forth a while. Vincenzo was getting angrier and angrier. Yves and Hector pretty much stayed quiet. The argument became so heated that Vincenzo called for a time-out. The three men went downstairs to the bar. They talked amongst themselves for a little while before Yves and Hector got into their car and drove away, followed by six police cars. Vincenzo had two more drinks. This was early afternoon. As he drank, Jim again called his NYPD contact, Mike Spataro. Now he explained exactly what Vincenzo looked like, that he had an uncle who was connected.

Mike said, 'Let me think, let me think . . .' Jim could hear him rustling through paper files. Suddenly, Mike let out a whistle.

'I got it! I know who this is!'

41

SPIDER'S WEB

His name was Vinnie Lore. He was a made member of the Gambino crime family. Coincidentally, quite amazingly so, his uncle was Frankie Tuminaro, who was murdered alongside Frank Gangi's father. His other uncle was named Angelo Tuminaro. Both were principals in the French Connection Case; Angelo had been a fugitive for over 20 years now. Vinnie Lore had been indicted in the same case as Gene Gotti, Angelo Ruggerio and John Carniglia and fled while on bail. The Bonannos and the Gambinos were close. As Eddie Lino was very close to Tommy Pitera, Jim Hunt had learned that Pitera and the Bonannos had supplied the Gambinos with heroin. This, Jim Hunt knew, clearly put Pitera in the drama on the stage he was now watching.

The plot thickens, Jim thought.

Jim knew what had to be done. He sat Maria down and looked her in the eye.

'Maria,' he said, 'I want you to get tough. I want you to yell and curse and show this Vincenzo guy no respect. You tell him you're not separating the drugs and you tell him it's the whole load or nothing. You understand?'

'Si, I understand,' she said, seeming to enjoy the role she was about to play, her face taking on a histrionic demeanour.

Jim said, 'Tell them the drugs are sealed in a trap in the van you drove up in and that you're not giving them up until the deal is carried out. You tell them that when they show up with the money, you'll give them the van and they can get the drugs.'

'OK, James,' she said, resolute, confident in James's words, confident that he'd protect her.

Word came that Vincenzo was on his way back. He seemed somewhat wobbly, came the report. No wonder, Jim thought, as he had been drinking since late morning. Everyone took his or her positions. There was a knock on the door and Maria opened it. Vincenzo walked in. He began with the same old rap.

Maria interrupted him and said, 'Listen to me, you spaghetti-bending, guinea motherfucker. I'm not doing it the way you said. I'm not doing anything that isn't what we agreed on. You give me the money and I give you the van and I'm not doing anything until that happens that way, you got it?'

Vincenzo Lore, a made man in the Gambino family, a killer, was obviously cowed by this fat, colourful Brazilian lady. When he began to protest, she let loose a string of obscenities and swore she would leave if they didn't live up to their end of the bargain.

'I ain't breaking open the seal to give you 20 keys,' she reiterated. 'That's bullshit. No one ever said I had to do that. Fuck that. I'm not doing it. My people know where I am and will have a hit team come up here and wipe you the fuck off the map.' She pulled out her cantaloupe-sized tit and violently shook it at him, saying, 'Here's my tit! Why don't you grow some balls?'

They looked at each other long and hard. Jim Hunt was ready to burst through the door for fear Vinnie would attack her. Everyone was tense. Vincenzo brought his hand to his forehead as if he had a sudden headache, obviously shocked by the appearance of her head-sized breast menancingly pointed at him like some kind of bazooka.

Maria had a pair of balls and they both knew it.

'I gotta go, I gotta do some thinking,' he said, rubbing his forehead. He got up and left.

Jim Hunt entered Maria's room and gave her a big bear hug.

'You were marvellous,' he said. 'Fantastic! Brilliant! The best performance I've ever seen anyone give.'

They all hugged her and shook her hand, all ten cynical Canadian cops and Tommy Geisel, too. She had been nominated for an Oscar and she had won hands down.

Now Hector and Yves the cop killer were under 24-hour surveillance. The Canadian authorities would not let these men out of their sight come hell or high water. Later that day, a very interesting turn of events came about illustrating just how deep La Cosa Nostra had their talons in the Canadian underworld. The authorities followed Vincenzo Lore to a popular diner. When he went inside, he met with Guy Mirot, who was the Godfather of crime in Canada. If there was a *capo di tutti capi* in Canada, his name was Guy Mirot. He was heavily into drugs and deeply immersed in the Bonanno family. Things were really heating up now, beginning to bubble.

Vinnie and Guy Mirot sat for an hour and Vinnie did most of the talking. Guy listened intently. He seemed to be agreeing with what Vinnie was saying. The meeting broke up. Vinnie went one way and Guy went another. Maria soon received a phone call from Vinnie. He told her that they would do it just like she wanted; that everything could be 'taken care of' the following day.

V-Day was here. Early that morning Jim Hunt and Tommy Geisel were at Mountie headquarters. They were 'guests', there only because of the goodwill of the Canadian authorities, so they could just make suggestions. A task force was rapidly put together. There was no reason to believe that Vinnie Lore was lying. The fact that Vinnie had met with Guy told them all, without a shadow of a doubt, that

Guy would be putting up money to facilitate the deal. They laid down how the bust would happen on a map of the area surrounding the hotel. There would be over a dozen police vehicles, 25 police personnel, with helicopters hovering overhead.

Later that morning, crime boss Guy Mirot left his house, went to a second home and retrieved two suitcases, placed them in the trunk of his car and drove on. There were no clouds in the Canadian sky. The sun shone. An unusually large flock of Canadian geese passed low overhead. Guy Mirot went back to the diner and, lo and behold, met with Vinnie Lore. Mirot put the suitcases directly into the trunk of Vinnie's car. In the suitcases, they all knew, was the balance of the money, some $1.6 million Canadian. Soon, Yves and Hector showed up at the diner. There was another man with them, a man no one could ID. It would later be revealed that it was Gilles Mallete, a particularly tough old-school Montreal gangster. Tension was in the air. A nervous kind of static. Cops checked their guns. They had every reason in the world to believe that Yves would immediately start shooting when he saw cops. They were sure he'd go down in a hail of bullets before being captured.

It was a warm, muggy day. Rubbery waves of heat rose from the ground. As the bad guys made their way over to the hotel, surveillance cars were following them, switching places as they went. The bad guys seemed to be oblivious to what was happening. They pulled into the hotel parking lot. The Mounties had a parked minivan ready with Florida plates, thanks to an agent who had recently been transferred from Florida. Vinnie Lore went upstairs first by himself. He knocked on the door and Maria let him in. He wasn't that friendly.

'You've been a very bad signora, a very bad signora,' he said. 'I don't know why I'm doing what I'm doing, but I'm bringing the money up here and you can hold it until my guys get the van. If everything is OK, you can keep it and we go.'

'OK,' she said.

'You've been a very bad signora,' he said again, half-jokingly, and went downstairs to get the others and the money. Quickly, Jim entered the room.

'Look, Maria,' he said, 'when we go to make a move, I'm going to call you on the phone and then you go to the bathroom. When the phone rings, pick it up, talk to me a second and then go straight to the bathroom. Got it?'

'Got it, James,' she said. Jim Hunt left. Maria stood there, tough and jaded, cynical and street smart.

Within minutes, Vinnie returned, the other three in tow. They put down the bags of money. Smiling, Maria told them they were doing the right thing, complimented them and gave them the keys to the van. She said, 'We had the material stashed in the chassis and welded over. All you have to do is open the seal and you'll have it.'

Yves, Hector and the third man left to retrieve the coke. Vinnie stayed behind. Calm and self-assured, his glock sticking out of his waistband, Jim Hunt knew it was time to act; he called Maria's room. The others got ready, drew their guns, got themselves in the right frame of mind. They knew Vinnie Lore was a dangerous man, that he had killed people – that he had a lot to lose. They all wanted to go home that day to their wives and families and none of them were about to let this mafioso miscreant take them down.

'Maria,' Jim said into the phone, 'go to the bathroom.'

'OK, OK, Jaime,' she said and hung up. She excused herself and went to the restroom. As soon as she was out of the room, out of harm's way, the hard-jawed Mounties, Jim and Tom burst into the room. Vinnie Lore barely had time to blink, let alone react. In split seconds, he was up in the air, slammed to the ground and handcuffed. His rights were read.

Jim said, 'What's your name?'

'Vinnie Mancino,' Vinnie said.

'That's bullshit,' Jim said. 'The game's up. You're Vincenzo Lore, and your pals Carniglia and Gotti each got 50 years this morning.'

Vinnie's face was the colour of the underside of a flounder, pale and bloodless. He knew he could not argue and didn't try.

Outside, Yves, Hector and the other man moved towards the van. As Yves opened the chassis of the vehicle, suddenly, out of nowhere, an army of police surrounded them, were on top of them, demanding they put down their weapons and get on the ground. Neither Yves nor the other two had any time to react. They were hit at such lightning speed. It was over. The bad guys had lost. No blood had been spilled.

The job done, it was time to go back to New York, to Gravesend. It was time to tighten the screws on the Pitera case.

42

1-900-FUCK-ME

Over the underworld jungle drums of La Cosa Nostra, word quickly spread from Montreal and Canada to Brooklyn, Gravesend and Bensonhurst, and Dyker Heights: Vincent Lore had been busted. The Canadian Godfather Guy Mirot took it on the lam and disappeared with the wind. Some $2 million was lost. It didn't take long for the Bonanno family to also hear the news, which soon passed to Tommy Pitera. It was the kind of bust he dreaded hearing about. It involved organised crime figures; it involved obviously good police work, infiltration, duplicity, informers, wiretaps; it also involved the loss of a lot of money. Pitera knew, felt in his bones, that it involved a rat.

It always boiled down to rats in his mind. Oh, how he hated rats. The thought of them made his skin crawl. He resolved to run his crew even more tightly. He'd be more watchful, wary and on guard of everybody around him; he would trust nobody, he vowed. Pitera felt that Frank Gangi was becoming a concern. He felt that Gangi was 'good people'; he knew the womb he came from, he knew that Gangi's blood was mafioso. What worried him about Gangi was his drug use, his drinking. He made a mental note to talk to him.

Meanwhile, Pitera applied good, sound business sense to the money he was making. He had this dream of building a spectacular palatial home for himself and, to that end, he bought a townhouse in a nice residential area of Brooklyn known as Bay Ridge. It was on Ovington Avenue. From the corner, you had a direct view of the Narrows and the Verrazano Bridge, the bridge that connected Brooklyn to Pitera's cemetery. It was a three-storey limestone property. He had the building completely gutted and was going to renovate it from the beams on up. He bought the best of everything for his home. He had marble brought in from Carrara, Italy. Pitera planned to buy more property that he could rent and make money from.

After the bust of Vincent Lore and Yves LeSalle in Canada, Jim and Tom's reputation grew by leaps and bounds. They had brought down particularly bad, heinous fugitives, one a cop killer, one a made man, in addition to Guy Mirot, *the* bad guy in Canada. They had also managed to recover $2 million in cash. What was also startling and unusual was that they had managed to do all this in a matter of days. No long drawn out listening to wiretaps; no endless surveillance.

Now, back on the ground in Brooklyn, Hunt and Geisel were back to the raw basics. They wanted Pitera. They focused their energy on Pitera. Whatever they asked for, whatever they wanted, was quickly given to them. A task force of some 13 agents would soon be trailing Pitera. He sensed their presence. Once in a while he spotted a pair of the agents, but for the most part they stayed out of sight. He had no idea from where they hailed, but he knew they were cops. He smelled the smoke, but he didn't see the fire that was slowly surrounding him, slowly enveloping him.

By listening carefully to the jungle drums resonating through La Cosa Nostra, the DEA had come to believe that Pitera was not only selling large amounts of narcotics but also killing people at random on a regular basis and chopping up their bodies for ready disposal.

Because of Pitera's intimate involvement with La Cosa Nostra, the DEA decided to bring in the FBI. Normally, the DEA do not involve other agencies. They want to work cases the way they see them. They don't want to argue or debate or fight over jurisdictional issues and, most importantly, who gets the limelight.

Likewise, Jim Hunt thought it would be a good idea to bring in the NYPD's organised crime unit. Perhaps more than any other government agency, they knew exactly what was going on in each family, who was who, what role everyone played. In that the task force had now two other agencies working hand in hand with the DEA, a virtual army was looking to nail Tommy Pitera to the cross. However, even with all this manpower, even with all the technical assistance, it was very hard to nail Pitera. Stymied, they watched Pitera meet with Frankie Lino, Anthony Spero and other members of upper echelon of the Bonanno family and go on walk and talks around Gravesend, speaking softly, Tommy most often covering his mouth as he spoke, making it impossible to record what he was saying. As one agent put it: 'The fucking guy looks like he's always playing a harmonica.'

The weak link: Jim kept wondering about the weak link. Judy Haimowitz, of course, would be helpful, but a good lawyer could minimise the impact she had on the case. They needed more. They wanted blood, bodies, large amounts of cocaine in Pitera's hands. Meanwhile, Judy Haimowitz was entertaining now not only the DEA but also the FBI and the organised crime unit. Her having phone sex while listening to the most kinky of recordings, orgasming out loud, the sound of the vibrator in the background, had become much-needed comic relief.

43

HE'S A REAL BAD DUDE

S hlomo Mendelsohn, also known as Sammy, was your basic lowlife, drug-dealing, hustling wannabe gangster. He was hooked up with the Israeli drug cartel that operated, for the most part, out of a slew of different lofts they owned in the West 30s in Manhattan. He was tall with high cheekbones, a strong jawline and a thick head of straight, black hair. He was so good-looking that he could have readily been a model or a leading man. He had stupidly got busted selling several ounces of cocaine to an undercover DEA agent and was now stewing in jail, pacing, mad at the world. Jail wasn't for him. He'd find a way to get out of this trouble. He'd be clever, not like all the other fools around him. Shlomo Mendelsohn would find a way to get out of this mess.

Shlomo was one of those people on the outside of the war who, apparently, never heard: 'If you can't do the time, don't do the crime.' *What*, he wracked his brain, could he give up? *Who* could he give up to get out of jail?

His mind kept going back to one person and one person only: the worst criminal he knew of. The Israelis that he knew were drug dealers and weren't even in the same category as the person he was thinking of. He paced his cell like a caged rat. He knew if he could get his freedom, he'd ultimately be able to leave the country, go back to Israel and there he would be insulated and protected . . . he was a Jew. The Jews protected their own. In Israel, he would blend in, become one of many.

Having made up his mind that he would become an informer, he reached out to law enforcement. What Shlomo knew, what Shlomo had to say was passed along and ended up on the desk of Jim Hunt. Hunt and federal prosecutor David Shapiro went to visit Shlomo in the Metropolitan Correction Center (MCC). David Shapiro was a thin, athletic man who stood about five-nine, a magna cum laude graduate of the State University of New York at Buffalo. He was thorough, likeable and had a profound understanding of the law and all its intricate nuances and shadings. Shapiro was regarded by Hunt and Geisel, and most other agents and prosecutors, as the best trial attorney in the Eastern District of New York. Neither Jim nor David Shapiro was impressed with Shlomo. Often Jim came into contact with people who had got themselves in trouble and were now offering up information. Often they were, in plain English, full of shit, so whenever Jim met a person in prison looking to give up something, he was wary, sceptical.

Doubtful, Jim Hunt listened to what Shlomo had to say: 'I know a real important guy in the Mafia who kills people. He's also a big drug dealer. I'll tell you everything I know; I'll testify in court . . . But I want to go home. I want to go back to Israel. If you do that for me, I'll give you this guy.'

Jim stared at him and he stared back. Shlomo added conspiratorially, as though he knew where the Holy Grail was hidden, 'He buries people. He kills them, cuts them up and then buries people.'

Alarms went off inside of Jim's head. Red lights began spinning.

'What's his name?' Jim asked.

'You've got to first guarantee me—'

'Hold on a minute. Nobody can guarantee you anything. If what

257

you say is true, if you help us from the beginning to the end, we can recommend that you'll get a good deal. We can recommend that you be extradited to Israel. We don't make guarantees.'

Shlomo thought this over. He stared at the two government men. Resolutely, Jim stared back. Jim was not playing poker. What he said was true.

'His name is Tommy Pitera,' Shlomo said, and Jim felt the hairs on the back of his neck stand up. Jim knew cases are frequently broken by information coming from the most unlikely of places. Just the fact that Shlomo knew Pitera's name was *very interesting*. Jim already knew that people in Pitera's crew, Pitera himself, were dealing with the Israeli mafia, buying drugs from them. Both the DEA and the US Justice Department were interested. They reached out to Shlomo's attorneys and a tentative deal was struck.

Shlomo was allowed out of MCC and placed in the Federal Witness Protection Program. During debriefings, he told members of Group 33, Jim Hunt and Tommy Geisel, what he knew about Tommy Pitera. He said he had been in the home of Moussa Aliyan when drug transactions went down during which Pitera bought large amounts of cocaine from Aliyan. He said, more importantly, more shockingly, that he was there when Tommy Pitera killed Talal Siksik. Pitera not only killed him, he said, but he also 'put the body in the bathtub, got undressed, stepped into the bathtub naked and methodically cut the body into pieces. Sick fucking stuff. I never saw a thing like it,' shaking his head in sincere dismay.

These words fit together like the last pieces of an intricate puzzle. Jim not only believed what Shlomo had just said, but also it so fit the modus operandi of Pitera that Jim suddenly realised he was sitting with a man who had actually seen Pitera cut a body into six pieces. This was shocking and eye-opening, but this might very well be the weak leak, the Achilles heel they'd been looking for. With his intelligent icy-blue-green eyes, Jim stared at Shlomo; he believed every word Shlomo said. Jim was an astute judge of character – especially characters coming from the street. He was so perceptive and adept at reading people, informers, that he could tell the truth from bullshit as readily as a lie detector.

'So, you were there?' Jim asked.

'I was there,' Shlomo confessed. 'Most horrible fucking thing I've ever seen in my entire life. And he did it with such . . . ease. It didn't bother him at all. It was like he was just taking a . . . a shower.'

'Step by step, I want you to tell me everything you saw,' Jim said. And Shlomo ran down the whole evening he had spent at Siksik's house.

When Shlomo finished, Jim said, 'This place you went to bury the body, where was it?'

'Staten Island,' Shlomo said, fear of Pitera creasing his brow, tightening the mini-muscles on his handsome face as he went on to explain how they had wrapped Talal Siksik in plastic and put him in suitcases and taken him out to some desolate place in Staten Island. 'Like in a forest,' Shlomo said.

'Do you think you could take us to this place?' Jim asked.

'I could sure try,' Shlomo said.

44

DAY TRIP

It was a hot day in late July. The humidity was 90 per cent. There were no clouds to offer any reprieve from the searing July sun. Jim Hunt, Tommy Geisel and Shlomo Mendelsohn were on a field trip of the most macabre, morbid kind. They were in search of a body farm, a Mafia burial ground. Under the best of circumstances, had Shlomo known Staten Island, been reasonably familiar with it, he still would have had a hard time finding the William T. Davis Wildlife Refuge. When he had been there previously, it was night-time. When he had been there before, adrenaline had been filling his body and he wasn't paying attention to exactly how they got there and where they went. He had disconcerting, horrible images seared into his brain, as though they had been branded, but they were a series of disjointed images that had neither rhyme nor reason.

That whole day, Jim and Tommy drove Shlomo all over Staten Island. They checked out most every forest, every place that would be good for burying a body. The more they looked, the more frustrated, anxious and out of sorts Shlomo became. He had only seen Staten Island that one time. To him, it was a foreign and distant place. He had no point of reference, did not know east from west or south from north. Both Jim and Tommy were becoming restless, tired. Though they didn't think Shlomo was lying, looking to get himself out of trouble, they were disappointed by his lack of understanding of the area. At one point he said, 'Maybe . . . maybe it was in New Jersey,' which really frustrated the two agents. It not only frustrated them but it also pissed them off.

Be that as it may, all Shlomo did was lead them up one blind alley after another after another after another that whole day and night.

However, just because Shlomo couldn't find this burial ground didn't mean it wasn't there, both Jim and Tommy believed. Hearing about the burial ground and seeing the fear that lived inside Shlomo motivated and drove the two agents on. There was high-octane jet fuel in their tanks. They would not rest until Pitera was nailed to the wall with long, sharp spikes.

Luck . . . it seemed that Tommy Pitera of Gravesend, Brooklyn, had an inordinate amount of luck. He had been getting away with all kinds of crimes: drugs, murder, dismemberment. Jim Hunt was going to make sure that Pitera's luck changed.

45

THE ROCK OF GIBRALTAR

Joe Dish Senatore was a career criminal. He had spent over 30 years of his life in jail, was an original tough guy. As a young man, he had been the head of the Persico gang in South Brooklyn known as the 'South Brooklyn Boys'. He was also Genovese capo Joe Jinx's driver. He knew every mafioso in Brooklyn. People liked him. People respected him. He was old-school tough. Now, Joe Dish was in the fall of life. He was greying, round-shouldered, not the energetic, tough dynamo he had once been, though of course Joe Dish still did what he was best at: impersonating a cop, a New York City detective. He had badges, he had guns, he had the walk, he had the talk. He began working with Pitera's gang in 1988. Several times over the years, he had managed to get Pitera's crew into the homes of drug dealers. He was so good that when they did one score, Pitera was so pleased that he gave him a gold Rolex watch, which had been stolen from the victim.

'This is for you from me. It's personal. It means something,' Pitera said, showing a rare, giving side.

'I appreciate it. Thank you, Tommy.'

'Don't ever sell it!'

'Of course not,' Joe Dish said.

Joe Dish did not like Pitera. He felt he threw his weight around, bully-like. He knew that Pitera cut up people in tubs. He had heard that Pitera had killed a girl and cut her up. This flew against Mafia protocol. It was something more a psychopath out of a B-horror movie would do, not a man of respect. The thought of doing that was anathema to Joe. Still, he'd keep his personal feelings to himself, inside. Over the years, in his life of crime, he had dealt with every type of unsavoury character. He'd smile and nod when he saw Tommy but inside he felt disdain, not warmth, not friendship, not that kind of netherworld bond.

Joe Dish would become one of those weak links Jim Hunt and Tommy Geisel and all the members of Group 33 had been looking for. What happened was that Pitera went to Joe Dish to get him to help set up Willie Boy Johnson. Willie Boy Johnson and Joe Dish went back. They were good friends. There was a genuine bond between the two men. No way was he about to set up Johnson for the likes of Pitera. When Joe Dish refused to help Pitera, there was a sea change between the two. Joe Dish believed it was just a matter of time before Pitera killed him. The fact that he had said no to such an important hit involving Eddie Lino and John Gotti himself was a death sentence. Number one: he had insulted Pitera by saying no. Number two: he knew that when Willie Boy Johnson went down, it would be Pitera's doing.

As if that weren't enough, Joe had also refused to help in the rip-off of the cash stash house in Howard Beach, the murder of the two female counters. Perhaps, in days gone by, Joe Dish could have gone to somebody connected who would speak on his behalf, but the truly connected people Joe had known were either dead or in jail. He was now on the far fringes of organised crime. He was an old-timer who had outlived a culture that had fallen by the wayside.

As it turned out, Joe Dish was not the old-time tough guy people perceived him as. He had actually been a police informer for quite a few years. He was one of those individuals who adroitly played both sides of the fence. He had been sharing information with ATF Special Agent Billy Fredericks periodically; giving him information about crimes he was involved in, about crimes he knew of. Essentially what Joe Dish was doing was playing both ends against the middle. This was another reason why he decided to tell all, tell what he knew about not only Pitera's crew but also Pitera himself.

He was the man Jim Hunt had been looking for. He was the door that would open out into the world of Tommy Karate Pitera. He'd become the crack in the Rock of Gibraltar that was the visage Tommy Pitera offered to the world.

In Joe Dish's mind, he was striking first. In Joe Dish's mind, he would prevail over Pitera because he had the sense to pull the trigger first. Joe Dish's idea, however, of pulling the trigger had nothing to do with a gun. There was no way in hell he would try to kill Pitera with a gun or knife or bomb. The only way he could get to Pitera, he knew, was through law enforcement, by turning the tables. Joe Dish called his contact and friend Billy Fredericks and asked for a meeting.

Billy Fredericks was a good friend of Jim Hunt. They had worked together on several cases. He was a tall, robust man with black hair and a twitch in his right eye. He was the type of man who was naturally fearless. He didn't like people in the Mafia. He thought they were back-stabbing punks. He had little respect for them. Fact is, all he had for them was animus. When he heard what Joe Dish had to say, he immediately called Jim Hunt. He knew Jim had been working on the Pitera task force.

When Jim received the call at DEA headquarters, he said he'd be happy to meet with Joe Dish. In fact, he had seen Joe Dish at the Just Us bar and knew who he was. They met in the parking lot of a shopping centre in Staten Island. Jim got into Billy Fredericks's car. Joe Dish was in the back. Introductions were made. They shook hands. Joe Dish began to tell his story. It was an interesting tale that immediately drew Jim Hunt in, but there wasn't the kind of proof, solid and irrefutable, that would hold up in a court of law. The crimes Joe Dish described were, as such, minor. They wanted Pitera for more – for murder. They wanted him for heavy-duty drug dealing. What Joe Dish was offering up was neither of those things. However, Jim Hunt knew Joe Dish would be a good witness, that he would surely bolster the case against Pitera. When Jim asked Joe Dish what crimes he was convicted of, there was a long list involving all sorts of larcenies, forgeries, etc.

'You ever commit a murder?' Jim Hunt asked, and Joe Dish told him that just recently he had been involved in a killing. He said it was a long, convoluted story, but it involved him and another guy named Jack McInerney going to rip off the partner of someone who owed them money. This individual's name was David Braun and he ended up resisting, escaping from his bindings and running out of the door of his house. Joe's partner Jack McInerney shot him several times as he ran.

'I felt terrible about it. I didn't want the kid to die. It was just one of those things, one of those spur of the moment things. I only went there to get what was due me. I swear I never thought about killing him,' Joe Dish said.

This, Jim Hunt knew, could put a damper on the viability of Joe Dish as a witness, but he had seen far worse characters used successfully, quite brilliantly, to put mafiosi away. Immediately, Jim Hunt asked Joe Dish if he'd wear a wire in order to get Tommy Pitera to start incriminating himself in different crimes. Joe Dish said Tommy was paranoid, suspicious of everyone.

'But,' he said, 'I'll try.'

Over the coming days and weeks and months, Joe Dish tried to get Pitera on tape talking about crime to no avail. It got to the point where he didn't want to be around Pitera because he felt that at any moment Pitera would pull a gun out and kill him. However, with the guidance of Jim and Tommy Geisel, Joe Dish was wired up and let loose on all the many players in Pitera's mob. Dish had the gift of the gab, was a consummate actor – a born con man. He was completely above reproach. He was an old-time gangster. Without much effort at all, Joe Dish managed to get Lorenzo Modica, the man who killed the two Colombians, Manny Maya, Frank Martini, Michael Cassesse and Pitera associate Jimmy February, amongst others, talking freely and openly and incriminatingly about their crimes. More importantly, Joe Dish got them to talk about the role Pitera played in a laundry list of crimes – murders and rip-offs and drug dealing.

46

THE MEATWAGON

It is amazingly difficult for the government to bug the car of a citizen. Even if that citizen is a notorious bad guy; even if that citizen is a mafioso killer; even if that citizen is a major drug dealer. Contrary to common belief, the government does not have unlimited power to eavesdrop on the American people. There are mandates, protocols, stringent rules and regulations that must be followed. Jim and Tom and Group 33 were intent upon adding to the growing amount of evidence piling up against Pitera: Shlomo Mendelsohn and Joe Dish Senatore. They wanted to get a bug in the car that he had recently started driving, a black 1984 Oldsmobile. With the help of Justice Department Attorney David Shapiro, papers were drawn up to get a listening device implanted in the Oldsmobile. The affidavit was over an inch thick and laid out the reasons why the government wanted the bug. In this case, what Shlomo Mendelsohn and Joe Dish had told the government and what they had learned via other informants was reason enough to demand the right to install a listening device.

Using the VIN number of the Oldsmobile (which Pitera had dubbed 'The Meatwagon', and as a result Group 33 had started calling it, too),

Jim went to the dealer that sold the car and was able, with the help of court papers, to get a duplicate of its key. Their plan was to take the car using the key to a place where a listening device could be cleverly installed in the car and return it from where they had taken it. On the night they were going to pull this off, a half-dozen agents were involved. They were tracking Pitera from early evening to well after midnight, hoping he'd park the car and finally go to sleep. While he slept, they would quickly do what needed to be done. Pitera was in his bar, the Just Us, the agents patiently waiting outside in an unmarked van and in Jim's black Cadillac. Hour after hour passed and Pitera did not come outside. Finally, near four o'clock in the morning, he exited with a couple of cronies in tow and they continued to talk outside.

Agent Dave Toracinta thought Pitera was so pale that he truly looked like a vampire. Toracinta was, in a sense, typical of DEA agents in that he had been in law enforcement in Dover, New Hampshire, but wanted more. He wanted to be part of the war on drugs, go up against the most cunning and dangerous criminals in the country. Like all the members of the Pitera task force, Dave was highly dedicated, highly motivated, would not rest until he knew the job was done, and done well. It was Dave who was taking most of the clandestine photographs of Pitera and the Bonanno people.

Dave and the others watched Pitera grab the lower rungs of the fire escape and effortlessly do chins. He was obviously in good shape, they noted. Finally, near dawn, Pitera left Avenue S, went and parked his car near where he lived and went upstairs as Brooklynites headed to work, went from one end of the borough to the other. Moving swiftly, the DEA agents absconded with the car, parking a government car in its place. They took it to the tech people nearby and a bug was installed in the car. They returned the Oldsmobile to the spot where Pitera parked it. A job, they thought, well done.

Unfortunately, however, the bug malfunctioned and didn't work, and all their efforts were for nought. It seemed Pitera's luck was still, to a degree, intact.

47

LION'S SHARE

Both Jim Hunt and Tommy Geisel knew that Manny Maya was a drug dealer; that he worked with Pitera. They were still looking for concrete proof, evidence, a way to turn Maya against Pitera. It was Joe Dish who revealed to Hunt and Geisel just how tight Manny and Pitera were – tight enough that Manny Maya and his garage could be used to undo Pitera. This was the garage where people from all the different crime families brought their cars to be detailed: cleaned up after a murder.

Manny was an average-sized man with short hair, dark skin, who was muscular. He was friends with a very successful, active pot dealer named Michael Harrigan from Ozone Park, Queens. Harrigan had an excellent grass contact in Texas. He and his associates would actually fly down, buy suitcases, fill them up with hundreds of pounds of pot and audaciously check the luggage on flights bound back to New York, according to Joe Dish.

This was many years before 9/11 and law enforcement were acting like wide-eyed innocents, so it was an easy task to fly hundreds of pounds of marijuana from Texas to New York on domestic flights.

Foreign flights, however, were another issue altogether. The luggage coming in from Italy, Turkey, Afghanistan was, as a matter of course, checked for narcotics. Be that as it may, luggage on domestic flights was not scrutinised, as such. Thus, Mike Harrigan and his associates were able to bring large amounts of grass in from Texas as though it were something as innocent and innocuous as clothing. They were making a fortune – hundreds of thousands of dollars every month. Harrigan had been working under the umbrella of John Gotti Jr, the son of John Gotti Sr. People in the know say that John Junior did not have the street acumen that his father did. This business between John Junior and his associates was a narcotics operation, so this was all off the books. It had to be.

Mike Harrigan did not like Gotti Jr or any of his cronies; he felt they were all over the top, loud and vulgar, in-your-face 'gangsters'. He felt that dealing with them, being associated with them, would eventually cause trouble. The trouble began when Michael Harrigan's ill feelings towards Gotti Jr and company spilled over. He didn't want to be involved with them any more. He vehemently complained to Manny Maya. Maya immediately suggested that they go to Tommy Pitera, that Pitera would welcome him with open arms, that Pitera would protect him, that Pitera wasn't afraid of anybody, least of all John Gotti Jr.

With that, Maya set up a sit-down between himself, Pitera and Michael Harrigan. Pitera well knew the fortune that could be made with a good pot business. He knew, too, that because it involved drugs he could freely co-opt the enterprise away from John Gotti Jr with few problems. There would not be any kind of sit-down regarding this matter, particularly in light of the fact that John Gotti Sr could not come to bat for his son over a matter that involved narcotics. Pitera played his cards with potent indifference to Gotti and company. Everyone knew, Pitera knew, that he was a killer. He was not just a man of respect, not just made, he was an *assassin*: he was the man who shot down Willie Boy Johnson; he was the man who cut up what was left of his enemies and adversaries and cleverly disposed of them somewhere out in the wilds of Staten Island and Long Island.

Now, he'd be happy to be in a pissing contest with John Gotti Jr.

Michael Harrigan was between a rock and a hard place. He was pleased to be away from Gotti and his associates, pleased to be working with Pitera now, but Gotti Jr was naturally irritated and angry. Gotti Jr felt he was being disrespected, was losing a lot of money; he felt, too, that something he had set up and nurtured was arbitrarily, unfairly being taken away from him.

'*Who the fuck does this Pitera think he is?*' were words heard frequently coming out of John Junior's mouth.

John Junior could not go to his father about this, as Pitera knew. What he could do was 'demand' a sit-down with Tommy Pitera. This sit-down would be like a quivering Chihuahua sitting down with a muscular Dobermann pinscher – the Dobermann was Pitera.

At the sit-down, John Gotti Jr showed up with an Albanian associate named Johnny Alite. Pitera had Michael Harrigan with him. Harrigan was there because he had a vested interest in the outcome; Alite was an unknown guy who had no legitimate right to be there. Pitera immediately let his feelings be known: he didn't want Alite there. Offhandedly, somewhat feciciously, Gotti bragged that Alite had killed six people. Pitera disdainfully snorted that he had killed over 60 people, in a way of qualifying him, his presence. Because both John Gotti Jr and Pitera were made, Pitera had every right to demand that Alite leave, to throw Alite the fuck out the door, which is exactly what Pitera did. Pitera knew that no matter how you cut it he had the upper hand, provided that he stayed within the confines and dictates of Mafia protocol. He could not, as an example, slap John Junior. He could not curse at him. He had to treat him with respect. That certainly did not hold true for Johnny Alite.

When Pitera sat down and settled himself, calmed down somewhat, he told Gotti Jr that Michael Harrigan now worked for him, that he was with him, and that John Junior could go and tell his father if he wanted. Pitera had outmanoeuvred him with ease. Like this, the matter was resolved in favour of Pitera, and thus the pot business was wholly his. He came, he saw, he conquered.

Naturally enough, Pitera turned to Billy Bright to unload the pot. Bright had been selling weight of marijuana for many years. With Bright's connections, all the pot they brought up from Texas was quickly sold, turned into hard, cold cash. Pitera, Billy Bright and Michael Harrigan made money hand over fist. Of course, no matter how you cut it, Pitera always got the lion's share.

Everything was going smoothly, with the precision of a fine, Swiss watch, until Greg Reiter, a particularly loud and vulgar associate of Gotti Jr, came to Michael Harrigan and began making waves. Greg Reiter was a muscular tough guy who wore gold chains and drove a souped-up red Corvette. He felt that a good thing had been taken away from him unfairly; that something he had developed with Michael and Gotti Jr and Alite had been usurped, suddenly gone with the wind. He went and found Michael and said, 'Look, what you're doing here is very unfair. I know you're with Pitera now. Everyone knows who Pitera is. Everyone is afraid of him, but there's a basic right and wrong, and what you're doing here is wrong. This was our thing, man. We made it happen. Michael, we're friends. How could you do this?'

Reiter's words fell on deaf ears. No matter how you cut it, Harrigan could not go back to the way things were. Pitera had his sharp talons deep into their business and there would be no turning back. Harrigan well knew that if he betrayed Pitera, if he lied to him, he'd be dead. Like everyone else, he had heard about Pitera's burial ground, that he cut people up, that he got naked and got into tubs with people and cut off their arms and legs and heads.

No – Michael Harrigan would not, in any shape, manner or form undermine Pitera's role in their pot business. Though Greg Reiter did not say anything overtly offensive to Michael Harrigan, he had opened a Pandora's box that would release something ugly and dreadful.

The following evening, Michael Harrigan sought out Tommy Pitera and found him at the Just Us. They went outside and walked along Avenue S. As they walked, DEA agents surreptitiously observed them, took pictures of them. Michael explained to Pitera that Greg Reiter had come to see him, had said that what he was doing was 'unfair'. With that, Pitera said, 'Why don't you do this? Set up a meeting with him and I'll come.'

'OK,' Harrigan replied, unsure where this would go, apprehensive. After all, Greg Reiter had a right to be unhappy. Not believing that Pitera would cause Greg any harm, that he was just going to 'set him straight', perhaps warn him, Michael reached out to Greg and said he would like to talk to him further. They agreed to meet in a parking lot in Nassau County, Long Island.

It was after 11 p.m. when they finally met. There were few people about. It was a cold night. Chill winds with long, bony fingers tore through the wide-open expanse of the parking lot unchallenged, unbridled – mean. When Pitera arrived, he had Billy Bright with him. Bright was there as a back-up gun for Pitera. In that Bright was a pot dealer, partners with Pitera in the pot business, he had a vested interest in what was about to occur. Pitera patiently, calmly explained to Michael that Greg Reiter had to go; that sooner or later, he'd become a problem. That right now was the time to nip it in the bud. Considering the amount of money involved, millions of dollars, Michael Harrigan knew Pitera was right. Greg could very well, as the next step, look to kill both Michael and Pitera. 'When he pulls up,' Pitera said, 'just act normal. Just act normal. Leave it all to me.'

With that, Greg drove into the parking lot, ensconced in his red Corvette, comfortable and confident, and pulled up to where Mike Harrigan and Bright and Pitera were standing. Serious-faced, he pulled to a stop and began to get out of the car.

With shocking speed, Pitera moved towards him, raised a sawn-off shotgun that seemed to come out of nowhere, as if by magic, and fired. The shotgun sounded like a cannon, a thunderous roar. The double-O buck blew much of Reiter's face, neck and collarbone into oblivion. What was left of his face was a sorrowful sight. With what was left of his countenance, he looked at Michael Harrigan and said in a weak voice, with blood bubbling from his mouth, most of his teeth missing, 'I thought we were friends.'

'If we were friends,' Michael Harrigan said, 'I wouldn't need him.' As he said this, he pointed to Pitera, as though he were some kind of robotic killing machine – not a human being.

Reiter's body was placed in the trunk of Harrigan's car. There were two shovels there already. Pitera, Bright and Harrigan drove to a wildlife sanctuary in Nassau County – another location that Pitera used to get rid of bodies. By the time they arrived there, it was close to one in the morning. A cold March wind tore through bramble and bush and trees stripped of leaves. The branches looked like bare, arthritic fingers quivering and shaking in the winds hurrying off the nearby Atlantic Ocean. Because it was March, digging was hard and arduous, though with the three of them, each a strong, powerful man, the hole was soon done and the body was dumped inside it. They covered the hole, patted the ground down carefully and left.

Michael Harrigan would never forget how quickly and with what ease Pitera had taken Greg Reiter's life. He'd never seen anything like it. Not even in a movie had he seen the likes of Tommy Karate Pitera in action. Though he was clearly associated with Pitera, a business partner of Pitera, he had come to loathe him. Over and over again, he had heard stories of how Pitera killed people who one day were his friends, one day were his partners, and the next day were dead as a doornail: murdered, by Pitera. He well knew that Pitera had killed Phyllis Burdi, had cut her into six pieces and buried her. He also knew about Pitera's private cemetery on Staten Island. Slowly,

Harrigan began to distance himself from Pitera. Whatever money he could earn via Pitera was not worth the creeps Pitera gave him, not worth the nightmares. It didn't take long for Pitera to sense that Harrigan was putting space between the two of them. Pitera sent out word that he wanted to meet with Harrigan, to no avail.

Without notice, Pitera showed up at the Canarsie beauty parlour where Harrigan's wife Anna worked. She was an attractive brunette who knew nothing about the world of crime her husband was involved in. However, she knew Pitera, had met him in passing several times. Pitera asked Anna about her husband, why he had stopped coming around, why he didn't return phone calls. He seemed . . . out of sorts, morose. Anna did not have the answers to Pitera's questions. Not knowing any better, not being a part of that world, Anna called up her husband, got him on the phone and handed it over to Pitera. Pitera asked Harrigan where he'd been, why he'd stopped coming around. Harrigan said he'd been busy, that his mother hadn't been feeling well, that he'd come to Brooklyn to see him asap. With that, polite and smiling, Pitera thanked Anna and left the shop, Anna still on the phone with her husband.

'Why the hell did you do that? Why'd you put me on the phone with him?'

'Well, did I do something wrong?'

'Yes, you did something wrong. I'm not returning the guy's calls because I don't want to talk to him.'

'He seems so . . . he seemed – lonely, like he has no friends.'

'Anna, he has no friends because he killed them all,' Harrigan said with an intensity and sincerity that unsettled his wife. Michael Harrigan did not like Pitera going around his wife. Fact is, he hated it. Pitera had no fucking right to bother Anna. But what could he do about it? Nothing, he knew, if he wanted to stay alive.

Though he didn't quite know it yet, Michael Harrigan's days were numbered.

48

DUI

The thin line between nightmares while sleeping and nightmares while awake, for Frank Gangi, had become blurred, indistinguishable. Tall and thin and beak-faced, Gangi was inexorably, inevitably speeding towards a granite wall. The murder of Phyllis Burdi, how Pitera had cut her up in front of him, the smell of her blood, the purple, rancid odour of her exposed organs had never left him, particularly the sight of her head on the edge of the tub, her hair stiff with drying blood, her lips askew, frozen in a perpetual scream. One eye had been open and the eyeball stared off to the left, unseeing and unknowing. The images had stayed inside his brain and soul and had grown and grown like a particularly vicious, malignant cancer, becoming more and more grotesque to the point that he felt as if he were living in a nightmare; a Coney Island house of horrors that, for him, had become a tangible reality.

Frank Gangi had never been cut out for the life. He didn't have the heart, fortitude, necessary calluses. True, he had come from the streets, knew the streets, but he was not cut out to be a true mafioso – like his father, his cousins and uncles. The only way Frank was able to get through the day, the night, was with the help of cocaine and alcohol. They became his best friends. The alcohol he used to come down, to get to sleep. He was now drinking on average two bottles of whiskey a day. He lost track of how much coke he was doing.

On the night of 10 April 1990, as Joe Dish tried unsuccessfully, with Jim Hunt and Tommy Geisel encouraging him, advising him, to find a way to set up Tommy Pitera, Frank Gangi was in his car driving on Bay 50th Street stoned out of his mind. More than high on coke, he was drunk. Frank was comfortable around women and women were comfortable around him, so he was often in the company of different females, as well as the woman with whom he was living, Sophia. This night was no exception. He had two guidettes with him. One talked like Rocky Balboa and the other like a Brooklyn dockworker. This night, Gangi was so stoned he was weaving back and forth as he went. His driving was so bad, erratic and sloppy that it was patently obvious to anyone who saw him driving that he was drunk. When he went through a red light at Bay 50th and Cropsey, a squad car was suddenly behind him, red lights spinning. Two cops were soon beside him, asking him for his licence and registration, unfriendly, unhappy, obviously aware that he was inebriated. They made him get out of the car. He reeked of alcohol. He tried to talk his way out of a ticket; he offered them money. Before he knew it, he was under arrest, handcuffed and in the back of a police car headed toward the 60th Precinct near Coney Island. He was booked and put in a stinking, graffiti-covered holding pen.

When Gangi was again confronted with the hardcore reality of steel bars, the smells and sights of jail, something in him began to change, morph, slowly evolve. He paced back and forth. He hated his life. He hated what he had become. He hated what had happened to Phyllis Burdi.

I could have stopped it. I could have done something. Instead what I did is I brought him to her.

There, in the bullpen at Coney Island, Frank Gangi made up his mind to make a life change. He was going to purge himself.

The detective who arrested him for the Guvenaro murder, Billy Tomasulo, had been kind and professional, a gentleman. Gangi now reached out to him, asked the desk sergeant to call Detective Tomasulo. He said he had a lot to say and he had to talk to Detective Tomasulo. At first, the desk sergeant took it lightly.

'Yeah, OK, I'll see what I can do,' he said dismissively.

'No, I'm serious. This is about murders, about terrible murders. About people being cut up. Get him here,' Gangi said.

Gangi's demeanour, the imperativeness of his words, the urgency of his tone, told the desk sergeant that something serious was afoot. He walked away, began making phone calls.

NYPD Detective Billy Tomasulo was a hardboiled cop from the mean streets of Brooklyn. He was smart, tough, though he was always a gentleman, courteous and polite. When he first arrested Gangi, in connection with the murder of Guvenaro, he was fair. He treated him so fairly that Gangi came away liking him even though he had locked him up. Tomasulo had pretty much seen it all. Murders, rapes, mutilations – you name it, he'd seen it, experienced it, was a part of it. Having said that, Billy Tomasulo was not ready for what was about to come out of Frank Gangi's mouth.

By the time Tomasulo reached the cell Gangi was being kept in, Gangi had sobered up quite a bit; he was more resolute than ever about what he was going to do.

When Gangi said the name Tommy Pitera, Tomasulo immediately knew who he was talking about. He, like most everyone else in law enforcement, had his ear to the ground and had heard about Pitera and what he'd been doing. His interest was piqued. He was tired, had had a long day, but suddenly he was wide awake. Gangi was a consummate storyteller with a very good memory for detail, times, names, places – he painted a thorough picture of what Pitera was about, of the crimes not only he had committed but also ones Gangi had committed with him.

Gangi was readily admitting to murder. Here he was admitting to having been there while people were cut up, while Phyllis Burdi was murdered and mutilated. Of course, Detective Tomasulo knew about Phyllis Burdi. Her family had been in the Coney Island precinct numerous times over the last several years. He was so familiar with her case, her disappearance that he had a clear picture of what she'd looked like in his mind, from the photographs the family had given him.

Gangi became visibly unhinged when he talked about Phyllis. The tough-guy exterior melted away. He began to cry. His hands shook. He stared off into the distance, seeing images so horrible his mind tried to deny them, push them away, bury them deeper than they already were buried – an impossibility. Gangi was branded for life. He told Detective Tomasulo about the night Phyllis died: meeting at the after-hours club, going to his house, blowing coke and partying, running out of coke. He explained that he had called Moussa Aliyan and that he and Phyllis had headed into the city for more drugs. There they began to smoke cocaine and minutes quickly slipped into hours. Time, when high on cocaine, moves with shocking celerity. He explained how Pitera called, how he answered the phone, how Pitera came rushing over with Richie David and Kojak Giattino.

Gangi said, 'When Pitera walked in, he said: where is she? I indicated the bedroom. He walked into the bedroom carrying a gun with a silencer on it. He opened the door and he shot her a couple of times. Then he took her in the bathtub and got his knives and things and he slowly cut her up.'

As Gangi spoke, he chain-smoked. His hands shook more and more, as though he was freezing. He unsuccessfully fought back tears. He went on to describe how Phyllis's head was on left on the edge of the tub; how the lifeless eye had stared at him.

'This is all too much for me. This is something I never wanted to get involved in or see. This guy is a fucking monster. A fucking monster,' Gangi repeated, as though talking to himself out loud, again seeing the horror before him.

Now, at this point other detectives were there quietly listening to Gangi's cathartic cleansing of his soul, his purging himself of his guilt. Now, he described the killings of Talal Siksik, Marek Kucharsky and Joey Balzano, how he had gone out to the burial site in Staten Island and buried Marek Kucharsky at the behest of Pitera.

'Could you find it?' Detective Tomasulo asked. 'Could you find it again?'

'Yeah . . . yeah, I could find it again,' Gangi said.

Detective Tomasulo knew this was big. He knew the DEA and FBI were trailing Pitera, were very interested in him, though they were having difficulty securing viable evidence, substantial and irreversible, that would hold up in a court of law. Detective Tomasulo would have bet his house that Gangi was telling the truth. Every nuance, the way his face moved, the tears in his eyes all spoke of truth. Detective Tomasulo knew what he had to do next, and that was contact Jim Hunt and the DEA. He went to a phone, took out Jim Hunt's card and dialled his number. Thus the crack in the Rock of Gibraltar widened a bit more. Jim answered the phone.

'Boy, do I have news for you, Jim!' Detective Tomasulo said.

49

REVELATIONS

When Jim Hunt heard that Pitera confidant Frank Gangi was telling all, spilling the beans, crying as he did so, he was elated. This was what Jim Hunt, Tommy Geisel and David Shapiro had been waiting for. This was what some of the agents involved in the task force had been praying for. They all knew Gangi was not only close to Pitera but also involved with Pitera on numerous levels. They had seen him go in and out of the Just Us; they had seen him in Pitera's company many times over; they knew he had lived with Judy Haimowitz for a while. They had often seen him riding around Gravesend and Bensonhurst and Coney Island and Dyker Heights – Mafiadom. They also knew who his uncle, father and cousins were.

Hunt and Shapiro got in the car and sped over to the 60th Precinct in Coney Island. Gangi was in sorry shape. He was pale, with dark circles under his eyes. His hair was a mess. He was smoking a cigarette and coughing all the while. A strange odour came from him. It was not BO, it was something else.

Open-minded, willing to let Gangi talk to his heart's content, Hunt and Shapiro and Detective Tomasulo sat down in a quiet corner of the squad room and listened as Gangi systematically and succinctly laid it out. What he had to say had been bottled up so long that he was like a pressure cooker – words poured out of him, names, dates, times, places, sights, sounds in a well-informed stream of crimes and murders and larcenies. Again, he talked about the murder of Phyllis Burdi. He then discussed, in detail, the other killings he had been a part of, privy to, committed himself.

Of all the things that Gangi spoke about, what interested the agents the most was unquestionably Pitera's burial grounds. Gangi said that he knew where the one in Staten Island was. This was the one Jim had been looking for with Israeli drug dealer Shlomo almost a year earlier. Gangi went on to say, however, that he believed there were more burial grounds than the one he knew of; that there was one out on the flatlands in Brooklyn and another on Long Island, in Nassau County. Wanting to see if Gangi would put his money where his mouth was, if he was really telling the truth, Jim asked him to take them – take them all to the bird sanctuary.

'Of course, I'll take you,' Gangi said, more relaxed, now a man with a mission.

Under the auspices of the Federal Prosecutor's Office, the DEA took physical control of Frank Gangi. They next hustled him out to a hotel near LaGuardia Airport. He was on the verge of being placed in the federal Witness Protection Program. At the hotel, as per agreements between the DEA and the Brooklyn DA's office, Frank Gangi began to be thoroughly debriefed by the government.* Over and over again, Gangi reiterated about how 'truly, honestly dangerous' Tommy Pitera was. The DEA, Jim Hunt and Tommy Geisel all promised they'd put him in the Witness Protection Program.

'My concern,' Gangi said, 'is my family. Sophia, the kids. You gotta protect them.'

---

* The Brooklyn DA's office got involved because Gangi had first spoken to NYPD detectives.

'We will,' Jim said. 'We will. I promise you.'

Gangi had every right in the world to be worried about his wife, Sophia.

After Gangi had been gone several days, Tommy Pitera became . . . concerned. He kept calling Gangi without response. He sent people to Gangi's house to no avail. Pitera's concern grew. Word spread around the Pitera camp that Gangi might have turned. Others said that he had been murdered and dumped somewhere. People all over Gravesend and Bensonhurst scratched their heads and wondered where Frank Gangi was.

On the morning of 7 May, Gangi's common-law wife Sophia Abbia was in a diner on Cropsey Avenue. Earlier, a mutual friend of her and Frank, Patty Scifo, had called the house and asked Sophia to meet at the Shorehaven Luncheonette. 'Patty Girl' was also intimately close to Tommy Pitera. As much as Frank could love anyone, considering his alcohol and drug abuse, he loved Sophia Abbia; he had made her children his children, though he had not officially adopted them. At the time of his arrest, he had several different apartments that he used to stash drugs and bed other women, but for the most part he lived with Sophia. Theirs was a strange relationship because of his drug abuse. He didn't come home for days at a time. When he did come home, he was in sorry shape. With him, life was a roller-coaster, but Sophia loved him for better or worse and was dedicated to him. Sophia had once been a vivacious, attractive woman, but the trials and tribulations of life as she had known it, of being married to Frank Gangi, had taken a toll on her. She was now overweight, worn and weathered beyond her years.

The luncheonette was crowded. Sophia and Patty Girl took a table towards the back of the place. As they began eating, the door opened and in walked Tommy Pitera, all gloom and serious-faced. He moved straight to their table. Without being invited, he sat down. Sophia's stomach knotted. She paled somewhat. Like most everyone in Brooklyn, Sophia was frightened of Tommy. Immediately, Pitera asked about Gangi. Had she heard from him? Did she know where he was? When was the last time she'd spoken to him? Sophia, knowing what was in the wind, knowing Frank was talking to the government, cooperating with law enforcement, said she had not heard from him in quite a while, that the last she'd heard from him he was going to California.

'California?' Pitera asked, incredulous, his icy-cold blue-grey eyes cutting into her.

'California,' she repeated.

She ate a bit of her lunch, thinking that Patty Girl had set her up, thinking that Patty Girl had put her in a precarious situation. At that moment, Pitera was paged. He used a payphone in the luncheonette. He came back to the table and asked more questions about Gangi and, without rhyme or reason, began discussing the pros and cons of the federal Witness Protection Program, particularly disconcerting for Sophia. He seemed to know exactly what was going on. This unsettled and frightened Sophia even more.

He said, 'Is Frank in the Witness Protection Program? Do you know?'

'I don't know. I know what I've told you,' she said.

Pitera soon got up, went outside and quickly returned with the always foreboding, menacing Kojak, thick and muscular, bald, with the face of an angry pitbull. Pitera now introduced Kojak to Sophia, saying she was Gangi's 'wife'. Sophia wasn't sure why Pitera was doing this, but she didn't like it. It frightened her; she wanted to get away from them. Pitera and Kojak left as abruptly as they had arrived. Sophia wanted to get away from Patty. She called for the cheque. Patty insisted on paying it.

'Did you set me up, Patty?'

'How do you mean?' Patty asked.

'You know exactly how I mean,' Sophia said.

And with that Sophia turned, worried for her children, worried for herself, worried for Frank Gangi. She went straight home, concerned about being followed. At the house, Sophia reached out to the office of the DEA. Her fear, what had happened, was immediately passed on to Frank.

Gangi complained to Jim Hunt. Soon after, heavily armed DEA agents picked up Sophia and the children and took them out to the hotel to be with Frank.

Jim was a hardcore, seasoned cop, not a social worker, but he came to believe that Gangi was more or less a man who had been in the wrong place at the wrong time and had got caught up in his surroundings. Jim came to view Gangi as essentially a nice guy who had made bad decisions. He believed he was not a stone-cold killer; he knew that he had a conscience, remorse. For the most part, Frank and Sophia had an on-again, off-again relationship. He had been caught up in a merry-go-round of cocaine and alcohol and women, cocaine and alcohol and women. Now that he was sober, he was . . . *himself.* Sober, he wanted to be near his family. Sober, he wanted to be with his wife. Sober, Frank Gangi was a different man. He was soft-spoken, reasonable, willing to listen. He felt like he had got a 2,000-pound load off his shoulders by purging himself.

Now, Frank Gangi was becoming who he really was; slowly, he was becoming the man he should have been.

Tommy Pitera was not a stupid man. As well as being particularly observant, street smart and well read, he had developed and ultimately honed a sixth sense as sharp as any scalpel. Now this sixth sense, as well as all his other senses, told him that there was trouble in the wind; that Frank Gangi had become an informer. He turned over in his mind what to do, how to combat this *rat.* Naturally enough, he thought about abducting Sophia. Ultimately, for now, he decided against that. He put out word to all his people to find Frank Gangi; to kill Frank Gangi. It was not just the Bonanno family that would heed this call. It was all the members in all the families, as well as the associates of each of the families. Soon, several thousand men were looking for Gangi, were sniffing the air, were listening to the drums that demanded Gangi's head be brought to Pitera on a silver platter.

Back at DEA headquarters, sitting at a large, oval-shaped table, black-and-white photographs of Pitera's surveillance on pin boards to the right, including many soldiers and capos in the Bonanno family, photos of Overstreets and Just Us, Group 33 strategised with the help of federal prosecutor David Shapiro. They discussed when to pick up Pitera. Before they moved, they wanted to make sure all their ducks were in a row, i's dotted, t's crossed. They wanted to verify what Gangi had said. In short, they were intent upon putting together a rock-solid case. To that end, David Shapiro, smart and cagey, a man who knew his way around a courtroom as well as he knew his way around his own desk, put together a war plan.

What they all agreed on was to keep Pitera off guard; that is, not give him wind of the law-enforcement firestorm slowly enveloping him. He and the agents discussed going out to the sanctuary in great detail. They knew that once they did that, Pitera would find out and be on guard, get rid of evidence, perhaps even go on the lam. Everyone there knew the Bonannos were deeply entrenched in Canada, had numerous contacts there, and that Bonanno star Tommy Pitera could very well disappear into the wide expanses of the Canadian borders, get lost amongst its various peoples, cultures, languages. This was a very realistic concern – after all, they had just picked up Bonanno fugitive Vincenzo Lore in Canada. Bonanno boss Carmine Galante had lived in Canada for many years while he set up the Sicilian-Canadian-US heroin conduits.

As the days went on and the DEA put together an airtight case against a seemingly unknowing, unaware Pitera, the crack in the Rock of Gibraltar grew deeper and wider.

* * *

Pitera knew Frank Gangi's drinking, his drug abuse, made him a large neon deficit.

Again, he demanded of his people: 'Find fucking Gangi!'

To no avail. It was as though Gangi had been swallowed up by the earth, sucked into a pit of quicksand.

Now that the DEA had a full picture of who Pitera was – names, places and times; who, what, when, where and why; the ghoul he was – they kept a very close watch on him. They would not let him get away. Over the years, numerous mafiosi had run away when the time came for them to face the music. They were wealthy, they were fearless, they were, for the most part, the type of men who readily would go to a foreign place and make a new life for themselves. As the evidence the DEA, NYPD and FBI gathered against Pitera was put together, as the wheels of justice methodically turned, as the pros and cons of different witnesses and pieces of evidence were debated, it was decided that it was time to get Pitera. It was time to act. By now it was 3 June 1990. They couldn't take the chance of him fleeing, disappearing into the wilds of Canada, its sophisticated cities.

That morning, Pitera had volunteered to drive his girlfriend Barbara to visit her son. Apparently, the boy had not taken any of Pitera's many lectures seriously. He had got arrested for attempted murder and was now sitting forlorn and angry in the Brooklyn House of Detention on Atlantic Avenue.

For Tommy Karate Pitera, the clock was ticking.

When he left his house that morning, he had no idea that there were some 15 heavily armed law-enforcement professionals trailing him, watching him, getting ready to pounce. It had been a long, drawn-out case and they were all glad it was finally coming to fruition – especially Jim Hunt and Tommy Geisel. It was decided that Jim and Tommy would actually put the cuffs on Pitera, bring him down. After all, they had initiated the case.

It was a hot day. The skies over Brooklyn were blue and unblemished. It was so warm that Jim and Tommy Geisel were forced to keep the air conditioner on in the car. Both Jim and Tommy had been waiting for this moment for many months now. They had come to hate Pitera, what he did, what he represented, who he was.

After Pitera dropped Barbara off, he headed east on Atlantic Avenue. This part of Atlantic Avenue had become a Middle Eastern enclave. Here, there were crowded Middle Eastern restaurants and sweet-smelling food shops on both sides of the busy street.

The task force decided to move. It was time to break open the Rock of Gibraltar. Pitera was stuck in traffic. Jim and Tommy pulled their car just up behind him. They had decided when the moment came to arrest him they would bang the back of his car, get out with lightning speed, guns drawn, their badges clearly visible, hanging from chains around their necks. When there was a bus in front of Pitera and he was boxed in, they made their move. Hunt accelerated – bang – and rear-ended Pitera's car. Surprised, caught off guard, Pitera, believing a hit was about to take place, thinking he was going to get shot, ducked, looking to avoid bullets, slamming himself down onto the car seats.

With shocking speed, Jim Hunt burst from his car and ran to the driver's side of Pitera's car. The door was locked. Jim could not open it. Meanwhile, big, powerful Tommy Geisel pulled open the passenger door with such force he nearly tore it off of its hinges. Jim Hunt vaulted over the hood of the car as though he were a champion gymnast. As Jim hit the ground, he grabbed Pitera. Though both Jim and Tommy had shouted, 'Police! Police!', Pitera was still not sure if it was a hit or if these were really cops. Pitera resisted. Jim tried to get him to lie down on his stomach, to cuff him. Because he resisted, Jim pushed him so hard that Pitera's face slammed into the hot, black tar street, giving him a broken nose and two large black eyes, injuries that would be clear in Pitera's mugshot photo taken later that day. Hunt put the cuffs on him and read him his rights.

Pitera was thrown into the back of Jim and Tommy's unmarked car. Sirens blaring, red lights spinning, they headed towards Manhattan, DEA headquarters on West 57th Street.

What, Pitera wondered, over and over again, *do they have against me?*

Pitera hated having been arrested. In the world that he came from, being busted was – failure. Getting arrested was for miscreants and wannabes; certainly not for the likes of him – a man with his street acumen, wherewithal; a man who could readily see trouble coming a mile away. Immediately, Pitera suspected Gangi, but had no proof yet that Gangi was the cause of it.

When he got over the initial shock of the arrest, his mind began to work defensively. Seething inside, Pitera thought about good criminal attorneys, the best ones available – how to get out of this. He thought about making whoever the witness was disappear. He would fight this, he would win this. As he was being driven to DEA headquarters, he stared with disdain at Tommy Geisel and Jim Hunt. He had no idea of Jim Hunt's family history in law enforcement – that Jim Hunt Sr had arrested Carmine Galante, the Chin and Vito Genovese, too – but none of that mattered to him. Hunt was a cop and he represented all that Pitera disdained. Pitera thought of cops as bullies with badges. Respect – he would never show these people respect.

Outwardly, Pitera appeared friendly, made light of the arrest, acted as though Jim and Tommy were just doing a day's work, nothing more, little less. Pitera was an omnipotent power: he'd beat them through his iron will, his guile, his power over life and death.

At DEA headquarters, he was fingerprinted and photographed and put in the holding cell. Agents Dave Toracinta and Timmy McDonald tried to make small talk with him. Initially, he was tight-lipped, but after a while he said that he was not going to talk about the case in any way. They said that they understood he had been given his Miranda Rights and had nothing to say. He, in turn, said that he'd be willing to talk about things in general 'to pass the time'. At one point, Pitera said to Agent Dave Toracinta, 'Hey, why don't youse guys write my story and we will split profits on the movie rights? I'll provide all the gory details,' laughing as he said it, amused. For a streetwise mafioso, Pitera was talkative. He had got over the initial shock of being arrested, the earthquake of it, and his mood had lightened somewhat. He spoke about the Mossberg and Ithaca shotguns, how they easily took a human head 'clean off' if you shot right above the collarbone, he said.

As a matter of course, correct procedure, Jim Hunt brought prosecutor David Shapiro down to meet Pitera. Standing outside the cell, Jim introduced the two.

'Are you going to be my prosecutor?' Pitera asked.

'Yes . . . yes, I am.'

'I have absolutely nothing to say to you.'

'Fine, no problem. I understand.'

'But if I did talk to you, what would you want to talk about?' Pitera asked.

'Well, what about Willie Boy Johnson?'

'Ah, there's a rat for you!' Pitera said, clapping his hands, smiling. Pitera went on to say, regarding Willie Boy Johnson, 'Remember the guy who ran over Gotti's son? Willie Boy did that for Gotti; cut him up in three pieces . . . Gotti would kill me if he knew I was talking to youse guys like this. Don't get me wrong, Gotti is a gentleman and a man of honour and Willie Boy is dead. What's the difference?'

Pitera again withdrew into himself, became tight-lipped. Shapiro asked him another question or two about Johnson, but Pitera had nothing more to say. His attention moved to the small screen television. Jim and Shapiro soon left. Jim had assigned agents Dave Toracinta and Timmy MacDonald to watch Pitera round the clock. They did not feel he was a suicide risk, but he might talk, he might have more to say that could help them and hurt him.

Several hours later, during that night, Pitera – surprisingly – began to talk about Phyllis Burdi. He asked Dave Toracinta if he had heard of Burdi.

'Nope, I'm not familiar with that name,' Toracinta said.

Pitera continued. 'Wherever Phyllis is, she can come back to the city. I won't bother her. She didn't do the right thing by my wife, though. She gave my wife drugs that made her overdose and die. She knew my wife had overdosed and she didn't take her to a hospital or anything. It's like if someone's riding in your car and you have an accident – if that person gets hurt, you take them to a doctor. Phyllis didn't even do that.' He said this with a candid disdain that surprised them. Both the agents were startled that he had talked about Burdi. He seemed to be trying to use some kind of reverse psychology. He brought her up before anyone else did, as though he were an innocent babe in the woods. It seemed, at face value, he was being sly, at least trying to be.

The following day was again hot and humid. People all over New York City went about their business. The rat race that is New York City didn't miss a beat because of the arrest of Tommy Pitera. After a particularly good night's sleep, Jim Hunt went straight to the holding pen where Pitera was being kept when he arrived at DEA headquarters. Though he truly doubted it, Jim was going to see if Pitera would be willing to cooperate, tell what he knew, expose the inner workings of the Bonanno clan and their narcotics operation . . . Hey, you never know. From what he had heard so far, Pitera hated rats, hated informers. He had heard about Pitera's not allowing anyone in his crew to don moustaches because they looked like whiskers and only rats had whiskers. When Jim arrived, he asked Pitera if he'd like some breakfast. He said sure. Pitera said he'd be willing to talk about anything but information regarding the case. It seemed, Jim thought, that he wanted to come across as the right guy, as 'approachable'.

An agent named Barber returned with an egg and cheese sandwich. Pitera opened the bag and smiled. 'How did you guys know that I liked these? You been following me?'

'We've got warrants for your houses,' Jim said.

'I figured that. How are you going to get in?'

'Break in, if we have to,' Jim said.

Pitera offered to show him which keys belonged to which locks on his key ring. He didn't want the agents breaking down the doors of his homes. He said, 'Look, when your guys go to the house on Ovington, tell them to be careful about the floor. I dug up the basement to make the ceilings higher and we were doing work on the roof and it's not so stable. I wouldn't want to see any of your guys hurt.'

'OK,' Jim said, surprised by his seemingly sincere concern. It was in sharp contrast to the monster he knew Pitera to be.

Jim soon went back upstairs to his desk and called the guys in the field. He wanted to let them know that he had keys to the properties at 342 Ovington Avenue and 3030 Emmons Avenue. John McKenna, the agent at the scene, replied, 'It's too late. We already broke into 3030.'

The apartment Pitera had shared with Celeste at 3030 Emmons Avenue was, for the most part, empty, but in a large closet they found Celeste's panties and bras neatly laid out with little signs that labelled each: 'favourite panties', 'favourite bra'.

'Fucking weird,' one of the agents would later comment.

Pitera had been paying rent on it because he didn't want to give the apartment up, lose the memories; plus, he had heard that the building would go co-op and he wanted to get an insider's price. When agents executed the warrant at his address at 2355 East 12th Street, they found a treasure trove of interesting, incriminating evidence: books, hundreds of them, related to martial arts, books on how to kill, how to maim, surveillance and police interrogation tactics and, also, very tellingly, books on how to dismember bodies. Titles included *Mantrapping*, *Kill or Get Killed*, *Getting Started in the Illicit Drug Business* and *Torture, Interrogation and Execution* by infamous French Revolutionary figure Maximilien Robespierre. This book was of particular note for it was obvious that Pitera had read it with great interest; the pages were dog-eared and well worn.

Motivated and spurred on by these findings, the agents found 'every type of knife imaginable' – samurai swords, bayonets, stilettos, ice picks, razor-sharp hunting knives. There, too, was an impressive collection of shotguns, and there were different parts of pistols, automatics and revolvers. None of these parts made a whole gun and therefore Pitera was not charged with illegal possession of handguns. The shotguns were legal in New York State. Pitera's 'working guns' were in a duffel bag in the ceiling of Billy Bright's house off Bath Avenue. Here, there was a wide assortment of over 60 autos and pistols. The DEA did get a warrant to search Bright's home, but since Frank Gangi had disappeared, Pitera had had the guns in Bright's house removed to an unknown location.

Most incriminating of all, most unsettling of all, were the autopsy kits they found in Pitera's home – these contained razor-sharp scalpels, small handheld saws, some for large bones, some for smaller bones. There were also hack knives for cutting through sinew and tendon.

They found a safe and were able to break into it. Inside, they found jewellery, which, as it turned out, belonged to various murdered people. There were watches and rings, necklaces and earrings and gold chains. Included in this cache of jewellery was Sol Stern's wedding band. Interestingly, they found women's jewellery there, too. Again, in a classic sense, these items could very well have been perceived as trophies, totems. There, too, were funeral cards . . . funeral cards that would turn out to belong to victims of Pitera's, according to Jim Hunt. This, the government agents felt, was, 'morbid, macabre, unsettling'.

They didn't find anything at Pitera's house on Ovington Avenue. Agents discovered that it was essentially a construction sight. There were slabs of expensive marble, beautiful Italian tiles. It seemed Pitera had big plans to turn this building into an upscale townhouse – a place to be proud of. The DEA, in conjunction with the Justice Department, would move to confiscate the house as a result of criminal enterprise.

All during that day, 4 June, 25 other Pitera associates were arrested, including Vincent Kojak Giattino, Thomas Carbone, Lorenzo Modica, Manny Maya, Michael Cassesse, Frank Martini, Luis Mena, Angelo Favara and Richie David.

They were offered deals. Anyone willing to cooperate would be treated with leniency. This had become the standard operating procedure for the government. Federal prosecutors, the United States Justice Department, had learned to manipulate and pit one defendant against the other, thus ensuring they would get the bigger of the two fish. They used Sammy 'the Bull' Gravano to nail John Gotti and some 36 other mafiosi (though Gravano never testified against anyone in his own crew); they used Phil Leonnetti in Philadelphia to convict several busloads of wise guys and send them packing off to jail, all grumbling, all fit to be tied, all swearing murder and mayhem – revenge; they would use, shockingly so, Mafia royalty Joe Masseria to unhinge the Bonanno family.

Now, the person they wanted the most, the person they were focused on, was Tommy Karate Pitera. The debriefings began. The questioning of Pitera's people was long and tedious.

With Pitera and his gang safely behind bars, Jim Hunt and his people decided it was time to see if they could find the bodies, Pitera's victims, the graveyard. Finding the bodies would be the *coup de grâce*; finding the bodies would put everything into perspective.

When Gangi's partner Billy Bright got wind of what was happening, he took off. Billy was adept at leaving Brooklyn quickly and adapting to new surroundings. He had been on the lam several times before. Because the bust caused such media attention, Billy Bright ended up on *America's Most Wanted*. With his distinctive looks, dark hair and large eyes, he was recognised and identified, and quickly arrested in Las Vegas. Unlike some, including his childhood friend Frank Gangi, Bright refused to cooperate with the feds. He would, down the road, plead guilty to the murders of Solomon Stern and Richard Leone, which took place at Overstreets, and drug conspiracy, and would serve a 17-year sentence. Had he gone to trial, he would surely have been given a much stiffer sentence. At face value, one would think that the story of Billy Bright was now over, said and done, but that proved to be untrue.

Incorrectly believing that Billy Bright had murdered his son, Greg, Mark Reiter wanted revenge, wanted blood. No matter how you cut it, he felt his son had been unjustly and unfairly killed. Though Greg's body would never be found, his father Mark knew he was dead. Greg, his brother Michael and his father were all close. No way in hell would Greg stay away for so long and not contact his father or brother. The first to feel the wrath of the Reiters was Michael Harrigan. Michael and Mark Reiter knew that Greg was going to meet Michael Harrigan that evening and they never heard from him again. Michael Reiter stalked Mike Harrigan and when Harrigan went to use a public phone outside a grocery store in Howard Beach, Queens, an unknown, nameless, faceless killer walked up behind him and blew the back of his head off. The Reiters were pleased that Michael Harrigan was gone, but they were not satiated.

They believed that Billy Bright had killed Greg Reiter, and Mark Reiter – coincidentally housed in the same facility as Bright – took out a murder contract on Billy Bright's life. He turned to the lethal, deadly Aryan Brotherhood, paid them $5,000, numbering the days Billy Bright had left on this planet. Billy felt all his troubles were behind him and that he could walk around the facility with a clear head. Unaware, innocently, a year after he had been sent to the United States Penitentiary in Atlanta, Georgia, Billy Bright was making his way across the common yard when two Aryan killers approached him, one from behind and one from upfront. Each of these men was a three-time loser with a life sentence, who would never see freedom again. They had nothing to lose. Billy Bright, innocent of the murder of Greg Reiter, was suddenly and viciously attacked from the rear and the front. Each of the muscular, animalistic killers had homemade shivs, long metal blades sharp as razors, pointed as pins. Billy was repeatedly stabbed in the back, in his chest, mercilessly, until he was dead. These two Aryans were like bone-cracking, hysterically laughing hyenas – pets of the grim reaper himself. Like this, Billy Bright's life came to an end.

PART 4

TRAUMAS AND TRIALS

THE WILLIAM T. DAVIS WILDLIFE REFUGE

It was now time for the task force to look for bodies in earnest, to find Pitera's private burial ground. It was 6 June 1990. A caravan of cars left for Staten Island. In these cars were stoic, hardboiled, seasoned, cynical NYPD organised crime detectives, DEA and FBI agents. In that the Pitera case had been a multi-agency effort, Jim Hunt was obligated to involve all the different agencies on this day. Frank Gangi was in a light-coloured Plymouth with black wall tyres with Jim and Tommy Geisel. Because Gangi had only been to the burial site at night, it was difficult to find the bird sanctuary. But now he'd been sober for weeks, had his head screwed on his shoulders properly, and, with a little luck, managed to find the right turns and the William T. Davis Wildlife Refuge. They all got out of their cars. The sky was clear that day. The sun shone strongly. The sound of birds came from many directions at once. The agents and NYPD detectives faced a wall of deep green, the smell of flowers and summer foliage coming to them.

'You sure this is it?' Jim asked Gangi.

'I'm . . . pretty sure,' Gangi said, looking at the forest spread out before them, nodding his head in the affirmative. Everyone there that day donned disposable white jumpsuits. They wore these so as not to contaminate the crime scene in any way. Anxious, curious, they moved as one into the forest, tall and gangly Frank Gangi leading the way. A gaggle of residential crows made a lot of noise. They were annoying, distracting. All that day, the task force, with Frank Gangi's directives, looked for bodies; searched the ground for some indication that a body was buried here, or there. Curiously, they sniffed the air; curiously, they scrutinised the ground for some sign that human beings were buried in this dirt, in this place.

That first day, they had no luck. Even the second day, upon their return, they came up with nothing, zilch, a big zero. They brought in happy-to-please, tail-wagging cadaver dogs, pretty certain they'd do the trick. The dogs weren't able to find any cadavers. The cops began thinking that there weren't any bodies here. The third day they brought a man who had a machine that, supposedly, could find bodies. That proved to be a wash also. It was on the third day that the task force began using four-foot metal probes with a T-shaped handle to probe the ground. Working in pre-assigned grids, walking in straight lines shoulder to shoulder, they probed the ground, looking for cadavers: no luck. Prompted by Agent David Toracinta, they discussed using the telephone poles with street lamps as a starting point. His reasoning was that Pitera might have used the ambient light from the pole to make his way into the foliage at night. Thus, he said, the bodies could be buried perpendicular to the poles. It was a good hypothesis, but in reality Pitera had used flashlights to guide the way.

It was on the fourth day, with the help of NYPD Detective Bobby Povone and the old-fashioned metal probe, that they hit pay dirt. The day was coming to an end. Long shadows appeared. Birds chirped insistently. The task force had just finished taking a break. Bobby Povone was sitting on the stump of a tree. When it was time to get back to work, as he made his way back to the task-force line, he absently probed the ground as he went and struck something . . . odd. He called out to his colleagues.

'I've got something! Hey, over here! I've got something!'

It was decided for the sake of expediency and proper protocol that they would wait until the next day; they would reach out to the Medical Examiner's Office and use the light of a new day to continue their ghoulish task.

That night there were no celebrations, no toasts, no back-patting. Feeling whole and accomplished, that many months of hard work had panned out, Jim Hunt went home to Queens. Hunt was a confirmed bachelor. Work, his dedication to it, his involvement in it had taken the place of a wife and family. The quintessential professional, he went to sleep quickly, woke up when it was still dark and headed back out to Staten Island. As he drove across the elegant expanse of the Verrazano Bridge, as a fiery dawn lit up the eastern horizon, Hunt wondered how many other mafiosi had crossed this very bridge, this very way, for the purpose of getting rid of bodies.

CHEAP SUITCASES

Using oval-shaped, long-handled shovels, the agents slowly, carefully, uncovered the object Bobby had found. In the nascent light of 9 June, the task force regarded a large, chequered suitcase, the cheap kind that you could buy on 14th Street; the kind that people filled with jeans and camera equipment, contraband, to take back to their respective Third World countries. The agents gingerly lifted the suitcase out of the hole. Everything about it seemed normal except for the horrific smell that issued from it: unmistakably, the stink of human death, they all knew. The Medical Examiner's Office had been contacted. An ME and a morgue wagon had been dispatched by the New York City mortuary on 1st Avenue and 22nd Street. As the gloved hand of the medical examiner struggled with the rusted zipper, slowly opening the case, the smell became worse and worse still. Surrounding the suitcase in a neat circle stood the members of the task force, engaged and curious, quiet and solemn – as though in a church, engrossed in prayer – so very pleased that their efforts had worked out. Because of the thick summer foliage, they stood in a solemn, dappled light.

They were looking at what was left of Marek Kucharsky. Off to the left, the crows returned and incessantly cawed, distracting everyone, annoying everyone.

'Wish I had my shotgun,' one of the agents mumbled.

This was the boxer with the rugs whom Pitera, Gangi and Moussa Aliyan had murdered in Moussa's loft. By pure happenstance, he was found first. Kucharsky had been put in the ground some 34 months earlier. In the suitcase were his severed head, trunk, arms and legs wrapped in one of his nice Oriental rugs . . . the rugs he had died for. He'd been in the ground for so long now, the flesh had dried and shrivelled up. The once-thick muscular arms were mere remnants of what they had been; now, they were brown and wrinkled, parchment-like, and the bones were clearly visible.

Now that they had struck pay dirt, that they knew bodies were truly here, a newfound energy, a pump of high-grade adrenaline affected the task force. Again they made lines and again started probing the ground, invigorated by the hardcore, horrible, homicidal reality of Marek's body. It didn't take long for more bodies to be found off to the left, off to the right, all some 30 steps from the road. They seemed dispersed without rhyme or reason, here, there and everywhere. The only placement they had in common was the distance from the road.

The fifth body found at the sanctuary was that of a woman – Phyllis Burdi. Finally, Phyllis had been found; Phyllis would have justice. Phyllis, of course, was the main reason Frank Gangi had turned on Pitera. She had been cut into six neat pieces. Now, as her remnants were filmed by the task force for evidence, as Jim Hunt described who she was and what had happened to her to the camera, there were only five pieces in the suitcase . . . two arms, two legs and a torso. She had died almost three years earlier, and her breasts were shrunken, barely discernible. Even though the flesh was as dry as a raisin, bullet holes in her chest, between her shrunken breasts, were still visible. Though Phyllis Burdi was barely recognisable as a female, a woman, the fact that she was a woman had a clear effect on all the detectives and agents there that day. She could have been any one of their daughters or sisters, they all knew. She was helpless and defenceless – and the thought of her in the hands of Tommy Pitera was unsettling and disconcerting and affected them in a way the bodies of the men did not at all. Silently, privately, a few of the men there that day said prayers for Phyllis.

Next Sol Stern and Richie Leone, the two men killed at Pitera's club, Overstreets, were found. As the body of Sol Stern was laid out in the field by the medical examiner, it was obvious that he had shat in his pants, no doubt because he was terrified, they all knew.

This little observation, insight, gave all the agents and medical examiners, forensic people, pause. They had come to despise Pitera. They had come to view his crimes as being particularly frightful and heinous, but he had a mean-spirited audacity that they had grown to loathe. He killed at will, tortured, stole from people, sold drugs, and on top of everything he was a woman killer. They worked cohesively, as silently as though they were in a mortuary. The branches and leaves that canopied the area where they worked gave the whole scene the ambience of a funeral parlour – a funeral parlour designed, built and decorated by nature herself.

Even though there had been no official announcement yet to the media, reporters got wind of chopped-up bodies, a Mafia burial ground. As though vultures zeroing in on the smell of carrion, curious, nosy reporters showed up at the dig. The streets leading to the spot had been cordoned off with yellow police tape and reporters learned little. However, over the ensuing hours and days, press releases were given out and detailed feature stories appeared in all the major New York papers. *Newsday* ran a two-page feature story. All the local television stations covered the story extensively. Tommy Pitera was suddenly famous.

At autopsy, in the Medical Examiner's Office in Manhattan, Phyllis Burdi's remains were laid out on a gleaming aluminium table. Giant fluorescent lights illuminated what was left of her. As her chest cavity was cut open and peeled back, the medical examiner noted for the autopsy report that she had been shot with Glaser rounds – bullets that contained small BB-like pellets that caused horrific wounds inside her chest. The medical examiner noted with interest that all the cuts severing the limbs from the torso were neat and precise – professional-looking. He would later comment that whoever did it had experience; whoever did it knew what he was doing.

THE EXECUTION OF
TOMMY KARATE PITERA

All the officials who worked the Pitera case, were involved in the task force, were involved in Pitera's prosecution, wanted him to die.

'If ever someone deserved the death penalty,' federal prosecutor Elise Liang said, 'it's Tommy Pitera.'

Elise Liang was a small, soft-spoken, attractive Asian woman who was an excellent prosecutor, was very good at her job. She, like everyone else involved in the case, was appalled not only by what Pitera had done, the ABCs of what he'd done, but also by the fact that he'd done it with such aplomb; that he could be so blatant about it had outraged everybody. Here was a criminal who acted as if he had a God-given right to kill. Regardless of what anyone's feelings were, more importantly there was a federal statute known as the Drug Kingpin Law that would clearly make Tommy Pitera eligible for the death penalty. As lawyers in the Justice Department put together a case against Pitera; they scrutinised the viability, mulled over the realities of a death-sentence case. They came to the conclusion that

Pitera's crimes warranted the death penalty and legally he could be given a death sentence based upon the nature of the crimes. Due to date conflicts, however, the only charges that carried a death sentence were the murders of Richard Leone and Sol Stern, which had taken place in Pitera's club.

It was announced by US Attorney Andrew Maloney that the United States Justice Department would officially be seeking the death penalty for Tommy Pitera. When Pitera heard the news, told to him by his lawyer, he said, with a smirk on his face, 'Bring on the firing squad.'

At the Justice Department, Pitera had become the focal point of its collective energies. He was one of the most heinous criminals it had had to prosecute in modern times. No resources were spared, any overtime necessary was quickly allocated. All the manpower needed to build the prosecution case properly was provided with alacrity. To further the government's quest to execute Pitera, DEA and FBI agents again began, in earnest, talking to co-defendants in the case, looking for people willing to turn; looking for people to become informers. They already had Frank Gangi and Joe Dish aboard. Judy Haimowitz also readily agreed to cooperate. As it happened, very little loyalty was shown to Pitera. Just about everyone arrested agreed to cooperate. The ones who didn't were Vincent Kojak Giattino, Billy Bright (Billy Bright's case had not been adjudicated yet; he had not yet been placed in a federal prison) and Richie David. When Jim Hunt spoke to Richie, Jim said, 'Look, Richie, this guy is a first-rate scumbag. You don't owe him anything. There's no doubt about that. Why in God's name do you want to go down with him?'

Richie responded, 'Look . . . I understand that, but you don't understand. This guy is insane. Sooner or later, he will get me. I know he will, sooner or later.' And with that Richie David decided to plead guilty to a laundry list of charges and take the heavy sentence recommended by the government.

Kojak decided he would take his chances at trial; he would not testify against Pitera.

A shroud descended over Gravesend, Brooklyn. Any innocence the neighbourhood had was lost with the revelations of what Tommy Pitera had done, how brazenly he had done it, what he had done to Phyllis Burdi, that he had cut her up in six pieces, that her head was never found.

Gravesend would never be the same, thanks to Pitera.

In the Mafia hangouts throughout Gravesend, Bensonhurst, Coney Island and Dyker Heights, mob guys discussed Tommy Pitera. For them, what Pitera had done was all about business. What he had done to Phyllis Burdi, though, was something else. The killing of a woman, the killing of a woman that way – all cut up like that – was something out of the ordinary even for them; beyond the pale, even for them. However, they discussed in detail how Pitera had warned Phyllis to stay away from Celeste over and over again, how Phyllis wouldn't listen to reason. In the end, they decided Phyllis had got what she deserved. The next big question they discussed amongst themselves, as though they were an assembly at the UN debating important world issues, was whether or not Pitera had turned. They knew that most of the people he had working for him had become rats. This did not bode well for Pitera. It was a given that Pitera would be able to offer up his boss, and even the head of the Bonanno family.

Would Tommy Pitera talk?

Would Tommy Pitera divulge the secrets he knew about the inner workings of La Cosa Nostra – details, names and places; who killed whom, when, where and why; the Bonanno family's extensive dealing in narcotics? Those were the questions they asked themselves in Mafia clubs throughout Mafiadom, as they sipped strong espresso laced with homemade anisette, smoked cigars, discussed all the different aspects of all the different businesses they had their well-manicured fingers in.

53

TIGHT-LIPPED PITERA

Authorities did try to get Pitera to talk, to share what he knew about the inner workings of the Bonanno family, the Mafia. In the world Tommy Pitera came from being a rat was the lowest form of life, anathema. He not only felt that way in a very real, cultural sense but also in his heart and in his soul; he felt that betraying colleagues, partners in crimes, was the worst sin of all. Pitera hated rapists and child molesters but, for him, rats were even lower on the totem pole of criminals.

No, he wouldn't talk, he resolved with all his being. No matter what they did to him, he would not talk. He would die, quite literally, before cooperating with cops.

The arrest behind him, Pitera prepared for war. He'd find the best attorneys; he'd put on the best defence he could. But in reality the case the government put together against him was voluminous, air-tight, monumental: there were not only many live, hands-on witnesses but there were also tapes and drugs that Jim and Tommy Geisel had bought from Angelo Favara and Judy Haimowitz. As Group 33 had always known, Judy Haimowitz would turn the moment she was given the opportunity, and turn she did. She, like the others, would cooperate wholly and fully, truthfully and sincerely.

Pitera hired sharp criminal attorney Matthew Mari and the battle between Tommy Pitera and the federal government began in earnest, a no-holds-barred street fight, no quarter given, no quarter asked.

THE UNITED STATES
OF AMERICA v PITERA

Thomas Pitera was tried in a well-lit courtroom at the Brooklyn Federal Courthouse located at Cadman Plaza, beginning on 6 May 1992. It is a modern-looking, austere building and silently tells interested observers: serious business goes on here. In truth, America's worst enemies are tried at Cadman Plaza.

A jury was chosen; opening statements were made and battle lines delineated, weapons loaded and cocked. Federal judge Reena Raggi would be presiding over the trial. This was one tough jurist. She had sat on the bench during many organised crime proceedings. Nothing cowed her, nothing frightened her. She was highly respected by both prosecutors and defence lawyers. Judge Raggi had straight, shoulder-length brown hair, a somewhat severe triangular face with high cheekbones and particularly intelligent, piercing brown eyes. She was nominated to the bench at the tender age of 35 by President Ronald Reagan. Prior to becoming a judge, she was a highly respected prosecutor, with stints as the chief of narcotics and chief of special prosecution. Jim Hunt would later explain, 'She's the best jurist I ever worked in front of.'

Esteemed criminal attorneys Matthew Mari, Cheryl Mackell and David Ruhnke, hired as a death penalty expert, sat on the left with Pitera between them. Pitera seemed bemused, as though the trial, the seriousness of it, were all about somebody else, not him. Pitera had gained weight from the jail starch diet and his hair had receded, but otherwise he seemed fit and ready to do battle. On the other side of the courtroom sat the prosecution team: Elise Liang and David Shapiro, amazingly well prepared, anxious to get this trial started, so very ready to put Tommy Pitera way for life – or, better yet, put him to death. Execute him. ASAC Jim Hunt would also be an intricate part of the prosecution team. Anything the prosecution team needed, he would facilitate, manage, appropriate.

The prosecution team made Jim Hunt their first witness. The bailiff called the court to order. Jim Hunt was asked to take the stand. He was dutifully sworn in. He was easy-moving, sure of himself, names and dates as familiar to him as the fingers on his right hand. With great detail, Federal Prosecutor David Shapiro used Hunt to paint a portrait of Pitera's crimes for the jury. With Shapiro guiding Jim Hunt, little by little, in simple detail, the case was laid out for the jury. Anyone watching the direct examination was stunned by the number of details Jim Hunt had in his head. On occasion, he referred to notes in a small black book, but for the most part it all came from his head. It was obvious, too, that the jury's attention was caught and held by what Jim said. Any of the jurors who thought this would be a boring, time-consuming pain in the arse were soon enraptured by the case, chopped up bodies being found in Staten Island, huge amounts of drugs being passed from hand to hand. It was, in reality, more like some Martin Scorsese movie than real life, but this was real life and the jurors and spectators and press were all wide-eyed and hypnotised, mesmerised by Jim Hunt's words. When Jim Hunt finished his testimony and slowly stepped from the stand, you could hear a pin drop.

* * *

Methodically, David Shapiro called witness after witness. One after the other a colourful rogue's gallery took the stand and in no uncertain terms, pointed their fingers at Pitera and told what they knew. Billy Fredericks, Frank Gangi, Judy Haimowitz, Andrew Miciotta, Luis Mena, Billy Tomasulo, Joe Dish Senatore, family members of Pitera's victims, and a long list of forensic and technical experts took the stand to bolster and clarify the evidence presented to the jury. As each witness took the stand and was sworn in and testified, the crack in the Rock of Gibraltar grew and grew. As Tommy Pitera sat there, watching witness after witness indict him, point at him, he glared back with the deadly indifference and cold countenance of a great white shark. Regardless of the dirty looks Pitera gave the witnesses, however, he could do nothing to mitigate the damage their words did. With each witness, the words coming out of their mouths, long, pointed shiny nails were being hammered into Pitera's coffin.

When Frank Gangi, tall and thin and sure of himself, took the stand, Pitera was visibly angry. He moved uncomfortably in his chair. He doodled on a pad. His mouth twisted into a snarl. Gangi turned out to be an excellent witness – he was sincere and matter-of-fact. Again you could hear a pin drop. He was so sincere, wrapped up in the words he spoke, that he began to cry there on the stand. All the jurors were moved. Jim thought Gangi was one of the best witnesses he had ever seen.

Pitera hated Gangi. He felt he had been nothing but kind to Gangi, a friend to him, had tried to help Gangi out, and here he was telling all like some schoolyard crybaby punk.

At one point, during a break, as Gangi passed Pitera at the defence table, Pitera taunted him by saying, 'Are you going to cry again?'

Gangi knew, had accepted, that his life was forever altered; by doing what he had done, his fortunes had been irreversibly changed.

When Gangi testified about the murder of Phyllis Burdi – when he talked about Pitera shooting her and getting in the tub with her, cutting her up, putting her head on the edge of the tub – he, in fact, again started to cry. If he was acting, it was an extraordinary performance – certainly worthy of an Oscar. The jury was visibly shaken by not only Frank Gangi's heartfelt testimony, tears, his description of that night, Phyllis being cut up, but also the grave-site photos of the bodies. This would unsettle the most hardcore war veteran, let alone the John Q. Citizens of whom the jury was made up. You hear about such things in the papers, see them in horror movies, but the reality that these things happened in real life, people were murdered and cut up, people were buried in bird sanctuaries in the dead of night, was truly what nightmares were made of: unsettling. Shocking. Afterwards, some of the jurors admitted to having nightmares on a regular basis because of the testimony, the crime-scene photos, the grave-site photos of this horror film they had unwittingly found themselves cast in.

Never, not once, did Pitera show any emotion, any sign of remorse, empathy or sympathy. He may as well have been made of stone, a statue with black hair, a wide white brow, and those chilling, icy blue eyes of his taking it all in, bored, indifferent – even hostile.

As the prosecution presented its case, the defence cross-examined their witnesses expertly and thoroughly though they managed to do little to the wall of guilt the prosecution had slowly and expertly built around Pitera. They managed, to a degree, to undermine Gangi's testimony when they had him admit to drug and alcohol abuse, to trying to kill himself, to lying repeatedly in order to manipulate the system. They managed to portray Gangi as the murdering three-time loser he really was, but no matter how many holes they shot in his truth and veracity, the photographs of Phyllis Burdi cut up, the photographs of Phyllis Burdi while she was alive, spoke volumes and made any of Gangi's many vices null and void.

At one point in time, the prosecutor put on the stand Phyllis Burdi's sister, Antonina, Toni, and she said how, when her sister went missing, she went to the Just Us bar and asked Pitera where her sister was and he said, 'I hear she's prostituting herself in Coney Island,' knowing full well that he had not only killed her sister but also cut her up and buried her in the bird sanctuary on Staten Island. Antonina was one of the few people who showed no hesitation, no fear when she pointed at Pitera and said what she knew. All her words were laced with venom and hatred. When she looked at Pitera, her stare had the malevolence of a razor-sharp knife.

All 470 pieces of evidence presented, 143 photos shown, all 66 witnesses having testified, direct and cross-examination finished, the two sides made their closing arguments succinctly and well, and the case was left to the jury. The evidence and dozens of witnesses overwhelmingly pointed towards Pitera's guilt. The government's case was so strong and well put-together that Pitera's attorneys put up scant defence. The best they could do, they knew, was to try to save Pitera from the death sentence.

Interestingly, during the defence's closing argument, Pitera's attorneys called Frank Gangi, 'a pimp and a parasite'.

55

YEA OR NAY

It took six days for the jury to find Pitera guilty on 18 out of the 19 counts he was charged with. Pitera was convicted of those 18 charges on 25 June 1992. He was not charged with the murder of Greg Reiter because Reiter's body had never been found and the only witness to the murder, Michael Harrigan, had been killed. The one charge they found him innocent of was the murder of Willie Boy Johnson. The jury apparently felt that because there were no witnesses and only subjective suggestion that they should give Pitera the benefit of the doubt. However, they convicted him of killing Marek Kucharsky, Phyllis Burdi, Joey Balzano, Solomon Stern, Richard Leone and Talal Siksik. The prosecution, David Shapiro and Elise Liang, and Jim Hunt and Tommy Geisel, all believed the jury made a large error regarding Johnson, but they still felt they had hit a home run. Eighteen out of nineteen was excellent, reason to celebrate. No matter how you cut it, Pitera was off the streets.

Now came the most important, essential part of the prosecution: the penalty phase, whether or not Pitera got the death sentence. If he were given the death sentence, he would be the first man convicted under the Drug Kingpin Law in New York and only the second in the country. It would be a milestone. Now, the jury was given the delicate, very difficult task of determining, one: if the death sentence was warranted; and two: if it should be given to Pitera. Both sides succinctly made their arguments. Family members were called to testify to Pitera's character. Pitera's aunt, sister-in-law and two cousins all testified about what a good son, brother, cousin, friend Pitera was. Judge Raggi charged the jury with their task, according to the strict regiments of the law, according to the guidelines set up by the government to meet the criteria for death.

As the jury slowly filed out of the courtroom, looking at Pitera, some in fear, some with hostility, as if he were a dangerous animal caged in a zoo, Pitera turned to Jim Hunt, who was sitting behind him and said, 'I bet you they don't have the balls to kill me.'

'We'll see,' Jim said.

The deliberation for the death sentence took less time than the one for the guilty verdict. The jury was made up of six men and six women, all good American citizens who abided by the rules and regulations of society, who wanted to contribute what they could. They were . . . civilians. They were, as Pitera would put it, 'squares'. As such, the killing of a man, any man, was for them a very difficult task to decide. They all knew that if they did give him the death sentence, it would be as though their fingers had pulled the trigger of the gun that killed this man. Many, particularly God-fearing people, think of the death sentence as something barbaric, unfair, meted out in a way that flies against logic and reason, fairness and the rule of law.

Apparently, this jury was a godsend for Tommy Pitera, for they refused to vote in favour of the death penalty. They debated heatedly. Ultimately, ten were for the death penalty, two against. They argued for four and a half hours. They shouted at one another. When they were finally finished with their deliberations and returned to the courtroom, that number was the same. As the forewoman read the sentence, obviously shaken up, tears rolling from her eyes, emotionally embroiled in what was happening, Pitera turned and addressed his own attorney directly, Jim Hunt and David Shapiro indirectly. 'They didn't have the balls to kill me,' he said, in his high-pitched voice – a voice that might very well have been the beginning of the end for Tommy Pitera, a voice that put him at odds with society and all those around him as far back as he could remember.

Still, regardless of his voice, the painful barbs and abuse, slings and arrows he had suffered because of it, Judge Raggi gave Tommy Pitera of Gravesend, Brooklyn, seven life sentences in addition to four terms of twenty years' imprisonment and five terms of ten years' imprisonment. Three of the life terms, two of the twenty-year terms, and one ten-year term run consecutively.

No matter how you cut it, Pitera would spend the rest of his days behind bars, in a steel cage. True to his beliefs, Pitera never tried to make a deal with the government for any kind of leniency. He remained loyal to La Cosa Nostra culture and mindset, to his pledge of omerta, to the Bonanno family. After the sentencing, two burly guards cuffed Pitera's ankles and wrists. Taking small, stilted steps, walking slowly towards his destiny, Tommy Pitera had his shoulders back, his head high and his thin-lipped mouth shut tight.

EPILOGUE

As of this writing, Tommy Pitera is being held at Allenwood Federal Penitentiary in Pennsylvania. He is a voracious reader with very eclectic tastes. He particularly likes books of epic proportions involving war and famous battles, martial arts and killing. All those in his family come to visit him; he receives mail and books from friends and family.

Today, Jim is working as the second-in-command at the DEA's New York office on 10th Avenue. He's still single and as physically fit as ever. When possible, when he can get away from the busy office, he heads down to Florida, where he enjoys playing golf.

Today, Frank Gangi is still in the Witness Protection Program. He is miserable. His family has completely disowned him. He still has a drinking problem and smokes two packs of cigarettes a day. When, years after it happened, he talks about Phyllis Burdi, he still cries. He is a man without a country, without a home, regretful.

Tommy Geisel retired from the DEA and is CEO of SunBanc Corp. He very much enjoyed his career and equally enjoys his current work and the colourful bounty that life has afforded him.

Bruce Travers has undergone 14 operations to restore his face. Today, for the most part, he looks fine. He still works for the DEA and is presently the head of their office in the United Kingdom. He is happily married and has three children.

After he quit the US Justice Department, David Shapiro was immediately hired by the Boies, Schiller & Flexner law firm in San Francisco – one of the best law firms in the country. (Attorney David Boies would argue on behalf of Al Gore to continue the presidential vote in Florida in the 2000 election.)

After the Pitera trial, Judy Haimowitz also entered the Witness Protection Program and disappeared.

Joe Dish also disappeared into the Witness Protection Program.